Turning the Century

Personal and Organizational Strategies for Your Changed World

by Robert Theobald

Resources for Creative Personal and Social Change

Knowledge Systems, Inc.

© 1992 by Robert Theobald

Published by Knowledge Systems, Inc.

For a free catalog of resources for personal and social change, *Guidebook for the '90s,* or ordering information for this book call (317) 241-0749, fax (317) 248-1503

 or write Knowledge Systems
7777 West Morris Street
Indianapolis, IN 46231 USA

Library of Congress Cataloging-in-Publication Data

Theobald, Robert.
    Turning the century : personal and organizational strategies for your changed world / by Robert Theobald
        p.   cm.
    Includes bibliographical references and index.
    ISBN 0-941705-25-0 : $12.95
    1. Social change. 2. Organizational change. 3. Quality of life.
I. Title
HM101.T473   1992
303.4--dc20   92-33414
                                                                  CIP

Contents

Preface

"THE WORLD WILL CHANGE WHEN THINGS GET BAD ENOUGH." I have listened to this statement throughout my career. Every time I hear it, I get more disturbed.

This common belief ignores the fact that human beings can adapt to almost everything. What was intolerable all too easily becomes the norm. There is a chilling parallel in biology. If you place a frog in cold water, and you raise the temperature very gradually, it will fail to jump out and will eventually boil to death. Similarly, if one leaves an alcoholic alone, the course of the disease will eventually destroy the individual and the family.

If we were thinking clearly, we would realize that we are already in the middle of a massive breakdown. Who would have believed that parts of New York would descend to third world levels of sanitation? Who would have thought that American citizens today would have to live with nightly shootings? Who would have dreamed that we would give up on our commitment to provide opportunities for all Americans? Who would have believed that our political process could be so ineffective?

On a world scene, there is little sign that we know how to provide a rapidly growing population with even minimal standards of food, clothing and shelter. Plagues which we had thought banished, such as cholera and tuberculosis, have returned. The splintered Yugoslavia and Russia are plagued by violence between intermixed ethnic groups and this process of fragmentation is certain to spread.

We must therefore stop waiting for the event which will catalyze a commitment to fundamental change. Rather we must join together now to create an "intervention" which will enable us to recognize the ever-growing breakdowns around us and to develop the processes which will grasp the extraordinary opportunities of our times.

I use the word "intervention" because of the precise parallel with the approach which has been developed for alcoholism. We have learned that it is possible to convince drinkers that they need help before their lives, and those of the people around them, are destroyed. The session which achieves this result is unpleasant and painful. It almost certainly involves threats that the support of family and friends will be withdrawn. When done successfully, however, it changes lives for the better.

Fortunately, interventions to help people recognize the breakdown of society are often less painful. It is my experience that a significant percentage of the population is already perfectly aware of the extent of the problems in the culture. But they fear they are alone in their understandings. Perhaps the most common reaction to my speeches is a heartfelt, "Thank you for convincing me I'm not crazy, Bob."

Turning the Century is for those who recognize that they are not at all crazy but rather are facing up to the new realities of our time. It calls for a global culture built on honesty, responsibility, humility, love and a respect for mystery. It provides a framework and context in which you can make sense of the radically new world in which we are living. Margaret Mead said long ago that, "We are all immigrants into a new time." We are now beginning to recognize the profound truth of this statement.

Turning the Century develops the directions and suggests the institutions which we must develop to live in a new period of history, which I choose to call the compassionate era. We are called to live with passion, to care about ourselves, others and the world. It is only as we accept these challenges that we can bring a viable culture into being.

I am writing for "courageous realists." I want to support those who are willing to face the world as it is, rather than pretending that problems do not exist. And I want to encourage people to see where they can make a difference, given their own situation and skills.

Courageous realists are neither optimists or pessimists. They do not believe that the world will necessarily move in either a good or a bad direction. On the contrary, they understand clearly that the future is determined by the actions of all of us alive today. It is our choices which determine our destiny.

I shall concentrate in this book on what we can do to provide a high quality of life for people throughout the world and maintain the viability of the ecology for ever. My emphasis on this subject often leads to misunderstandings. Some who listen to me believe that because I point out possibilities, I am convinced we shall choose them.

This is not the case. If I look at reality as an objective analyst, I am convinced that we shall fail to cope with our crises. Indeed, our current reality is so bad that it is "reasonable" to conclude that nothing can be done. Many people have withdrawn from participation in our society, choosing to concentrate on their own lives and trying to forget the decay in the society around them.

Despair is destructive, however. I choose to believe that enough people will commit to changing the world that we shall succeed. I know that success is possible. The challenge is to you, the individual. We all make a difference by what we do and what we leave undone. You are inevitably one factor affecting the future.

I am writing this book out of a life-time commitment to discovering how and why the world has to change in order to grasp its opportunities and manage its problems. I have participated in the rollercoaster ride of American attitudes and directions since the late fifties, when I came from Europe. It sometimes seems as though I have had several lives, so different have been the attitudes and behaviors in these different periods.

The sixties were the decade of challenge. They were the years when the industrial era started to unravel. It had become obvious that three forces would change the world radically. There were the impact of computers and robots, the dangers of modern weaponry and the demand for human rights. Later in this decade we became aware of the ecological challenge.

In 1964 I was one of the principal authors of *The Triple Revolution.* This document called for recognition of the inevitability of fundamental change and got front-page coverage across the country. It also received a large amount of negative editorial response because it proposed the adoption of a guaranteed income. This idea, popularized in my book *Free Men and Free Markets,* was later introduced by President Nixon as his Family Assistance Plan.

I spent the sixties making speeches across the country. I naively thought that people were ready to look at the radical ideas I and many others were proposing. I later discovered that we were the "clowns of the culture." It was fun to listen to wild ideas as long as one was sure that the world in which one lived would not really be turned upside down. People could think "objectively" about proposals because they knew that the world would remain stable.

By the beginning of the seventies, the dangers were beginning to become more obvious. The seventies were the decade of denial. People became convinced that our situation was hopeless. One of the causes of this gloom was the report *The Limits to Growth.* There was a growing sense that nothing could be done. Those who spoke and wrote, like I did, about the possibilities of our time seemed increasingly naive.

The title of my primary book during this period said it all from my point of view. *Beyond Despair* was a call for action based on realistic hope. I argued that despair would numb our senses and prevent intelligent decision-making and action. The call was not heeded. People continued to try—vainly—to put old systems back together so they would meet new needs.

In some senses the 1980 election was a conflict between realism and denial. President Carter challenged us to look ahead at the real issues of the future. President Reagan offered us denial. We chose Reagan. This does not mean, as is so often assumed, that we also chose denial. The election was not decided on the issues but rather on the fate of the prisoners in Iran. President Carter lost because he could not free them.

The eighties are already being seen as a weird aberration. They were a time when the real forces were ignored and denied. The economy was propped up by encouraging debt at all levels from the personal to the governmental. The cold war was heated up by President Reagan's use of the term "the evil empire."

But even before President Reagan left office his themes were losing their power. The economies of both Russia and the United States were in disarray and the two superpowers were in trouble because of their excessive military spending. Reagan failed to grasp the ecological challenge. He tried to deny the ever-growing evidence of fundamental change. He supported the decade of the rich and the famous.

My work in the eighties was to encourage people to grasp that there were choices to be made if the human race was to survive. I was the main writer of *At the Crossroads,* published twenty years after *The Triple Revolution.* This pamphlet showed that we had two routes into the future. We could continue along the same lines and this would inevitably be disastrous. Or we could take advantage of humanity's new knowledge and create a compassionate society.

The Rapids of Change published at the end of the eighties took the argument further. It helped individuals, and groups, recognize the challenge which had to be met. It was a base from which to do new thinking. (*Rapids* is a tool for introducing people to the need for change; *Turning the Century* assumes that people understand this reality and goes on from there.)

President Bush inherited a system which was collapsing of its own weight. Trying to please everybody, he has frustrated more and more groups. He has aimed to compromise when dramatic reconceptualization is needed. He hopes to preserve a world which has gone forever. He has failed to grasp the mood in the country which demands new thinking.

The nineties should be a wonderful time to be alive. Mainstream groups are interested in the ideas that many creative people have been developing since the sixties. Institutions which have been trying to solve their disputes through power and law are looking for new forms of communication. Individuals want to learn to support each other rather than fight.

This break in the trend, from trying to maintain the past to welcoming the future, happened at the end of the eighties and has been strengthening as we move through the nineties. The first time I saw it clearly was in Anchorage, Alaska. I was talking to some of the power structure prior to a speech to their mainstream club. They were griping about how they were ignored by the lower 48 states. I challenged them to change this picture by acting in new ways. My challenge was accepted and I had an opportunity to do some work which helped change dynamics so that Alaskans were more willing to set their own directions.

I have had a growing number of opportunities of this type in the nineties. I have worked in the River Bend area across from St. Louis, in Louisville, with the U.S. Army Corps of Engineers, in Spokane, Washington and many other places. There is a single paramount theme in all my work. How can we cope with the breakdown in our systems? How can we set up decision-making processes which work?

You will not get the point of this book if you try to force it into a "left" or "right" viewpoint. I believe that this dichotomy is now totally outdated. The issues before us require that we move beyond this debate. Today's critical conflicts have very different polarities. On the one hand, there are a growing number of people who believe in a society based on the values of honesty, responsibility, humility, love and a respect for mystery. These people know that the fundamental changes of our time require us to change our priorities.

On the other side, are those who believe we can maintain current styles and ideologies. These are the people to want to protect past patterns even though they are now counter-productive. The most dangerous people are those who support their ideologies with fundamentalist beliefs which reject all new ideas as dangerous, if not sinful.

I have now stated the core themes of *Turning the Century*. The following paragraphs provide an extremely brief "executive summary" of the book. They permit you to choose which chapters are most important to you. Obviously the book is most powerful read in the order in which it is written but the various parts are more or less self-contained. You can therefore skip around if you are short of time—and who isn't?

The book has four parts. The first provides an overview of the challenge which faces us. It has the fewest new concepts although there are, of course, a number of novel ways of making old points.

Part II examines the economic issues. It shows that we must abandon the goal of maximum economic growth and labor force participation and provides policies to support this direction.

Part III shows that we must move from our current educational systems to a commitment to learning to learn on a life-long basis—making the creation of "learning societies" our primary goal.

Part IV looks at collective decision-making, or politics. The directions I propose go far beyond what is currently considered acceptable, denying the validity of the concept of national sovereignty. In addition, they argue that majority rule is not a satisfactory base for the compassionate era.

There is a common structure to Parts II, III, and IV. The first chapter sets out the situation. The second chapter looks at the social changes which are required. The third shows that there are actions which individuals can take to alter their conditions. As you would expect, the boundaries between the sections are fuzzy—material could sometimes be placed in several chapters. Because of this reality there is inevitably some repetition, although I have tried to keep it to a minimum.

Chapter 1 states the forces which have damaged industrial-era structures and have made decision-making ineffective because people no longer agree on the best route into the future. The dangers of modern weaponry, ecological limits, changes in our perceptions of human rights and responsibilities together challenge all the strategies we took for granted in the middle of the twentieth century.

In the past I have underestimated the inertia of economic, social and political systems. Institutions have continued to use approaches which obviously damaged their potential. Today, the inadequacy of current approaches is so obvious that people and groups no longer have the option of continuing in the same direction if they want to survive.

Chapter 2 argues that we have now passed through the eye of a hurricane and the winds of change are blowing from a different direction than has been the case in the last fifty years. The industrial era is ending and is being replaced by the compassionate era, which will be based on a profoundly different set of values.

Our survival requires that we struggle with the driving forces humankind has set loose. We often think and act as if we can choose to respond to our changing world or fail to do so. This is not a realistic way of seeing our situation. Our two options are either to take advantage of the overwhelming opportunities or be buried by the dire dangers.

Today's challenge is profoundly new. The extent of the change we are undergoing is no more extensive than the shift from hunting and gathering to agriculture or the shift from agriculture to industry. But the speed at which profound alterations must take place is without parallel in human history.

In Chapter 3, I coin the word *mindquakes* to describe the process we must all accept and understand. Each of us has to face the need to shake up our current belief structures and to abandon many of the ideas which have been central to our past sense of purpose, and even our understanding of who we are.

The word mindquakes is coined as a deliberate parallel to earthquakes. Earthquakes are least destructive when they are small-scale and frequent—so are mindquakes. Each of us needs to be open to new knowledge so we prevent our idea-structures from hardening and then having to break them open with great pain.

Chapter 4 takes up the subject of economics and economic growth. It proves that the commitment to maximum growth and maximum labor force participation must be abandoned in order to ensure humankind's survival. It argues that the twin pillars of economic policy must be to permit the free play of market policies where possible but also to recognize that they must be subordinated to social, political and ecological realities when this is vital.

This chapter also demonstrates that free markets can only operate efficiently when four conditions—long known to economists—are largely in place. We need to limit the size of firms, reduce the power of unions, cut back the amount of law and regulation and improve the flow of information and knowledge so people can make good decisions.

Chapter 5 suggests the changes in policies which are required to reduce the pressures toward economic growth. A good deal of attention is paid to major shifts in taxation policy, a subject that began to be opened up in the 1992 election campaign. The key elements proposed are a national consumption tax with high levies on gasoline, an income tax which is only paid by those with discretionary income, the elimination of the social security tax and an increase in corporate taxes.

In addition, this chapter recognizes that there will be profound changes in lifestyles in the twenty-first century. Indeed, shifts have already started. People are setting different priorities for themselves. For more and more people jobs are no longer the center of life; many are prepared to accept lower income as a necessary price for more leisure.

Chapter 6 examines the way that individual actions can, and have, altered the way Americans live. It shows that each of us can change the products that are available, the ways the media report news, the types of entertainment that are developed and the amount of recycling that is feasible.

I also discuss the ways in which work and job patterns can shift so they are more attractive and effective. The phrase "right livelihood" is now used frequently to describe what happens when people earn their incomes doing work they enjoy. Obviously, this shift in work patterns also implies profound shifts in the ways that institutions are structured with people having more rights to make decisions about what will benefit them.

Chapter 7 discusses the difference between current educational practices and those which would exist if we committed to helping people to learn to learn on a life-long basis. It forces us to face up to the fact that people living in the compassionate era have very different needs than those who supported industrial-era patterns.

The challenge, then, is to alter not only the ways that we encourage people to learn but the very ways that we structure knowledge so that people can discover what they need to know. We have lived in a world which has concentrated on finding answers. Now we need to support people as they struggle to define the right question.

The challenge is for all of to be learners throughout our lives. The idea that one can learn a body of information in one's youth that will serve all one's life has become profoundly unrealistic.

Chapter 8 addresses the many social crises of our times. It shows that medical care must inevitably be rationed but that the standard of health can be raised as people take responsibilities for their bodies and society reduces environmental hazards. It revisits the issues of equality of opportunity and argues that help must be given to those in need rather than to certain defined groups.

It takes up the issue of justice and argues that the balance between the rights of criminals and citizens needs to be readjusted. It also argues that the cause of much crime today is prohibition of drug use and that little progress can be made until drugs are decriminalized.

It also recognizes the need to reduce the rate of growth of population and shows how past moral and religious dogmas are getting in the way of clear thinking about one of the most critical issues of our time. It also links population pressure to patterns of habitation by asking how many people need to live in urban environments and how should rural populations be supported.

Chapter 9 argues that much decision-making authority must move from the nation and the state to local communities. In the past, communities were unwilling to make the tough decisions and power drifted away from them. My experience indicates that the clearest thinking is now going on in the local areas.

The definition of a good community is one which grasps opportunities when they are available and prevents problems from developing into crises. This is a very different way of looking at the proper way to organize than has been the case in the past. It requires an acceptance of diversity and a willingness to cooperate.

This chapter provides a number of examples of how communities can get together to bring about constructive change. It also states several sets of rules which have been developed by people who aim to support positive processes.

Chapter 10 deals with politics—where there has been less radical thought than in any other area. It is only now that we are becoming aware that the underlying principles of democracy will not be enough for the twenty-first century. We need to move beyond democracy.

Our institutions are still based on the belief that it is appropriate to use power over other people. We have taken the old models which gave kings and priests power over others and diffused this power more widely. But the basis of our thinking is still based on the assumption that power must be exercised. Thus, within countries, the majority claims a right to control minorities. And on the international scene, might makes right.

I argue in this chapter that our only hope lies in moving to authority based on competence, knowledge and servant leadership. I recognize that this is an enormous shift to make but I also point out that changes of this magnitude have been made in the past. The greatest danger is that we shall lose our nerve and believe that the necessary tasks are beyond our skill and courage.

Chapter 11 proposes that the required goal for the twenty-first century is responsible freedom. People need to have the freedom to make their own choices but they need to make them within a realistic context so that what they choose to do will benefit others.

This goal of responsible freedom requires that we revise our thinking so that we believe that most people will want to be responsible most of the time if we give them a chance. This is the exact opposite of most of our current thinking which believes that we must develop regulations and pass laws to prevent people from doing wrong.

Our only hope is for the human race to move out of its adolescence into maturity. Today, we want leaders to fulfil our dual, but contradictory, desires of giving us orders but retaining our right to gripe because the orders are no good. The majority of people will need to be willing to make their own intelligent choices if humanity is to survive.

The final chapter discusses our personal role in changing directions. We all need to do what we can plus ten percent for risk. There can be no master plan because none of us are bright enough to know exactly where we need to go at the current time.

We therefore must hone our own skills but also learn to listen to those with whom we disagree. But all of us must commit to a value-based society. Both religious and system-thinkers agree that this is the requirement for survival.

In the end, the challenge of this book is to you the reader as an individual. I believe that each of us can be far more effective in supporting a more compassionate society than we recognize. If this book provides you with new insights that help you on your journey, it amply repaid the time taken to write it. If you want to tell me what you found helpful and where you disagreed, please write to me at 330 Morgan Street, New Orleans, LA 70114.

I want to acknowledge in closing the generous help I have had from a wide circle of colleagues who helped me through many drafts of the book. They are, literally, too many to mention without my risking leaving out key people. You all know how much you have done to help—please accept my thanks.

Robert Theobald
New Orleans

PART I

Entering the
Compassionate
Era

CHAPTER 1

The Revolutions of the Twentieth Century

THE CHINESE HAVE A CURSE: "May you live in interesting times." If we share their negative perceptions about periods of fundamental change, we shall see ourselves as fated to live tragic lives. But each of us can alter the way we look at the world. We can decide that we are immensely lucky to be alive at the time when the human race can grow up and become part of a positive evolutionary process working with, rather than against, natural forces.

The pace of change in the nineties is without parallel in human history. The nostalgia of the eighties, supported by President Reagan and Prime Minister Thatcher, seems decades away. The iceflows which accumulated during the cold war are breaking up. Events are moving faster than we can understand, let alone manage.

It is enough to hit the highpoints of the last few years to remind us of this reality: the fall of the Berlin Wall; the savings and loan debacle now estimated to cost more than $500 billion; the end of South Africa's stonewalling resistance to change; the revolutions in Eastern Europe; the Iraqi invasion of Kuwait, the American response and the environmental disasters which followed; the support of the Kurds despite infringements on classic traditions of sovereignty; famine in the Horn of Africa; donor fatigue in the face of escalating demands for help; banking and insurance failures; the collapse of communism and the Soviet Union; the breakup of Yugoslavia; the decision by the Soviet Union and the U.S. to stop supplying weapons to Afghanistan; the Mideast Peace Conference; the Judge Thomas hearings; the support for violent, extremist movements throughout the world; continuing recessions and high levels of unemployment; the rise of Japan and Germany as the possible leaders of Asia and Europe.

Behind these patterns, lie several continuing crises which American institutions are failing to resolve. Most children are not reaching their potential. Health costs continue to rise out of control: there is already "rationing" of health care although we deny this reality. A larger proportion of the population is in prison in the U.S. than anywhere else in the democratic world: one quarter of black males between 20 and 30 are dead, in prison or on parole. Social security systems throughout the world cannot cope with the inevitable aging of the population. The gap between the rich and the poor is widening. The infrastructure on which production and the quality of life depends is decaying.

The current failure to face these and other damaging trends is causing a paralysis of decision-making. Not only are systems becoming "hollow" as the number of personnel is reduced but we are using styles of governance which no longer fit the realities of our time. The survival of the human race demands larger changes than our media, our academic systems and our politicians have so far been willing to consider.

The rate of change we have seen in the early nineties will continue and, indeed, intensify. Our survival requires accepting the inevitability of rapid change and learning to deal with it. *Turning the Century* is centered on American realities, but also reflects the global situation. I am British and spend several months in Scotland each year. I have worked on issues of European integration and consulted with the United Nations on development issues; indeed, my first passion was how the poor countries could achieve a higher quality of life. It is my hope that this wider perspective will enrich the flavor of my arguments.

From my perspective, the real clash of the nineties is between "stories." Each of these stories has its own styles. The new story I am telling has no single hero or heroine. It rests on a call to all of us to play our part in building a new society for a profoundly different era that I choose to call the compassionate era. Compassion is a strong word; its meaning is "with passion."

The nineties provide a challenge to tackle the issues of our times with courage, imagination and joy. They demand that we use our intelligence to live within ecological limits. They require us to use all our capacities. The new story we must develop challenges the current beliefs which places things in the ascendancy over people.

My arguments will inevitably seem surprising to you at first sight because they deny the ideologies of both left and right. But they will make sense for those who are ready to face the gap between old truths and new realities. Concerned girl scout leaders and corporate executives, priests and rabbis, mayors and citizens, teachers and communicators, students and parents, nurses and lawyers will find opportunities for leadership described in this book.

There is a route into the future which will continue the human adventure, rather than end it. In these turbulent times, our individual and group choices do make a difference. None of us can change the world by ourselves. But the sum of our decisions does decide the way the world evolves. The tides of history are running with us if we are smart and committed enough to discover and move with them. A profoundly new vision and story is already emerging all over the world.

The last decade of the twentieth century coincides with an extraordinary change in conditions which requires that the human race leaves behind its adolescence. Fortunately, there is a natural tendency to examine the future as we reach the end of a century. This pattern is reinforced at the conclusion of a millennium. Our inevitable tendency to ask fundamental questions as we approach the twenty-first century therefore comes at the right time. It is this needed commitment which lies behind the concept of "turning the century." All of us must work together to "turn" society so we create a better world for ourselves, our children and grandchildren. How much of a turn is required? It is certainly not a U-turn. We cannot return to the past. On the other hand, a slight alteration in directions will not be enough. The need is for a shift of about 90 degrees.

In order to understand our times we must look at the four primary driving forces which are changing global systems so rapidly. I list them below in order of their understanding and acceptance in the culture. Some of them are already relatively well known: others are only now beginning to be understood. While much of the material I set out in this chapter will be well known to you, I often reach significantly different conclusions that those currently accepted. If you have kept up with the debate about fundamental change, however, you may want to skim, or skip the rest of this chapter.

Beyond violence

Violence has always been a major part of the human experience. It is a deeply personal issue as well as a major danger to the continued existence of the world. We all know people who have been mugged or abused as children, if we ourselves have not suffered these experiences. We are all aware of the casual violence of adolescence which currently seems to be mutating into something far more dangerous.

We are all most aware of the dangers from warfare. Immediately after the atomic bomb was dropped, a few people recognized that war—

the most visible form of violence—had become infeasible. The twentieth century therefore saw the development of a huge paradox. As weaponry became more destructive, its ability to determine the shape of events declined. Wars which involved America and Russia directly proved to be unwinnable. The struggles in Korea, Vietnam and Afghanistan resulted in stalemates or withdrawals. While the enemy could certainly have been defeated if nuclear weapons had been used, the cost in terms of internal and external public opinion was perceived to be too high and the risks of escalation too dangerous.

The Gulf War seemed, at first sight, to have created a very different pattern. Advanced weaponry systems provided an overwhelming advantage to the United Nations. A quick victory was achieved with very low loss of life on the UN side. Because America had dominated the coalition, the initial reaction was that America could stand tall again. There was little courage to raise the tough issues which victory swept under the rug.

Sober second thoughts have altered initial attitudes. The costs of the war proved to be far higher than was initially thought. The damage in Kuwait and Iraq was enormous: the bombs used in six weeks had more destructive power than those dropped on Germany throughout the Second World War. The accuracy of smart weapons proved to be far lower than was claimed when the war was going on. As many as 100,000 Iraqi soldiers were killed; some had been forced into the army against their will and were 16 or even younger. Huge amounts of resources were wasted which could have been employed for positive purposes.

There was enormous ecological damage in the Gulf waters because of oil spills and oil-well fires which exceeded anything which has ever occurred before in human history. During the war, it was argued that Saddam Hussein's tactics were unprecedented. "Scorched earth" tactics have, in fact, always been part of wars. Hussein did not start this pattern of behavior, he only continued it and showed how destructive it could be in an oil-rich area.

Finally, and most seriously, the Middle East is a more unstable place than it was before. It was doubtful even before the war whether Saudi Arabia and the other sheikdoms could survive into the twenty-first century. The only real hope was for a peaceful transition to more democratic forms of government. The chance of this development has been significantly decreased by the war because there is now increased commitment to keeping out Western ideas while the danger of fundamentalism has increased.

But in the end the Middle East is not the key issue. We need to look at global attitudes toward war. Now that the Soviet Union no longer exists, the possibility of a radical change in military philosophy is possible. In examining what is desirable, the attitudes of the U.S. toward the production and export of weapons becomes central to dynamics. This raises the question to what degree is America comfortable with wars.

Barbara Ehrenreich caught some of the issues in the following quotes from her essay "The Warrior Culture" in *Time* of October 15, 1990.

> "You must understand that Americans are a warrior nation," Senator Daniel Patrick Moynihan told a group of Arab leaders in early September, one month into the Middle East crisis. He said this proudly, and he may, without thinking through the ugly implications, have told the truth. In many ways, in outlook and behavior, the U.S. has begun to act like a primitive warrior culture. . . .
>
> It has not yet penetrated our imagination that in a world where the powerful, industrialized states are at last at peace, there might be other ways to face down a pint-size Third-World warrior state than with the massive force of arms. Nor have we begun to see what an anachronism we are in danger of becoming, a warrior nation in a world that pines for peace, a high-tech state with the values of a warrior band.

The Gulf War did not change realities. War is still obsolete as a way of settling disputes. The Gulf War was an aberration, not the beginning of a new world order. This is the lesson that must be learned if human survival is to be possible. The apparent low cost of a high tech war to the victors conceals enormous damage when the picture is drawn more widely. It was the decision to go to war which led to the massive ecological damage and the large-scale loss of life. There were alternatives but the U.S. did not have the patience or creativity to work them through. These alternatives would certainly not have been costless but would clearly have been less damaging than the war.

One of the primary arguments of those who reject wars is that they almost always leave the world more unstable than before and, all too often, sow the seeds of future violence. The reparations demanded from Germany, after World War I, made World War II essentially inevitable. There was no way that Germany could create a stable society if it had to pay large-scale reparations; the allies in World War I therefore planted the seeds from which Hitler inevitably grew. A few far-seeing individuals understood the dangers but the desire for vengeance was so great that their voices were drowned.

After World War II, on the other hand, America seemed extraordinarily generous. General Marshall was able to convince the

President and the Congress that it was in the best interest of the U.S. to rebuild Europe and Japan. Nevertheless, while American aid was given freely, we still need to remember that one of the primary motivations was to block the perceived danger from the communist world. The "cold war" developed as early as 1946.

The seeds of a new world war were once again sown in World War II. The tension between the East and West became so great that, if nuclear weapons had not existed, Russia and its allies would have fought with the members of the North American Treaty Organization at some time during the second half of the twentieth century. Despite the fact that we hate to admit this reality, nuclear weapons were "peacemakers."

The nineties have produced a situation without parallel in human history. The Soviet Union which had previously been seen as a "great power" is now revealed as an economically underdeveloped country where most people face hunger, and some may starve. In the past, this type of pattern has led to the rise of a dictatorship which enforces the discipline by which economic viability can be reestablished, the most recent major example was the rise of Hitler in Germany. Avoiding this danger should be the primary issue which preoccupies the leaders of the West in their dealings with the Republics which previously formed the Soviet Union—all other questions should be subordinated to it.

The fear of nuclear holocaust prevented the development of a major war for over forty years. But it also, however, permitted many areas of smaller-scale violence between countries and between ethnic groups within countries. New and profoundly difficult questions are emerging now that the stabilizing power of the cold war has been removed. How do we prevent the development of regional bullies? How do we deal with the rise of ethnic energies? How can the export of arms be limited so the capacity for violence within and between smaller countries is reduced?

We shall not understand the issue of violence, however, until we ask when conflict causes violence and when it does not. Conflict is inevitable in all societies. It emerges from differing perceptions and attitudes which always exist in a pluralistic world. There are, however, two very different possible reactions to divergent views. One is to argue that the other group is wrong and that force and violence should be used to subdue it. The alternative is to recognize that while there will always be clashing goals, more positive results can be achieved by creative problem-solving than by forcing agreement through coercion.

Conflict has highly positive aspects. The fastest way to learn is to discover a person or group which reaches totally different conclusions to your own when looking at the same reality. As you examine alternative views, your own understandings are inevitably enriched. You may not change your conclusions but you will certainly become more aware of factors which you have previously overlooked. This is the key toward new approaches to violence; it is further explored in Part IV.

Conflict is inevitable. At its best, it is a sign that people know what they want and need and are willing to challenge others to make sure their rights are respected. It becomes dangerous and violent when groups believe that their rights are more important than those of others and that they should impose their desires.

In this context, we need to recognize that much of the debate following Iraq's invasion of Kuwait was around a clash between industrial-era and compassionate-era rhetorics, although it was seldom defined in this way. Many of the world's leaders concentrated on the issue of responding to aggression or regaining access to Kuwait's oil. They wanted to "win." On the other hand, a few Senators adopted a compassionate-era viewpoint recognizing that there was no easy solution to a complex situation.

They pointed out that there were other nation-states which were interested in dominating the region and that the lessening of Iraq's power might well give Syria and Iran a freer hand. They reminded people that the only reason that Iraq had become such a threat was that the nations of the world, particularly America, had built it up to prevent the victory of Iran during the eighties war. Evidence which emerged after the war shows that the Bush administration was one of the major supporters of Iraq right up to the time of the invasion of Kuwait.

The debate around the Kuwaiti invasion was an argument between the past and the future. Those who argue for the future believe that dialogue is always worthwhile. They are convinced that the way to work through an issue may emerge anywhere and that it is only by truly listening to all those involved that a deadlock may be turned into hopeful movement. They believe that the range of circumstances in which power and force are seen as acceptable models for bringing about change must be dramatically reduced. It is only as this pattern becomes established that the waste of resources on weaponry will be significantly diminished.

One of the wonderful aspects of the twenty-first century is that human and environmental survival requires the progressive elimination of violence. The fact that we can only flourish if we move beyond violence does not, of course, mean that we shall take this step. We have a choice. We can decide to perpetuate historical patterns at immense cost to the human race or we can accept the challenge of moving forward, learning to live by spiritual values.

I am increasingly convinced that we shall achieve a positive future if we can abandon our ideologies and biases and learn to listen to each other. We must come to understand why individuals and groups see the same situation differently. If we fail to do so, the pace of technological change will drive ethnic groups and nations apart and cause a total breakdown both inside countries and between them.

Ensuring long-run ecological balance

It is now generally agreed that human beings are altering planetary ecological systems in unpredictable ways. The consequences of the increase in CO_2, the thinning of the ozone layer and the effects of acid rain all have global impacts. The most recent data show that the depletion of the ozone layer is proceeding far more rapidly than expected with "holes" showing up in the temperate zones as well as over the poles; probable deaths from skin cancer will therefore be far higher than initial projections.

Although nobody knows how to model the planetary ecological system, many analysts have concluded that global warming is inevitable. Donella Meadows stated some of the evidence for this thesis in an article in the *Annals of Earth*: "Winter snow cover in the Northern Hemisphere has been shrinking since 1978. The snow line is advancing south in the fall a little slower and moving north in the spring a little faster. . . . Globally 1990 was the hottest year in recorded history. . . . The seven warmest years out of the last one hundred and twenty were, in order of increasing temperature: 1980, 1989, 1981, 1983, 1987, 1988, 1990. The Freshwater Institute in Winnipeg, Canada reports that Canadian lake temperatures have gone up over the last twenty years by three degrees Fahrenheit." Since she wrote, many parts of the Northern hemisphere have had their warmest winter ever in 1991-1992.

While the reality of ecological overload is obvious, global warming is not the only possibility. Some fear that a new ice age can be triggered. Because we have essentially no knowledge about how major climate shifts take place, we should be extraordinarily careful when making specific projections. On the other hand, the growing evidence that sharp breaks in climatic patterns have taken place "rapidly" in the past should increase our determination to make intelligent decisions as soon as possible. Chaos theory shows that it is possible for sharp breaks in trends to occur rather than for there to be a steady process of change.

The highly dramatic consequences of atmospheric trends have drawn attention away from the excessive stresses on our land and water systems. These dangers are also critically important, however. The viability of the "enclosed" Mediterranean and Caribbean Seas is threatened by pollution. Underground water supplies are being infiltrated by surface run-off, community and industrial waste, pesticides, herbicides, fertilizers and deep-well injections. Chemicals and other noxious products are being exported to poorer countries and doing untold harm there because storage techniques are inadequate to the types of material they are receiving. Once water has been polluted, recovery to a viable state may take decades and even centuries. Rivers, lakes and even internal seas throughout the world, particularly in Eastern Europe, are dying.

As a result of the growing damage, water quality and supplies will dominate economics and politics in many parts of the world. Indeed, they could create greater problems than oil. Already, supplies throughout the Middle East are inadequate to immediately foreseeable needs. Behind the territorial issue, which dominates discussions between Israel and the Arabs, lurks the problems of allocating water supplies more fairly. In the U.S., the future of the water-shortage states, such as California and Arizona, is increasingly doubtful. Because rainfall is not regular from year to year, the inevitable future major droughts in various parts of the world will cause havoc when they occur.

Intensive cultivation of land throughout the world has led to the loss of much surface topsoil. Salinization of irrigated land is also a growing problem in many areas. Authoritative voices argue that the ability to raise food production fast enough to keep up with population increases is in grave doubt. Since 1984 persistent annual declines in per capita grain output—a drop of 14 percent—brought 1988 per capita food output back to the 1970 level. This reality is hidden by the fact that the rich countries are overproducing, the poor countries cannot however afford to purchase what is available.

Individuals respond in a variety of ways to this growing evidence of major long-run ecological stress. At one extreme, people deny that the problems are urgent, or indeed really significant. Those who react in this way believe that while there is certainly a need to limit environmental damage, there is no requirement to change the whole structure of our thinking and actions. This leads to a belief that it is possible both to pre-serve the environment and continue maximum growth strategies. Most governmental and United Nations thinking is still along these lines: the UN *Brundtland Report*, which is the current "bible" on this issue, supports this thesis.

The polar opposite view sees humanity as a plague on the face of the earth. Some individuals have gone so far as to welcome AIDS as a way to decrease population. It is also suggested that Gaia (a mystical concept for the earth as a living organism) knows what is required and will move in foreordained ways to achieve appropriate goals regardless of the actions of humankind and that trends will develop to limit the number of people who can live on the planet.

I am convinced that both of these extreme views are wrong. I believe that we must recognize that human beings are now one of the primary forces changing the planet and they will continue to play this role in either a positive or negative way. I am sure we can discover what we should be doing so long as we are willing to give up our attachment to old ways of thinking and past moral codes which developed when conditions were very different. Human beings must learn to be stewards of the earth. Denial of this fundamental requirement will continue to worsen our situation. The need is to look for directions which will lessen the stress on people while also ensuring ecological and social viability into the indefinite future.

One of the primary immediate needs is to recognize that mega-projects are normally too dangerous to build. We do not know how to model the impact of major changes, particularly when they may change Earth's ecosystems drastically and dangerously. For example, the building of the high dam on the Nile has fundamentally altered, and damaged, the Mediterranean ecosystem.

Unfortunately, there are still places on earth which are sufficiently far away from attention that megaprojects are still being planned and sometimes constructed. Many of the most serious past errors have been in the Soviet Union and Eastern Europe. Notable among future dangers are projects in the north of Quebec, Canada which aim to produce huge amounts of electricity and are even considering transporting large amounts of water from the north of the American continent to the south. Alaska is now considering a project at a similar scale.

Fortunately, we do not need to know the exact shape of ecological dangers before making the appropriate changes in direction. Cutting back on the level of production and waste will provide benefits whatever the shape of the specific dangers which may confront us. We need to quit arguing and move forward. This recognition is emerging in Sweden where a report has been issued which describes the degree of agreement about the need to minimize ecological damage rather than concentrating on the limited areas where people are still in doubt.

Human rights and responsibilities

The Bill of Rights is seen as the crowning glory of the American Revolution by a large number of thinkers. It reflects the true driving force which gave the revolt against Britain its edge. There was a fierce desire to curb the use of authoritarian, and often arbitrary, power expressed in the Revolutionary motto: "Live free, or die."

People wanted the right and the ability to make decisions for themselves. Strong individuals populated North America. Those who were willing to abandon hearth and home for the risks of crossing the Atlantic and homesteading a strange land at the other end of their journey came to the new continent. It is not surprising that they demanded the right to set their own directions.

De Tocqueville, the great French writer, saw and caught this mood when he visited the U.S. in the early nineteenth century. He understood that the cultural style of the country was very different from Europe despite the fact that it had been populated from there. The people who had moved were significantly different from those who had stayed home. Science-fiction writers have explored this same theme. Many stories are based on the belief that if human beings do gain the ability to travel to the stars, it will once again be the imaginative and the courageous who choose to travel. The fearful and the lazy will stay behind.

The drive toward individual rights made sense in the eighteenth century. The power of the state and the church needed to be broken. The rights of the individual needed to be affirmed and reinforced. The emphasis had been completely one-sided in the middle-ages, with the collective being seen as far more important than the individual. Despite this obvious imbalance, the intellectual giants of the eighteenth century did recognize future issues with remarkable prescience. They aimed to honor both the power of the state and the rights of the individual.

Unfortunately there was one force which could not possibly have been grasped at the time they were working out their grand schemes. They were not aware of the corrosive effect that capitalism would have on societal commitment. In their time, economics was very much a creature of the state, designed to serve state purposes.

The idea that it might break free and become the driving sector of society, rather than being subordinate to the power of the state, would have seemed the wildest fantasy to the founding fathers, and indeed to Adam Smith. While Adam Smith did believe that an invisible hand caused firms to do what was needed, he never thought for a moment that economics should drive all decision-making processes or considered the possibility that such a situation would develop.

Despite American individualism, most people still saw themselves as embedded in their communities in the eighteenth century. The idea that individuals should do what seemed best to them, regardless of consequences for neighbors and employees, developed in the nineteenth as Adam Smith's idea of the invisible hand spread teaching that social good is created out of individual self-interest. Many people came to believe that because competition was beneficial, it was all right for some people to be hurt because the overall impact of selfish behavior would automatically be positive.

This approach to economics really took hold in the mid-nineteenth century when lawyers decided corporations were permanent entities with rights similar to those of individuals. Most of the larger-than-life figures who ruled their companies believed they had the right to make the largest possible profit. One of the most powerful of these tycoons, William Henry Vanderbilt, when challenged about his behavior, made it clear exactly where he stood. He announced without any hesitation: "The public be damned." The anti-trust legislation of the late nineteenth and early twentieth centuries that aimed to control predatory capitalism was the direct result of his type of attitude and behavior.

Unfortunately, the anti-trust bills did not tackle the central issue: business's claim that it could do what it wanted in the economic field without considering social consequences. Joseph Schumpeter, a great Austrian economist, who has never received the attention which was his due, showed that the emphasis of the corporation on profit, and the desire of individuals to serve their narrow self-interest, would destroy the ties required for any society to function.

Schumpeter was very aware that societies can only flourish if there is a strong sense of interdependence. His fears that this sense of mutuality would be destroyed by capitalism have been proved true by developments. The most obvious evidence of this reality is the language we use as we pitch capitalism to the poor countries and Eastern Europe. We inform them that it is only if people are permitted to gain great wealth, and others are thrust into poverty, that the capitalist system can be expected to function properly.

We have become so used to this way of looking at the world that we fail to recognize its essential injustice. It is certainly true that absolute equality is not possible or desirable. But it is equally true that the degree of income disparities which have now developed, particularly in the eighties and nineties, will be destructive of our future. As people become aware that they are being left behind in the economic race, they are responding by demanding their rights. More and more groups believe that they are being treated unfairly.

The demand for equal rights was essentially started by the blacks in the sixties. It was followed by women. Now every group has adopted the same strategy. Chicanos, Asians, gays, the handicapped and many other sub-groups believe that the way that they can get what they deserve is to organize separately and fight society, and each other, for their share of the pie. William Raspberry, a columnist for the *Washington Post,* spends a lot of time on campuses. This fragmentation of directions is one of the trends which worries him most because it is breaking the solidarity of the culture.

The easiest way to understand the danger of this approach is that whites and males are now organizing to counter the claims of other groups. They increasingly see themselves as being unfairly treated because of the advantages which minorities and women are being given. Patrick Buchanan's popularity results from his abilities to tap into this anger of whites, particularly those who are poor and male.

The essential difference between the white movement and that of minorities is that the former can win at the polls because it is in fact a majority even though it defines itself as a mistreated minority. Non-whites must rely on whites for justice; whites can dominate the system and exclude others. Pushing whites to the point where they feel that they are being mistreated is therefore counterproductive for they can prevent the essential movements toward social justice.

Central to any new way of viewing the new social contract must be the understanding that there can be no rights without responsibilities. One of the easiest way to grasp this truth is to look at the way in which the discussion about weapons has been so greatly abused. The second amendment to the constitution, on which the debate is based, states: "A well-regulated militia being necessary to the security of a free state, the right of the people to keep and bear arms shall not be infringed." The National Rifle Association has used this amendment to claim an absolute right for citizens to possess any form of weapon. They ignore the obvious truth that the right of the people to bear arms is clearly subordinate, in the original amendment, to the security of a free state.

Modern weaponry has changed the nature of the world so profoundly that having modern weapons in the hands of citizens damages the security of a free state rather than enhances it. People need the ability to prevent the abuse of power but the dangers of the late twentieth and early twenty-first century cannot be controlled by weapons but rather by the force of ideas and personal courage.

It was not weapons that changed the course of history in Eastern Europe. It was the will of the people. The movement into the future has to be driven by a profoundly new covenant between all those who live on our small and overcrowded globe. The story which supports this covenant will have to provide us all with rights and demand that all of us our fulfil our responsibilities.

Impact of new knowledge

It may seem strange to list new knowledge so far down the list of driving forces, given that I stated at the beginning of this chapter that I would list the driving forces in order of our degree of understanding. After all, everyone is increasingly aware that computers and robots, biotechnology and nuclear energy, engineering and medical skills, and information and communication technologies have been changing the world in which we live throughout the second half of the twentieth century.

Harold Linstone, editor of the journal *Technological Forecasting*, wrote in the late eighties:

> Technological advances continue to trigger much change. Information technology is moving at a remarkable pace. By 2000, information will be processed by computers a thousand times more powerful than our current ones. . . . Other fields of rapid technological change include production automation (robotics), the creation of advanced materials (ceramics, bacteria-based polymers, genetically engineered drugs), the use of superconductivity to improve magnets, and fossil fuel substitutes.
>
> We recognize that this unprecedented pace of change is not matched by social rates of change. Indeed, the gap between technological and societal rates of change is becoming ever wider. The U.S. is approaching the twenty-first century with a 19th century institutional structure while subject to a dizzying pace of technological advance.

Owen Paepke has developed another way of raising the same critical issue. He notes that 60% of the labor force used to be needed to produce food in the developed countries and the number is now down to 5% or less: further decreases will not be really significant. He then notes that, used effectively, only a small proportion of the lifetime of each person is required to produce goods and services. Human beings need not be tied to production as they have been throughout human history. This is true not only in the rich countries but in the developing world. Modern technology decreases the demand for labor and makes an economic development strategy based on full employment impossible.

This type of understanding is increasingly common. We have, however, concentrated our attention on the ways in which this increased knowledge could provide a higher standard of living through dramatic increases in productivity. We are only now looking at the social and political implications and beginning to understand the inevitable shifts in the styles, approaches and systems by which we have lived during the industrial era.

Some of the most dramatic developments result from the impact of computers and robots. The basic reality is that if the nature of a task can be fully defined, then it is possible for the activity to be taken over by a computer, or a machine which is controlled by a computer. When judgment or intuition is required then computers, at least as currently structured, cannot take over from human beings.

The challenge, therefore, is to educate people so they can do more than computers or machines controlled by computers. This means that our current educational goals which aim to turn people into "efficient" workers are counterproductive. Students are still taught to do what they are told rather than learning to think for themselves. The creativity they need to be full human beings, and that is required to enable their institutions to cope with rapid change, is therefore stifled. We can only deal with this profound danger by committing ourselves to developing learning to learn systems which encourage imagination and creativity.

Will this be enough, however? Many front-edge thinkers believe that computers will develop the skills to deal with unstructured situations in the twenty-first century. This naturally leads to the fear that human beings will be unable to keep up with computers and will ultimately be replaced by smart machines. This fear is only valid so long as one remains caught in industrial-era patterns of thinking.

There is no "absolute" set of understandings which can be learned by a computer, which will permit it to operate without error or ambiguity. If computers gain the skills to deal with real, complex situations, they will be no more certain of the results of their actions than human beings are able to be. The idea that there can be an all-knowing computer died when we realized that knowledge is not objective but perceptual. The results from computers will be no more certain than those of human judgment.

There is another area where our growing knowledge is changing our norms and standards rapidly and dramatically. Growing medical and biological information is shifting the way human beings think about their bodies. It is also challenging our beliefs about life and death in ways which are deeply troubling. The 1991 referendum in Washington state which aimed to increase the right of doctors to help people choose death has led to deep splits in both medical and religious groups.

Death is obviously a part of the life cycle, but this reality has been denied in Western countries and particularly America. In primitive societies, however, there was no way to practice the deceptions which are now so common. For example in the Eskimo culture, where survival was always in doubt, the individual who could no longer support the tribe was expected to chose death in order to ensure the survival of the group when scarcity threatened.

The development of medicine set us off on another track. Doctors took an oath to support life. So long as their powers were limited, this oath was essentially benign. People were enabled to live longer and the quality of their lives was improved. The developments in medical technology in the second half of the twentieth century have shifted the situation dramatically. Today, death has to be chosen by more and more people. Society is still trying to keep this difficult truth at bay by defining death as the ultimate enemy.

We need new definitions if we are to make sense of today's patterns. I would suggest that life is the ability to develop and help others to develop, death occurs when this is no longer possible. I am arguing that we can only make sense of our choices if we adopt a subjective definition of life and death rather than the objective measures of the failure of heart and brain which we use today.

I am, of course, aware that we shall only be able to benefit from this new definition if we can develop a far greater level of personal and group maturity than in the past. We must learn to value life, helping those in unreasoning despair to move beyond their darkness—whether it results from their teenage fears, the aftermath of pregnancy or the fear of old age. We must also recognize that a time does come when death is an appropriate option which can be welcomed as the appropriate end to a good life.

The cross-cut between medical and societal challenges is even more complex. We are now in the process of deciphering the genetic code. We shall be able to determine the types of diseases which are genetically based and likely to be passed on to children. A growing number of people therefore argue that it will be possible to delete a dangerous gene from a human being so that the quality of life of their children will be better.

The problem with this approach is that we do not know, and will perhaps never totally know, the linkings between genes. We may aim to improve the qualities of the next generation but introduce, instead, new problems. As options of this type increase, how should parents make these choices? Indeed, there may be a prior question. Will the state try to take away the freedom of people with inheritable serious diseases and deny them the right to have children?

Some people want to go still further and start programs to "improve" the human race. They argue that the human race should be bred to achieve certain patterns. But what should we choose? Some would want longer life. But do we know that older people can maintain a high quality of life until their death? Others might want to choose intelligence as their goal. But this is a tricky concept. Do we mean the ability to absorb book learning? Or should we be interested in creativity? These are not necessarily linked and, indeed, may require very different qualities.

Human beings have been successful because of their diversity. They have not specialized as animals into a specific niche. Some people have therefore always been able to see the advantages of new directions. A genetic program which worked to decrease this diversity might well prove to be a severe disadvantage.

The last issue I want to take up in this section is the impact of communication technologies. Only a hundred years ago Carnegie build libraries in many cities. These libraries provided people with a chance to enter the world of ideas for the first time. Today, our problems are totally different from those of the past. We are besieged with more messages than we can possibly absorb or process. We are overloaded with information. And more and more of this information is designed to manipulate our thinking rather than help us see clearly.

The majority of the messages we receive today are screened by others before we receive them. All of us have had the disconcerting experience of being at an event and then watching it on the news and feeling that what was reported did not reflect what we experienced. Part of the problem comes from the fact that each observer sees a different picture. In addition, however, the media know what "news" is and inevitably distorts what goes on to fit into the norms they normally use.

This problem is going to worsen in the immediate future. New technologies, such as "virtual reality" which enable people to act within a totally created world, will further challenge our abilities to understand and make decisions about our lives and societies. It will only be as we understand why it is important to help people learn to learn about reality, and as we can provide ourselves with a story which makes sense of current conditions, that we can hope to break out of current confusions and frustrations.

Looking forward

The primary forces which are currently driving our world emerge from past commitments. People decided that they wanted to achieve certain goals and they succeeded in doing so. The human race has not failed. It has succeeded. It is therefore difficult to understand the grim despair which controls so many who propose fundamental change. Those who deny the capacity of human beings to deal with present crises are turning their backs on the overwhelming evidence that proves that individuals can grow and help others to grow. They are denying the intelligence and resiliency of human beings.

My frustration at the negativity of many professional change agents is only equaled by my disagreement with those who believe that because one has been successful in the past it is possible to continue in the same direction for ever. The mindless optimism of growth-oriented economists and politicians, which denies all the obvious evidence, is deeply depressing. The unwillingness to face any of the major questions of the day, opting instead for diversionary issues, makes it easy to despair.

Fortunately there are millions of people who operate in a quite different mode. These courageous realists look at the changes which are going on in the world and do what they can, in their own situations, to improve dynamics. They are well aware that positive directions do not develop as a result of orders from the top of the society, but rather emerge as a large number of people do a wide variety of things a little bit differently.

This group appreciates the viewpoint of William James, the well-known author, who wrote, "I am done with great things and big things and great institutions and big successes, and I am for those tiny invisible molecular moral forces that work from individual to individual, creeping through the crannies of the world like so many rootlets or like the capillary oozing water, yet which, if you give them time, will bend the hardest monuments of human pride."

When operating as a courageous realist, one sometimes sees oneself as a salmon swimming upstream against a current which is too strong. To break out of this discouraging feeling we need friends and colleagues. The purpose of this book is to help courageous realists find each other. We need to recognize that the essential conflict of the nineties is between those who are prepared to imagine and create fundamental change and those who want to maintain a status quo which is more and more dangerous.

Changing Success Criteria

INDIVIDUAL AND GROUP SURVIVAL IN THE TWENTY-FIRST CENTURY requires fundamentally different behavior compared to the twentieth. All of us need to rethink our current understandings of the world and learn to see it in new ways. This is the only way life can be attractive in today's conditions.

Traditionally, each of us aims to outdo others using the success criteria of the past. We try to go beyond our ancestors. For example, during the industrial era most people have tried to be wealthier. This is still the goal of most people. But now it is being realized that this goal is obsolete because ensuring maximum rates of economic growth is no longer desirable. Rather, we need to ensure ecological balance for as far into the future as we can see.

Changing our success criteria is always a challenge but there are parallels from the past. People had different goals in hunting and gathering societies than in agricultural times. Similarly, the desires of individuals and groups were different in the agricultural period as compared to the industrial era. And now we must move out of the industrial era into the compassionate era.

The need to change success criteria is therefore not new. The fact that each of us has to change our success criteria within our lifespan is, however, totally novel. The current moment of choice is unique. Every previous generation was constrained by the need to toil for a living. Only now, when we have developed effectively unlimited productive and destructive power, do we have the ability to choose life or death for ourselves and our beautiful planet. Each of us influences the route our culture will take by our thoughts and our decision-making which may maintain old patterns or create new and positive ones.

Future generations will envy those of us who have the opportunity to be involved in this process of choice. Our grandchildren will ask us what we did in the nineties and will not understand if we "slept" through this immensely challenging decade. They will wonder how we missed the opportunity to be involved in the creation of a new order.

Patterns of change

I have been discussing the issue of change for forty years. Perhaps the most common response to my ideas has been that I'm saying nothing new because change has always existed and is, indeed, the only constant of human experience. At one level, this is absolutely true. Even hunting and gathering tribes had to cope with seasonal fluctuations and varying weather patterns. Nevertheless people lived out their lives in a known environment where patterns changed slowly because existence was controlled by natural forces and stable cultures.

City-states, based on agriculture, began to have more options. Priests and kings gained power and the lives of the masses were subject to increasing upheavals. But the underlying rhythm of the seasons remained and the sense of vulnerability to natural forces persisted.

The industrial era was based on a fundamentally different concept of change. The idea of controlling nature developed. People began to see how they could benefit from supporting and investing in new ideas and technologies which would alter the conditions in which people lived. A growing gap developed between the young who saw the new conditions as desirable and the old who wanted to preserve the past. Shifts took place as the old died and young people with new ideas took their places. This process was able to keep up with shifting realities because life expectancies were still short and older generations died off before their blocking became too destructive.

This industrial-era generational pattern of change can no longer respond to today's dynamics. Lifespans are now far longer. Much technological development occurs in months rather than years, let alone decades. You and I can therefore no longer afford to complete our lives using the ideas we learned when we were growing up. This is one of the fundamental revolutions of the current period of history. It is also the reason why we must all continue to learn throughout our lives.

An image will help us understand why the nature of our challenges is altering so profoundly. Think about the eye of a hurricane. On one side of the eye, the storm hits from a particular quarter. If a craft passes through the quiet eye, the wind then hits it from the opposite side as it moves into the turbulence again. We can think of our culture as passing through the eye of a cultural hurricane.

The industrial era created a storm of modernization and materialism. The eighties were the eye of the hurricane. Maximum economic growth, national sovereignty and the importance of weaponry were supported most strongly just as their realities were fading away. This is not unusual. Frequently in history a set of beliefs is most discussed, and used, when it is losing its vitality. People cling to old beliefs when they feel they are being overwhelmed by new realities.

The world is now moving out of the eye on the other side of the turbulence. The commitment to maximum growth is being replaced by a desire to increase the quality of life and to preserve the environment. The danger of the growing split between the rich and the poor, within and between countries, is increasingly perceived as both intolerable and highly dangerous. The gender gap is growing as more women than men sense that the time has come to abandon violence against other people and the environment; this gap is increasingly visible in voting patterns.

Given these fundamental alterations in perception, many people are now looking for shifts which will move us in the opposite direction to those which are still being proposed by almost all academics and politicians. Most intellectual and establishment decision-makers have not adapted to the fact that the move through the eye of the hurricane is essentially complete. They are still proposing directions which were appropriate in the past.

Unfortunately many people who are most aware that we face very new challenges are ineffective because they conduct their discussions at a very high level of abstraction. All too often their arguments are stated in ways which make the general public feel incompetent to grasp the realities of our time. I use a very different style. One of my colleagues, Joseph Coates, keeps telling me why he feels my work is unique. He says I am the only futurist he knows who is both concerned with the big issues and also wants to communicate their meaning to citizens.

The stance I take is obviously related to the way I see the world. I do not believe a small elite group can manage the change process. I am convinced that a much broader range of leaders must be willing to support the new directions society so urgently needs. I am deeply in tune with the statement which was taught me many years ago: "At the end of every intellectual journey lies common sense."

I have therefore spent much of my life encouraging people to develop new leadership styles based on knowledge and skills rather than power and manipulation. This work has been immensely rewarding at one level because I have seen people develop and grow. At another level, it has been frustrating because all too often those with whom I have worked have chosen to remain on the margin of the society rather than impacting its core dynamics. The need to become involved with the mainstream is growing rapidly as the scope of crises continues to broaden.

One of the paradoxes of the nineties is that the poor countries can move from the agricultural to the compassionate era with far less trauma than the rich if they are willing to face up to the requirements of the twenty-first century. This route can only be taken, however, if the poor countries are willing to challenge the agendas of the international institutions which are dominated by the rich countries.

An historical perspective

One of the major surprises of the coming compassionate era is that there is a real similarity between the views of people who lived in hunting and gathering societies and the views we need in the future. The common thread is that we need to see ourselves as embedded in nature.

In hunting and gathering societies the natural order was viewed as permanent. It was believed that nature should be propitiated and its functioning could be influenced by the proper activities of shamans and witchdoctors. Life was dominated by tradition. The cult movie classic *The Gods Must be Crazy* explored what happened when a coke bottle was found by a primitive tribe. In a world where there were stable patterns, and everything was shared, the bottle disrupted a long-run balance among individuals and groups in the tribe and therefore had to be destroyed despite its utility. The comedy in the film came from the adventures and misunderstandings which developed as primitive and modern mind-sets came into contact.

Industrial-era human beings, on the other hand, began to believe they could overwhelm nature. Our existing buildings, agriculture, and our very way of life proclaim the belief that human beings are invincible. Nature was squeezed out of the picture until Rachel Carson started its renaissance. As we move toward the twenty-first century, we are recognizing that natural forces are far more powerful than the most massive of humanity's efforts. Earthquakes and hurricanes dwarf the power available to human beings even today. We are learning that we shall either collaborate with natural forces or the feedback from them will prove increasingly disruptive and destructive.

The best scientists are learning that human actions can affect the direction of events but not control them. They are also aware that small triggering events can have huge consequences when the time is ripe. Large efforts, on the other hand, may have no significant impact if they aim to overcome dominant trends. These modern views are totally incompatible with the mechanical cause and effect universe which dominated the industrial era, where a given cause was always assumed to have the same impact.

Order was preserved in the industrial world by the belief that the people at the top of systems were knowledgeable and could therefore be trusted to do what was right. So long as people accepted this way of thinking, the system worked. The people in charge made mistakes but most of them were never visible because the establishment held together and covered up its weaknesses and its mistakes.

One can see the differences between today and the past by considering how differently Presidents are treated. President Roosevelt was hardly ever photographed so that his wheelchair was visible: it was thought by all concerned that this decreased the dignity of the office. Today the media dramatizes the failures of every public figure, from their sexual behavior to their tumbles down aircraft steps.

We have reached a "breakpoint," to use a term created by Beth Jarman and George Land; the approaches which served us in the past damage us today. What then is the way forward given that current models and approaches are not only obsolete but destructive? The first step is to recognize that in any given situation people will inevitably approach a subject from many different viewpoints. Nobody ever has all the truth. Our views are distorted by our past, our genes, our sex and our age.

One of the emphases of our time must be to help people really listen to others rather than to wait for the moment at which they can get their own ideas into the debate. This change of style is of course difficult because most individuals and groups are more interested in supporting their directions than in searching for the truth. The need for this shift is, however, inarguable.

A far more difficult question emerges from the fact that everybody's perception is not of equal relevance. Dialogue requires more than a search for consensus; it demands a drive to find the truth. In all groups, some people do not have the facts to make an informed judgment. Some think in cause-and-effect terms rather the system style which is required for clear understandings. Some ignore the fact that "wishing does not make it so."

While dialogue styles are indeed essential for the future, they can nevertheless lead to all sorts of dangerous errors. The two most destructive lie at different ends of a continuum. At one end, it is argued that all perceptions are equally valid—that there is no way of distinguish between the relevance of ideas. This first pattern of thought leads to the belief that all forms of thinking are equally valid. Visionary planning becomes impossible. We become lost in a maze of individually expressed thoughts, none of which seems to have any greater meaning than another. Purpose and vitality are lost beyond recall.

The other danger results from people who accept that all reality is perceptual but then claim that their own perceptual ability is always superior to that of others; this approach may seem internally contradictory but I know of many people who believe it is valid. Effective dialogue is also destroyed by this approach because one of the people in the group claims the absolute right to decide how the discussion should go.

Dialogue styles are difficult because those who practice them need to walk a tight-rope accepting that our ideas may be wrong but we must advance them until they are changed by better input. The people who are most skilled in compassionate-era activities are therefore confusing and threatening to those who use industrial-era styles because the two groups see the world totally differently. Industrial-era leaders believe they must control people and dynamics. Compassionate-era leaders are most effective when they support people who are ready and willing to be active. They nudge and encourage, rather than force, positive directions whenever possible.

It is extremely difficult to write about the shift between the industrial era and the compassionate era without seeming to imply that the industrial era was an error. It is therefore important to state that the industrial era was not "wrong," anymore than adolescence is wrong. Nevertheless, our new stage in human evolution requires the abandonment of industrial-era ideas and their replacement with more complex thought patterns. The simplicities of the past are inadequate to the realities of the present.

To be effective in the future, society must abandon the conventionally easy responses which are used when actions do not achieve desired results. One common pattern today is to put more energy behind the same actions. For example, nearly everybody now agrees that the schools are not meeting the needs of students but the response in almost all areas of the world has been to affirm existing systems and to do more of what has been done in the past. Another common response is to put "band-aids on cancers" which are, after all, depressing and ugly! Small, cosmetic changes are made but the breakdowns continue to expand in scope because the real difficulties are being ignored rather than faced.

There is an old image which is still helpful. A town kept on finding bodies at the bottom of a precipice near the edge of the community. The community divided itself into three groups. One wanted to improve the response times of ambulances. A second wanted to build a fence around the cliff so people could not fall over by mistake. A third favored changing peoples' attitudes and skills so they would not be tempted to play near the cliff nor to climb it without adequate skills. Only the third approach holds any hope for the future.

Today's industrial-era planning is based on data and information. Actions are determined—in theory—by objective approaches. The dominant appeal is to logic and rationality. The first step in the transition to the compassionate era is to accept the importance of intuition. One discovers what seems worth doing as an individual or group and then puts together the skills and resources to move from visioning to reality. In doing so, people recognize that they are themselves part of a solution.

I remember talking to a group of school superintendents in Wisconsin. One of them, in particular, had given up hope despite the fact that he had been a "radical" in the sixties. Facing the reality that positive visions were possible was very difficult for him. He had to abandon the despair which had governed his life for years and, indeed, made it tolerable! He had built his life around attacking others for their failures rather than thinking about what he, himself, could do effectively.

If I am right in my belief that many people are ready for fundamental change, why does so little seem to be happening? Many positive shifts are actually taking place but our culture is looking at the negatives, particularly in media attention. I have been promoting the idea of a news segment called "It's Working" for many years. I have been delighted to see NBC Nightly News adopt a similar idea: I am now sometimes able to get communities to pick up the concept on a local level. Reporters then comment on what is going right in the community rather than reporting on the breakdowns, the rapes and the murders.

We are suffering from the problem of "the competent, but isolated, many." Most people today feel alone in their efforts to improve the functioning of the culture. This makes them less willing to take risks and reduces the overall effectiveness of the movement toward new attitudes and directions.

A useful image for understanding how change could take place in these circumstances is to think of the current society as a forming crystal in a super-saturated chemical solution. The crystal can grow rapidly under these circumstances. Unless conditions are exactly right, however, additions to the crystal will not take place or will be flawed. Organizational processes for fundamental change activities must therefore be planned very carefully in their early stages if they are to attract the people who know enough to support the desired goals, rather than disrupt them. Later on, the process becomes almost automatic and self-generating.

Beyond the American dream

Where do we go from here? One of the most important shifts is to commit to environmental balance rather than economic growth. Many problems can be reduced by limiting the amount of energy and materials usage, and above all, waste. The more we invest and consume, the greater the impact on the environment. The less we use and waste, the better the situation.

E. F. Schumacher made this point clearly in his influential book *Small is Beautiful:*

> An attitude to life which seeks fulfillment in the single-minded pursuit of wealth—in short materialism—does not fit into this world, because it contains within itself no limiting principle, while the environment in which it is placed is strictly limited. Already the environment is trying to tell us that certain stresses are becoming excessive. As one problem is "solved" ten new ones arise as a result of this first "solution." The new problems are not the consequences of incidental failure, but of technological successes.

Perhaps the most visible challenge is the ever-increasing use of the automobile. I am old enough to remember when the first dual-track roads were introduced into Britain just before World War II. We all marvelled at the potential for car ownership and higher speeds. Today, roads continue to be built although there is clear-cut evidence that traffic increases to fill the available road space and that the average speed of automobiles continues to fall in cities.

The automobile was originally a luxury. It quickly turned into a necessity. Now it is becoming a burden. The Los Angeles area has faced up to this evolution and begun to come to grips with the realities of both limited energy resources and ecological threats. Unfortunately, most of the homes and businesses in the state have been built in a way that relies on cars. It will take a long time to change habitation patterns so that people can once again live in their neighborhoods, only leaving when they want to do so rather than because what they want is not available within walking distance.

California has the excuse that their major choices of habitation patterns were made before traffic patterns were really understood. The Seattle area, on the other hand, is doing most of the damage after the costs are far better known. They are moving toward gridlock throughout the metropolitan area. Citizens complain but politicians seem unable to come to grips with the issue. They are, indeed, more or less powerless.

Many of our current problems are related to an American constitution which was written when the population was small. The thought that mobility might have to be limited to preserve the quality of life would have seemed ridiculous to the founding fathers. It is only today that we are beginning to recognize that densities may become so great that they can destroy the quality of life—Oahu, the most populous island in Hawaii, provides a perfect example of this dilemma. In addition, the major fires in Santa Barbara and Oakland, California confirm the dangers of ignoring ecological limits. The continuing drought has made death-traps of desirable homes.

Let me now move from a large-scale issue of system design to one where each of us can make an immediate difference. There is today a major controversy as to whether paper sacks or plastic in landfills are more dangerous to the environment. A case can be made by both sides. The extraordinary fact is that few people have yet realized that both paper and plastics are far more destructive than an available alternative. Most Europeans carried cloth bags or wicker baskets in the past and a large number still do, thus reducing the need for either plastic or paper.

This brings up the broader subject of packaging. All too often packaging today is bulkier that the product, and sometimes seems more valuable! There is a need to rethink the way in which goods move, how far they move and how much protection they really require. Those who are going back to buying in bulk are discovering just how much of the cost of groceries reflects the excessive cost of modern packaging.

Waste is currently so much a part of our lives that it is often invisible. One major reason for unnecessary use of materials is accelerated obsolescence. Products are not made to last the optimum length of time. Even when they are, advertisers still often try to convince people that the "new" model makes it essential for them to replace their current one earlier than is required from an economic or technological viewpoint. Fortunately, this pattern is changing. The snoozing Maytag repairman used to be an oddity—now the advertisement reflects the reputation many firms would love to possess. More and more cars are boasting of their higher quality and the increased resale value due to their longer life.

People are becoming more and more aware of the problems associated with excessive waste. As landfills close and water supplies are threatened by chemicals, there is increasing understanding that it makes sense to throw less away. Cities like Seattle are charging households on the basis of their garbage *weight*. People are learning to be more careful in creating waste and even to take pride, as people did in earlier generations, in how little they have for the garbage collector. Unfortunately, municipal waste is only a tiny proportion of the total waste stream, maybe less than 2%. Real recycling progress depends on changing the behaviors of producers and the military—fortunately shifts are developing here also.

The real issue, of course, is changing the underlying habits, principles and values by which we live. Most of us have been brought up to believe that we always need 10 to 25% more than we already have or can afford! We are always striving to do more, to have more, to travel to new places. The brass ring is always just out of reach but we "know" it can be obtained if only we try a little harder, or are lucky. So long as we hold this view, production and waste will inevitably increase.

The American dream has spread throughout the world. When people complain that it is no longer available, this statement usually means that they are unhappy about the slow rise in the standard of living and, in many cases, its decline. We are still encouraging young people to believe they can have it "all" despite the contrary evidence and the fact that many teenagers already recognize that they will not be richer than their parents.

E. F. Schumacher caught the heart of this issue also:

> The cultivation and expansion of needs is the antithesis of wisdom. It is also the antithesis of freedom and peace. Every increase of needs tends to increase one's dependence on outside forces over which one cannot have control, and therefore increases existential fear. Only by a reduction of needs can one promote a genuine reduction in those tensions which are the ultimate causes of strife and war.

We have to learn to live with "enoughness." Accepting what one had was the norm before the expansiveness of the industrial era. People had a different vision of the "good life" or, perhaps, the feasible life. Most people did as well as they could with what they had. The idea of finding the "pot of gold at the end of the rainbow" emerged during the nineteenth century. Consequently the idea of "enough" is perceived as constraining freedom, forcing people to give up their dreams, to settle for less, to fail to reach one's potential. But there is another far more positive side to the concept of "enoughness." It can be a way of reducing the clutter in one's life, of deciding what is truly important and working to attain it.

Overload patterns, which frustrate us increasingly, develop because we want it all. Are we really better off when we are always rushing after the latest sensation rather than enjoying the tried and the true? Surely moments of quiet are worth struggling to maintain through all the busyness which the culture thrusts upon us. Is it good for kids to have everything they want at an early age and to discover later how difficult it is to maintain these high standards for themselves?

Across the country people are choosing to cut back. Dennis

Hammond of Minneapolis put it this way:

> All humans of every color seek happiness, but most of us don't know
> what it is or how to get it. Happiness is . . . not having and having
> and having. There's nothing wrong with goods, but they've become
> the focus, and the spiritual aspect is more important if we want to
> know peace and contentment.

Enough is not scarcity. Nor is it excess. Enough lies at a quiet
balance point which each of us must find in the light of our own energies,
lifestyles and the overall resources of the world in which we live. The
vast majority of those in the rich countries will have to learn to live with
less as we move through the twenty-first century. On the other hand, the
poor in the rich countries and the vast majority of the people in the poor
countries must be able to move out of the extreme scarcity which
destroys so many of their lives.

If we are to achieve the necessary balancing, the process of learning
must inevitably go both ways. The rich countries must discover how the
poor countries manage with what appears, from the outside, to be a
totally inadequate amount of resources. The poor countries can benefit
from the knowledge created in the technologically advanced world
without dreaming they can adopt lifestyles which are no longer
sustainable. All of us can then have a higher quality of life. We can learn
to value other experiences besides consumption and live by a different
set of values than those which dominated the industrial era.

Avoiding breakdowns

There are two options for bringing about change. One is to enable
people to educate themselves so they can keep up with the changing
needs of the world. The alternative route is to reinforce the current legal
structures and make them increasingly draconian. For example, the
government in China imposed population control because densities are
already so great that further increases would clearly decrease the quality
of life.

Open systems are more desirable and effective over the long-run. But
they only work if people understand the realities of the time and are
willing to make the hard choices necessary for survival. Maintenance of
free and open systems will be impossible if the strain on human, energy
and ecological systems is so high that people are unable and unwilling
to learn new ways of looking at the world. Indeed, this is the central
danger of our time because most people are so overstressed that they feel
that the problems we face are insoluble.

Perhaps the most urgent and difficult issue is the need to shift our perception of success. The rich countries have come to define success in terms of greater production and consumption. In an ecologically limited world, this vision cannot be maintained. The rich countries must cut back in order to make space for greater production in the poor.

It is easiest to demonstrate this issue in the field of energy. The U.S. currently uses far more energy per person than other nations. One inevitable reason is the huge distances compared with Europe. Another factor, which can and should be changed, is the unwillingness to tax fossil fuels at rates which have been accepted almost everywhere else in the world. Energy is too cheap in the U.S.

Many of our problems result from careless thinking. Most analysts still concentrate on miles per gallon rather than considering the amount of energy used from the time the automobile is built to the time it is scrapped. There is strong evidence that it is better to keep using a gas guzzler for as long as possible—to avoid building a new car—although this conclusion may change when the impact of pollution is added.

The energy cost of having to build a new car to replace a scrapped vehicle is far higher than any potential savings from better gas mileage. People are therefore recognizing that it is cheaper to keep a car far longer, even though energy analysts have still not caught up with this trend. The average age of automobiles in the U.S. has risen dramatically in the past decade: indeed this is one of the reasons for the slowdown in the growth of economic production.

A decision to raise the price of energy to European levels would dramatically change the shape of American life over the next twenty years. Travel would inevitably decrease because people would change their priorities. Decisions currently being made about needed airports and highways would inevitably be dramatically altered by an irreversible decision to increase energy costs as I propose in Chapter 5.

It is still believed by many that because total fossil fuel energy reserves in the world are high, there will be no energy problem for centuries. It is also argued that technology will inevitably develop new energy sources during the time which is available before fossil fuel resources run out. There are two profound flaws in this style of thinking, which taken together, demand radical changes in analysis and action during the nineties.

First, the relevant concept with which society must deal is not total energy reserves but rather net energy reserves. It always costs energy to obtain energy. The deeper the wells and the tougher the environment where wells are dug, the smaller the net energy which will be generated. The decline in net energy yields in the U.S. has already been dramatic.

The magnitude of the problem can be shown by the fact that the break-even cost to get a barrel of oil out of the ground in much of the Middle East is often under $2 per barrel while United States producers need a stable price near $20 to make a profit.

When looking at potential production, it is first essential to remember that some fossil fuels are present in forms which are unlikely to yield net energy at any time in the future. Oil shales, for example, which were seen as a possible savior for the energy hunger of the Western world in the seventies, now seem to hold little potential. The amount of energy needed to free the oil shales from the rock in which they are held is so great that past experiments have cost energy rather than gained it. Indeed, even if it were possible to produce net energy, the effective use of these "resources" remains very unlikely because their processing is water-intensive and deposits are located primarily in the West where surplus water is almost non-existent.

The net energy ratio will therefore continue to worsen over time as oil and gas have to be sought in less and less favorable conditions. A similar, although less dramatic, pattern exists for minerals, although there are still untapped reserves of some of them for many centuries. Nevertheless, the richest and most easily accessible ores have already been used up. This issue again relates to energy. If there is less net energy, and if the cost of working minerals is also rising, then the ability of societies to afford the extraction of metals will decline.

Unfortunately, President Bush sees no reason to limit energy demand and continues to concentrate on increasing supply. In the light of declining U.S. oil production and the inevitable instability in the Middle East, it is not surprising that President Bush's initial 1991 energy proposal was characterized by Senator Albert Gore as "breathtakingly dumb." Wilfred Kohl, director of the energy program at the John Hopkins School of Advanced Energy Studies, described it more temperately as "terribly mistaken."

The other reason for limiting fossil fuel usage is the danger of atmospheric degradation and climatic change. Cutting back on global levels of fossil fuel usage will, however, be very difficult. Any reduction in use in the rich countries will be swamped by increased needs in the poor country unless patterns of development change dramatically. The dangers are increased because most poor countries are still not widely aware of the necessity of planning in ways which reduce the dangers from fossil-fuel emissions.

The possible problems are demonstrated in a decision by the Chinese to provide families with refrigerators. Unfortunately their design was extremely inefficient and required the burning of far greater amounts of coal to produce energy than was theoretically necessary. Because China's coal is extremely dirty, the consequences for the atmosphere of China, and indeed the whole of the world, will be very serious.

World-wide decisions to reduce fossil fuel usage would raise two central questions. First, how much can energy usage be cut while maintaining, or improving the quality of life? We are beginning to recognize that better results can be achieved using less resources. Analysts like Amory Lovins have shown us that we are wasting huge amounts of energy. There have already been extraordinary gains in energy efficiency following the oil shocks of the seventies; these show what can be achieved. A study of energy use at the Lawrence Berkeley Laboratory "found that energy use in the U.S. per unit of activity or output fell 21% between 1973 and 1987."

We should certainly use the knowledge that is being developed by the Lovinses and others to limit throughput. (Throughput describes the total amount of energy, materials, goods and services which flow through the economy.) Indeed as one broadens one's perspective, it becomes clear just how significant the reductions could be. For example, if people decided to live on a vegetarian diet, the usage of fossil fuels would decline dramatically. It has been estimated that it takes 78 fossil fuel calories to get one calorie of protein from beef as opposed to only 2 fossil fuel calories to get one food calorie from soybeans, a food which is also high in protein. Movement in this direction will increase as people recognize that they can be healthier if fewer of their calories come from a meat diet.

A great deal can therefore be done by increasing efficiency and changing lifestyles. But there is still a second, very difficult, issue. So long as we maintain a commitment to maximum economic growth strategies, any gains in efficiency will be overwhelmed by the impact of increased production. Dr. Len Brookes, former Chief Economist of the UK Atomic Energy Authority, made the point this way: "One has to be absolutely clear about whether one is trying to improve economic performance or whether we are acting to reduce carbon emissions to avoid a global catastrophe. If we are trying to reduce carbon emissions, then we will have to reduce economic activity on a worldwide scale. Don't kid yourself that an easy solution like energy efficiency will reduce the total demand for energy, it just doesn't work this way." So long as our current economic system continues, the energy which is saved in one part of the system will be used elsewhere.

Significant progress can only be made after we recognize that a commitment to balancing ecological systems cannot coexist with a continuance of maximum economic growth policies. The *Brundtland Report* to the United Nations on the environment failed to face this reality. We shall therefore have to examine which of the activities and structures we created in the industrial era can be supported in the future.

In order to make these choices, we must make realistic assumptions about the maximum amount of energy which will be available to support each human being in the future. The three major currently visible alternatives to fossil fuels are first, conservation; second, renewables such as solar, wind, biomass, etc.; and, third, nuclear. Even with maximum advantage taken from conservation, there will still be a gap which has to be filled from new energy sources to maintain current standards.

The net energy available from solar, winds, tides, biomass etc. is still a matter of great controversy. While gross energy can obviously be generated, the net energy to be gained is still uncertain. There are two issues which need to be clarified. First, what are the maximum potential yields from various natural systems? This is a matter of analysis where answers can be reasonably accurate. Many of the euphoric estimates which were based on the amount of solar energy striking the atmosphere have turned out to be far too optimistic in terms of actual available energy on earth.

The second is what are the best technologies which can eventually be devised to take advantage of the energy which is available from renewable resources. Unfortunately, this type of research has been starved in the Reagan and Bush years and there is little idea of the degree to which costs can be reduced for various types of natural systems. It is easy to produce energy flows once systems are set up: it is far harder to prove that significant net energy can be generated in this way if one takes full account of invention, production and maintenance costs.

The final major existing possibility is from nuclear power. Attitudes in various parts of the world are very different. The French now get a great deal of their energy from nuclear power and do not seem to be too troubled by the safety issues which have traumatized the U.S. The British also have placed greater faith in nuclear than America. If the developed countries want to maintain a reasonable quality of life, and if the developing world hopes to achieve it, the nuclear issue will have to be reopened. Some believe that the options will be stark. Use nuclear and be able to maintain a reasonable level of comfort. Abandon it and watch a rapid slide in standards as fossil fuel use is restricted to meet the needs of future generations. This fall in standards could create such high levels of social tension that the possibility of moving toward responsible freedom would cease to exist.

The extreme views on nuclear energy are clear. Opponents see it as too dangerous and environmentally damaging. Proponents paint it as the most effective, non-polluting technology. Nobody would deny that past practices in the nuclear industry, based on fission, have been sloppy and dangerous. There is, however, considerable evidence that standards can be dramatically improved in the future. The question is whether this will be enough to make the technology safe and cost-effective. I do not know the answer to questions of fission, but I am certain that it is only as opponents and proponents listen to each other that clarity can be achieved.

Other analysts believe that fusion should be the goal, arguing that it will produce cheap, clean, abundant energy. Apart from the fact that fusion has not yet been proved to be feasible, critics of this answer remember that this is the same type of slogan which was initially used to justify fission. Fission was going to produce electricity which would be "too cheap to meter." Human beings like to believe that the next technology will be the one which works perfectly but the record shows that they are always problems and side-effects.

Relevant discussion of possibilities on any subject must always cover the unexpected. Is some totally new energy technology waiting in the wings? What about some of the technologies which are already being discussed, such as the potential of hydrogen power? The obvious problem with relying on new technologies is the crises which will develop if they do not arrive on time. The urgent need is for open-minded energy analysts to provide citizens with the clearest possible statement of options and choices which can then be used to determine appropriate directions in the context of already-developing environmental stress.

An overview of the recent past

There have been extraordinary changes in our general situation as we moved out of the fifties, through the sixties, seventies, and eighties and are now entering the nineties. In the fifties, we lived in a society which believed that things were just about as good as they could be. Rapid economic growth was occurring after the second world war. People were trading up. Shortages and rationing were ending throughout the developed world. President Eisenhower presided over a period of complacency.

In the sixties, President Kennedy opened a challenge. His recognition of the need for social justice led many people to struggle to advance the conditions of blacks, women and the young. The sixties were an exciting decade when it appeared that conditions were ripe for massive change. This was a false dawn, however. Many people were prepared to talk about far-out ideas but only because they "knew" they would never be taken seriously. I was involved in promoting change at this time.

The seventies were a period of withdrawal. People found themselves threatened by both the pace of change and by worsening economic conditions. Apart from the successes of the black and women's movement, there was a general feeling of withdrawing into one's shell, hunkering down and looking inward. People changed from being apathetic to being frightened. Unfortunately most change agents continued to talk about the problems, rather than the solutions, thus driving people further into disillusionment. President Carter tried to warn us of the need for change but we preferred to go on a final binge.

This was exactly what we did in the eighties. We overspent. We ran up debts both internally and internationally. We acted as though tomorrow would never come. We admired the rich and the famous and ignored the disadvantaged. We put off the bills until later. We thought that the yuppies, who represented 2% of the population, were the wave of the future and failed to see the deepening poverty.

In the nineties the bills have come due and the attitudes of the general public are changing dramatically. The sense that America is off course is shared by a growing number of people. It is my strong belief that, as a result, positive energy is available in the nineties, just as it was in the sixties. People are altering their perceptions of their self-interest more rapidly than we realize. Obviously, this positive energy must be expressed in different ways if it is to be effective.

Unfortunately, these new patterns of thinking all too often clash with past attitudes and laws. As positive adaptations to new hopeful realities occur, some people are threatened. They then cling more and more strongly to attitudes, structures and beliefs that have been made obsolete by technological changes. The clash today is between those who are able and willing to move with the positive potentials of our times and those who would deny the desirability of profoundly new systems.

It is not difficult for those who oppose change to organize. All they have to do is claim that innovations are undesirable and unnecessary. Proposals to return to the past can be stated in clear-cut ways and require little of those who support them. For example, all of us find it difficult to cope with the implications of new biological and medical knowledge. The opposition to rethinking birth control, abortion and the right to death stem from a desire to cling to attitudes and value patterns which made sense when human beings had less knowledge.

Those who want to break out of the past face a more challenging task. For the first time in history, human beings must consciously examine all the fundamental directions they support. Nothing can remain unquestioned. There are no longer any certainties except the need for a commitment to a moral, value-based culture. We are being challenged to take a further quantum leap in our understandings of responsible freedom.

The learnings we must achieve are not, however, new. They have been taught us in the past by the great religious and spiritual traditions. We must become honest, responsible, loving and humble and understand that there will always be mysteries in life we must respect.

Traditional spiritual understandings are today supported by modern secular knowledge. There is no longer a clash between advanced theology and intelligent intellectual thinking. It is therefore time for people from these two groups to come together, challenging humanity to develop the behaviors which are vital for the twenty-first century. Forward-looking people must look for allies in new ways. The key to alignment is a willingness to listen and learn together. The new coalition will be between all the people who believe in cooperation and a value-based culture. This is the wave of the future.

It is particularly critical that we move beyond the belief that "they" won't let us do it. "They" typically means the people in power. The tragedy I have found in many situations is that the majority of people in a system may want change but still be unable to get together because of their distrust for each other. Take a typical school situation. All the players—the teachers, the school board, the management, the parents, the staff, the children—assume that it is the other groups which are preventing forward movement. In fact, my experience shows that if these groups would only talk to each other, there would be shared interest in a profoundly different system which would enable kids to learn more effectively.

The argument about "they" and "them" sometimes gets carried to ludicrous extremes. I have been in situations where groups have argued that something cannot be achieved because "they" won't allow it. I have had to remind them that they are talking about themselves; they are the people who have the responsibility and the power to take the steps which they claim are impossible because of outside opposition!

Given the magnitude of the problems which confront us, how can I believe that we shall seize our possibilities rather than be overwhelmed by our problems? I remain positive because I know that people have already changed their perceptions of their self-interest. They know they should save the environment, limit violence, promote justice and redesign the socioeconomy. They are looking for ways to do this cooperatively. It is our joint responsibility as leaders to provide ourselves with the opportunity to be effective.

Change at the required scale has not been achieved because there is no sufficiently broad picture which permits a variety of positive groups to develop a common cause. There is still a great deal of unnecessary disagreement between those who understand that there must be fundamental alterations in patterns. We need to weave a coherent story and vision so that our various activities will be seen as moving humanity in the same direction rather than being competitive for scarce resources.

Because there have already been so many profound changes in technology and the way we perceive reality, major future alterations in the way we think, behave and act are inevitable. Whether the changes are positive or negative depends on our individual and group actions. The nineties will be the decade in which the main patterns of the twenty-first century will be set. This book provides a framework for action so that we can be ready for the twenty-first century.

If I were still thinking as a rational analyst, who must be all too well aware of the strength of inertial forces in cultures, I would necessarily be profoundly pessimistic about our future. Fortunately, I have given up this style of thinking and become a courageous realist. I know that fundamental change is possible and that many people are ready to support it. We do not need to begin a change in directions. Our task is easier. We are challenged to support the process which is already moving forward, and to do it as intelligently as we can.

Mindquakes

RADICALS WHO AIMED TO REMAKE THE WORLD drove the turbulent sixties. They were uninterested in real conditions and the complications posed by existing systems. They believed that moving the people in charge out of power would be enough. They lacked sensitivity to the saying that "If the devil should become God, he would have to act like God." They failed to see people are constrained by their positions and until their responsibilities are altered the potential for different behavior is minimal.

Change in the nineties, if it is to be successful, must be brought about by fundamentally different processes. We need people who are sensitive to the needs of people and systems and who realize the difficulty of changing the minds of individuals and the patterns of institutions. The people who will cause change in this last decade of the twentieth century do not come from one particular class or group. They are scattered through the society. Some of them have power and position, some of them work in the "trenches."

Change happens most effectively when those struggling in the trenches have the attention of the visionaries who are developing ideas and action plans to share with the general public. If society is to change fast enough to keep up with the ever-shifting realities of our time, we must discard the distrust of the creative thinker for the activist, and of the activist for the thinker. Both groups can then struggle to find out how to work with each other, talking through emerging perceptions of what will be effective.

In addition, both creative thinkers and activists need to seek out those people who can provide the necessary skills to make their thinking and actions effective. While many professionals are wedded to old styles of behavior, others are looking for ways to support the birth of the compassionate era. Wanting to do good is not enough; the approaches we use must be appropriate to the realities of today's world if we are to have the impact we so urgently need.

If the people who are committed to equity and social justice fail to move soon, there is no doubt that negative forces can seize the energy which is being created by the imbalances throughout the world. There have been all too many examples in history of positive energies turning sour when their potentials have been denied. For example, Patrick Buchanan hoped to capitalize on the desire to avoid the continuing development of diversity and the consequent creation of pluralistic forms of government. It is critically important to understand the Buchanan phenomenon because he excites voters while most other candidates seem "boring." For many years, most people have chosen their politicians because they were the lesser of two evils. Neither political party has seemed relevant and a growing number of people have chosen not to vote. Others, while wishing they could use the Russian system which permits them to vote "against," have chosen the candidate who seemed least intolerable. Buchanan breaks through this model by promising a return to a past, which seems rosy in retrospect.

Similarly, Ross Perot gained a great deal of commitment even before there was any clear idea what his directions would be. People were looking for somebody other than President Bush and Governor Clinton. The fact that they did not know what he stood for seemed unimportant compared to sending a protest message.

Those of us who want to create a compassionate era will only be able to do so if we help people understand and support fundamentally new directions, which currently often seem threatening, but actually promise great progress. We must therefore learn how to deal with mindquakes. A "mindquake" describes the process by which our fundamental ideas change to keep up with the ever-shifting world.

I coined the world mindquake as a deliberate parallel to the processes involved in earthquakes. Just as a series of small earthquakes is less destructive than a large one, a process of gradual steps which changes the way we think toward the new realities of our time, is better than a massive shift. Understandings must be flexible enough so we can continuously revise them as new realities emerge.

Considerable knowledge already exists about managing mindquakes. Unfortunately it is not yet fully used. All too often we react to change by trying to restore the patterns of the past rather than keeping up with the implications of change. For example, we ask how people can find jobs rather than consider wider questions such as what work which will be available as computers develop further, how tasks should be structured and what sort of financial and prestige rewards will be appropriate for various kinds of activity. Similarly, many discussions about population continue to support behavioral norms which were conceived for an empty world and create tragic consequences in a crowded one.

Decades ago, the novelist Herbert George Wells argued that life is a race between education and disaster. His statement is more true today than when he first wrote because the scope of potential opportunities and disasters has increased throughout the twentieth century. To take advantage of them we must learn to support mindquakes rather than leave people frustrated by forces which they feel they cannot control.

I first started to develop ideas which challenged existing patterns of thought in the fifties. I naively believed my challenges would be welcomed. I went to the Dean of the Harvard School of Public Administration and told him about my new concepts. I left stunned because he told me, in effect, that if the ideas were new, they were not significant. Alternatively, he stated that if my ideas were significant, they were not new!

After long reflection, I have understood that I could not possibly have received any better introduction to the difficulties of altering thinking. Social change never comes easily. Facing the fact that people tend to maintain obsolete understandings is particularly important at the current time. For example, today's economists are no more willing to rethink their fundamental goals than their predecessors who caused the great depression of the thirties.

Sixty years ago, the goal of economists and politicians was fiscal responsibility and a balanced budget. Because of these theories, government activities contracted as revenues fell and the economy was therefore unable to rebalance itself: the great depression developed. So long as a balanced budget remained sacrosanct, the changing realities of the thirties were ignored and, in a very real sense, invisible. In the nineties, the key priority of economists and politicians is maximum economic growth and labor force participation, whatever the human and social consequences of these directions. So far, the evidence that this emphasis is inappropriate, and indeed, dangerous has hardly shaken the commitment to it at all.

Perceived self-interest is the driver of change

There is today an extraordinary clash between positive and negative trends. The negative trends are more and more obvious and are much commented—the increase in poverty, the rise in crime, the breakdown in health care, the failing infrastructure. But as one looks around in communities one finds all sorts of building processes that are healing long-term rifts and creating new processes and structures.

The challenge today is to increase our skills so that we can be more effective in supporting the, often invisible, positive directions. The prime reality we must grasp is that changes in thought and action take place as people alter their patterns of understanding. Each of us does what seems good to us given all the circumstances of which we are aware at the time we take our decisions. It is therefore essential to understand what motivates various individuals and groups.

Understanding motivations and communicating about them is inevitably difficult. I'll illustrate this at an apparently trivial level with a story which deals with the interactions between a cat and a human being. A frustrated home-owner was trying to deal with his cat which clawed at and damaged his curtains. Trying to show his displeasure, the man threw the cat out of the house each time she did so. The cat eventually learned that the way to get out of the house was to claw the curtains! If they could have talked to each other, they might well have used the classic phrase: "What we have here is a failure to communicate!"

People, and indeed all organisms, follow their perceived self-interest. The homeowner wanted to deal with a problem. He wanted to convey his displeasure about the cat's behavior and chose a route which seemed appropriate to him—expecting the cat to learn not to claw the curtains. The cat, who initially clawed the curtains because it satisfied an instinctual need, took all the data available to her, saw that clawing the curtains resulted in getting out of the house, and learned that the way to communicate to the man her need to get out was to claw the curtains. The cat's behavior pattern had been reinforced rather than changed.

When a person sends a message to another person or organism, there is no certainty it will be understood correctly. In most cases, indeed, the message will be significantly distorted. This is the lesson one learns in the game when people pass a sentence from one end of a line to the other. The final wording often seems to bear little relationship to the one at the beginning. Obviously the potential for misunderstanding more complex messages and interactions is far greater.

The essential bedrock for understanding reality is that each person, even the most mentally ill and the pathological, thinks and acts in ways which make "sense" in their own world and which supports their self-image. The great movie *Rainman* made this point clear. The film told the story of two brothers, one of whom was severely mentally handicapped, who came to love each other. The "healthy" brother, who was a manipulator and a borderline crook, eventually was forced to get inside the other's mind in order to survive behavior which originally seemed bizarre to him. Once he did this, he was able to benefit from the skills he discovered, making money from the mentally retarded brother's ability to remember cards in Las Vegas. In coming to understand why the limited brother behaved as he did, the manipulator came to love him and wanted to support and protect him. The tragedy of the movie was that this proved to be impossible.

In the summer 1990 issue of the *Noetic Sciences Review*, Elisabet Sahtouris demonstrated the significance of the differences in perception between people. She wrote:

> Perhaps the most important discovery of modern science is that there can be no single true and complete worldview. Like all species, we have only partial information about our world, and our information changes as our knowledge increases, as our inventions become more sophisticated and as we and other species actually change our world. We change the world even while we are looking at it, for we are never only observers—we continue being players.

We can therefore formulate two simple rules about human behavior. First, organisms, both human beings and those from other species, always operate in their perceived self-interest given all the circumstances of which they are aware at the time they make their decisions. Second, people, and indeed all organisms, change their thinking, action and behavior when they see the possibility for more satisfying choices.

At one level, both of the statements are self-evident. People do make appropriate choices in terms of their own self-understandings even though they may seem nonsensical when evaluated by individuals with more (or less) skills, knowledge or a different cultural viewpoint. Even "destructive" behaviors make sense when the world-view behind them is understood.

To make things more complex, nobody operates from a single, consistent view of the world. The action pattern you and I choose depend on the calculus which seems most relevant to us at a particular moment. Thus it may seem important to have a good dinner on a Saturday night to relieve one's frustrations; at another time one may wish one had kept the money to reduce one's debt.

Anybody who wants to be an effective change agent must fully understand that views of their own, and other people's, self-interest are perceptual and not objective. Differences in perceptions emerge not only in terms of the way people view the world and their place in it. There are also deep differences about what behavior is acceptable and valued. Thus, one individual will see the mugging of a stranger in the street as an acceptable way to get money. Another individual would recoil in horror and see this as destructive of their self-image, preferring to starve than to abandon their values. At the other extreme, some will see saving another at the risk of their own life as appropriate behavior. Others regard this sort of action as totally foolish, and indeed incomprehensible.

This inevitably means that when one talks to a group, writes a book or creates a video, the message received by each individual varies widely. Each person screens communications to a far greater extent than most of us realize. Individuals can draw extraordinarily different messages from a given presentation. I have sometimes tested this reality by asking people to tell me what they have learned from my speech, seminar or consultancy. I have been consistently amazed at the range of reactions. Learning to listen, so we do not distort what we see and hear, is one of the critical skills for an effective change agent.

Choosing directions

None of us has a complete and coherent view of our self-interest. We should aim to move up the spiral of understanding and behavior toward a more inclusive view and a longer time-span. This is desirable because it leads to higher levels of creativity and potential. It is also a requirement for global survival because, unless more people think and work at these higher levels, massive breakdowns are inevitable. It is the responsibility of our overall educational process, acting through families, churches, schools, colleges and the media, to enable people to understand why they should care for others and the globe.

Fortunately, committing to help others, rather than benefiting solely oneself, results in profound personal gain. In an effective helping relationship, the person who is providing support receives at least as much as the person who is being supported. If this is not the case, the relationship will usually be unhealthy. We should only take on commitments to others if we believe we will benefit from the interrelationships. Otherwise, we become frustrated and expect those who are being helped to acknowledge the effort that is being made on their behalf.

It is hard enough to need help without also having to thank the donor for the effort they are making: much of the benefit of the support is lost if it is not freely given. For many years, I asked myself how some people could give so much help without burning out. I now realize that they can do so because the importance of supporting others is part of their self-perception and their goals. They therefore gain from their activities rather than being drained by them.

As people learn to care for themselves, others and the globe, their view of their self-interest changes. Understanding this reality is critical as we face the issue of fundamental change. I have been told again and again throughout my career that existing decision-makers will inevitably block positive change. I reject this conclusion on the grounds that it is today possible to show people in the establishment that many of the ways they are acting are not benefiting them. As they realize this, and see their self-interest in new ways, they will support different directions. Indeed, I find at the current time that it is often mainstream decision-makers who are most willing to look at the world in new ways. I therefore find it more and more difficult to be patient with those who argue that those in power must be treated as the enemy.

The challenge, then, is to help people from all groups and classes see realities in new ways rather than to assume that some types of people are going to be helpful and others will always deny the potential of fundamental shifts. There are many examples where unlikely people have led the drive for new directions. At the personal level, many of the super-rich Rockefellers have supported ideas and directions which challenge the current goals of the very well-off. Organizationally, Scandinavian Airlines, Canon, the Corps of Engineers and United Way are shifting their success criteria significantly.

Indeed, the much publicized row about United Way salary and perks is an example of this shift. Behavior patterns which were the norm in the quite recent past are now seen as totally unacceptable. Members of Congress are also being caught by this same shift in values. We are coming to demand more of our leaders and those who do not keep up with this mindquake will pay a high price.

From time to time, I have been able to set up activities which have catalyzed significant changes in thinking. I remember a conference with a large number of people from the Young Presidents' Organization, which brings together heads of companies. Because those of us organizing the seminar had the right message at the right time, we were able to demonstrate that the environment was critical to them and their children. They went away with a significantly different way of seeing, thinking and acting.

A number of people were so impressed with their learning experience that they came to a follow-up. We showed them the same slide-tape presentation that had sparked the change last time. Because they had now learned its message, the presentation was dismissed as superficial and boring. Indeed many refused to believe it was the same material we had showed them the previous year. The ability to bring about change is always specific to a particular moment: the possibility of an "ah-ha" depends on catching an individual or group when they are ready for new insights.

The challenge today is to help large numbers of people through the required shifts in understanding. Today, as in the past, people perish without vision. The need to fully understand this reality is one of the primary differences between the industrial era and the compassionate era. In the industrial era it was assumed that the future emerged from past trends and the clashes between them. Now we are aware that it is our visions which affect our perception and that our perceptions determine what we do. Visions are "practical:" they are, indeed, the primary creator of the future we inherit.

Once people look at reality clearly, they can make effective choices. They can either continue to move in the same direction or they can look for new potentials. The Chinese understand this: their word for crisis contains two characters. One of them conveys the sense of danger, the other opportunity. If people have a sense of their own vision, then they are far more likely to perceive, and later work toward, the potentials of their situation.

Crises are times when we are challenged to face the inability of current systems of thinking and action to respond to real needs. When this moment of realization comes, we can choose to move forward beyond the blocks of the past. Alternatively, we can fail to transcend them and become more deeply mired in old models. It is in this sense that "timing is everything" and "insistence on birth at the wrong time is the source of all evil."

All too often people are unwilling to push events to the crisis point where something significant can happen. They prefer to come up with slick and easy answers to complex questions. They prefer to avoid facing the hard questions of their lives and their institutions. The only way that anything significant can be achieved is to continue to live in the question until a moment of illumination arrives which shifts the nature of perceived reality.

We can understand, in this context, why the most difficult people to reach and change are the ideologues. Ideologues are committed to looking at the world in a particular way: changing this pattern challenges their self-image. Economic or social entrepreneurs, on the other hand, are interested in accomplishing a task: seeing reality correctly helps them accomplish this. Today our greatest problems come from those who distort reality to maintain their comfortable illusions.

The leader's role

Society today needs leaders who can work for quiet, positive, sustainable change. We need people who can help others understand that thoughtful value-based behavior will benefit them and their society. To achieve these shifts, leaders must understand how to help people change their self-image and their view of their self-interest.

The most resistant realities are the ones of which we are "certain" as well as those which lie below the conscious level. Part of the challenge of our lives at the current time is to become more aware of the styles and factors which control our decision-making. Some of these are personal and idiosyncratic. Others are shared by all the members of our organizations and culture.

Indeed, the very language we must use to express our ideas highlights some parts of reality for us, and hides other parts. For example, the Western sense of time, which includes past, present and future, is embedded in our languages. Many other languages, such as that of the Hopi indian, suggest that the only "real" time is the present. Modern science seems to be suggesting that the way the Hopi are forced to speak and think by their language is more realistic than Western thinking, which require that we divide our experiences into past, present and future.

Language and culture therefore inevitably blind people to many of the more innovative possibilities around them. One way to break through this blindness is to live fully within different cultures. I have personally been fortunate because I have made my home in different places for extended periods of time, including India, England, Scotland, France and very different parts of the U.S.: the East Coast, Arizona and New Orleans. I know from these experiences how differently the world appears to human beings. Those who are unable to move around physically can immerse themselves in the arts and the movies of other parts of the world; these can help us recognize the very different ways various cultures look at reality.

A hundred years ago each of these cultures would have seemed fixed and permanent to those living within them. Now all of them are shifting with extraordinary rapidity. One of the most exciting realities is that positive alterations have taken place in response to new developments. The belief that nothing can be done, which is all too common today, does not fit the facts. The world is changing around us: the real question is whether each of us will pay attention or pretend that nothing is happening.

Let's look at the issue of smoking. I shall give away my age only too clearly when I tell you I remember clearly the days when smokers and non-smokers were mixed together on airplanes. Later there were small non-smoking areas which were steadily enlarged over time until the smokers looked as though they would be pushed out of the back of the plane! In 1988 a ban was placed on smoking on all short flights. At the same time, Northwest Airlines decided that they could make money by advertising that they were the first airline to ban smoking on all domestic flights. In 1990, smoking was banned by federal legislation on all domestic flights except those from and to Hawaii.

This change was achieved against the strong, continuing lobbying of the cigarette companies. But an aroused public opinion, backed by the commitment of the U.S. surgeon general, enabled legislation to be passed which is now backed by the vast majority of people. Smokers are beleaguered and unable to smoke in most people's homes, and sometimes even in their own. The evidence shows that most smokers would like to quit but their addiction has a very strong hold on them.

There is, however, a darker side to this picture which shows the way in which positive change all too often generates negative side-effects. The movement against smoking is clearly still largely class-based. The poor and the working class continue to smoke heavily: one has only to take the bus instead of planes to learn this lesson. Tobacco companies are therefore increasingly focussing their message on the disadvantaged groups in society such as poor working women and those in the ghetto—whitewashing of billboards to cover up tobacco promotions is a growing "guerilla" tactic to counter this approach.

The cigarette companies are also trying to make up for their loss of sales in the United States by promoting smoking in the Eastern bloc and the developing countries. They are even trying to force the United States to use its clout to prevent these nations from limiting the imports of cigarettes. Given what we now know about the health consequences of smoking, such behavior is totally unacceptable. There are those who compare the tactics used by the cigarette companies to those which were employed during the opium wars in the nineteenth century, when Britain forced China to continue to accept opium to benefit British traders.

To return to the positive side, however, the revolution in smoking policy is part of a broader shift. About twenty years ago, I participated in an effort to create the Hawaii health net, one of the very first groups which encouraged people to believe that they could improve their health by better diets, exercise and looking after themselves. The general feeling at the time was that such an effort was naive and quixotic. Americans, it was claimed, were wedded to their junk foods. This has turned out to be untrue. Those who have watched the transformation of the fast-food and packaged food industries are aware that the health movement has had a powerful impact on the way adults eat. Salad bars are now advertised. More and more promotional material stresses how steps are being taken to reduce fats, particularly cholesterol.

Along with the movement toward a health emphasis has been a growing acceptance of the inevitability of death. Instead of denying death as was the case in the middle of the twentieth century, people are finding ways to help their loved ones die with dignity. Hospice, an organization which works with the dying, is one of the extraordinary positive stories of the last two decades. During the row about the "suicide" machine in Michigan in the early nineties, John Chancellor argued in an editorial on NBC that clarification of the right to die is long overdue.

Our thinking about violence is also shifting; indeed mindquakes are particularly necessary here. This behavior pattern is so ingrained in human affairs that it certainly cannot be eliminated easily or quickly. Some would say that the tendency toward violence is inevitable because it is part of our brain patterns. Each of us must surely continue to be dismayed by the degree that mental violence remains a large part of our behavior patterns, even if we have moved beyond physical violence.

Nevertheless, I believe that our problems are largely caused by the fact that most people were brought up in ways which sapped their capacity to love. Their perceptions and interpretations are based on the belief that others intend to damage them even when this is not the case. Breaking through this type of patterning is always extraordinarily difficult because actions which are meant in one way by the caring person are interpreted totally differently by the other. Compassion appears to be weakness. Love appears to be intrusive.

Fortunately, violence can be controlled and limited in many ways. Gregory Bateson, one of the extraordinary thinkers of the twentieth century, did a great deal of thinking about this issue. He concentrated his attention on animal behavior. He showed that many breeds of animals had effective ways of showing their attitudes. When an animal was submissive, it would lie on its back and expose its stomach to be bitten. The dominant animal would see this surrender and turn away. He pointed out that a primary problem in human cultures is that a message of submission is all too likely to be followed by an attack, rather than accepted as an offer of peace.

He also showed that our difficulties are tied to the complexities of verbal language as compared to body language. Body language is unambiguous, he argued, while verbal language permits lying to be brought to a fine art. Human beings therefore have to be far more cautious than animals in their interrelationships. It is this problem which makes it attractive to keep up one's defenses at all scales from the personal to the international. It is altogether reasonable to be afraid that you may be stabbed in the back, given existing cultural attitudes.

The maintenance of violent systems also seems attractive because there seem to be fewer surprises in negative dynamics. For example, the world was more "controllable" during the cold war than it is now. A surprising number of late nineteen-eighties thrillers made use of this theme. The plots turned on American and/or Russian conspiracies to return to cold war certainties, both in order to perpetuate internal power and to have an understandable context for international relations. Reality, however, greatly exceeded fiction for nobody imagined that KGB units would disobey orders, an event which actually happened in the failed 1991 coup in the Soviet Union.

This issue of violence is one which leads to very deep levels of disagreement. There are some people who not only believe that it is impossible to get rid of violence but do not believe that it would be desirable to do so. While I know that we shall never eliminate violence totally, I am convinced that we should try to do so to the greatest extent possible because it is only after this has been achieved that human beings will develop their potentials fully.

Beyond right and wrong

Moving beyond violence and dictatorships requires that people be open to new ideas. It is almost impossible to really hear others, let alone accept new ideas, so long as you know you are "right" and others are "wrong." Listening requires an open heart and mind. This is the reason why most of us reject divergent views rather than be challenged by them.

Certainty closes down one's mind and heart. In today's changing world this is a recipe for personal and social catastrophe. Each of us must learn to listen to other views. This means, in turn, that we must be prepared to move beyond holding onto our own cultural understandings to relishing those of others. Until we are willing to do this, we will be afraid of images and ideas which challenge our existing belief systems.

The patterns of violence will only be broken as we learn to see the world more positively. We must learn to be attracted to, and even fascinated by, diversity rather than being scared of it. We must recognize that we can learn from those who have different visions of reality than we do. We must encourage people to develop their own way of seeing the world while respecting those of others.

Movement in this direction will be more rapid when people come to understand that the quickest way of learning new ideas is to talk with somebody who reaches a different conclusion than one's own. Such an individual is seeing realities one has missed. Diversity is therefore the best source of creativity. As one learns to listen to others, one discovers that there are alternative directions to those one has previously seen as necessary, and indeed inevitable. The world becomes a richer, and more exciting, place as the number of options in one's life enlarges.

A willingness to tolerate diversity, let alone to benefit fully from it, cannot, however, develop so long as most people continue to believe that right and wrong can be easily and clearly defined. I frequently appear on radio talk shows. Increasingly when I am asked whether something is right or wrong, I respond that it is hard enough for me to make up my own mind on tough questions without forcing my views on others. Most moral dilemmas do not yield to hard and fast dogmas—people should develop their own moral code based on how honesty, responsibility, humility and love can be effectively applied in their own lives.

The classic response to my statement is to take an issue like murder and to test me with a response like "surely murder is always wrong." I have learned not to fall into this trap! The taking of somebody's life without their consent should certainly be unacceptable in any circumstances. But if we believe that taking life without the consent of the other person is wrong, then war is also wrong. So is the death penalty. And what about those who choose to die: is this ever acceptable? And what about a social structure which creates situations where murder is a "cost of doing business" as in the drug trade?"

All of us should stand for "life." But how do we define life in a high-tech medical age. Are those in an irreversible coma "alive"? Should one try to save every premature child? Does one use heroic measures to keep people alive even if they are ready to die? We can only keep our tidy moral certainties by avoiding complications in our thinking and keeping our frame of reference very narrow. As soon as we look at the real world, certainties fall away and disagreements and conflict are inevitable.

Until people learn to live with complexity and uncertainty, however, non-traditional behaviors seem more and more threatening. One natural, but highly dangerous, response emerges when people grab onto a single issue and make that the core of their beliefs. People who disagree are then totally unacceptable and any method is justified to overwhelm or destroy them. In these circumstances, civility and honest dialogue vanish from the scene. This is a common pattern which lies behind much of the violence in the world today.

This danger is vividly demonstrated by the following story. An abortion clinic was consistently being picketed by right-to-life groups. One woman turned up all the time to help keep pregnant women out of the clinic. One day she was found inside the clinic asking how her daughter could end a pregnancy. When questioned gently she explained that while she still thought abortion was wrong, her daughter's situation made having a baby "impossible." But her empathy with her daughter's needs did not prevent her from being back on the picket line next weekend, trying to prevent others from getting the help she felt she had to have for her own child.

Those who want to stop abortions are winning the battle. They are putting so much pressure on doctors, often using illegal actions, that they are becoming unwilling to provide abortions. Indeed, they are also forcing people out of the whole field of obstetrics and gynecology: a crisis is therefore developing for the care of pregnant women in the U.S. It is time for the abortion issue to be rethought. The real issue is not whether people should have abortions or not but why so many women get pregnant who do not want to. We should stop putting pressure on those who have unwanted pregnancies.

The tragedy today is that those who care passionately about morality are arguing with each other and losing their effectiveness while industrial-era "pragmatists" are making choices for us. An alliance must be developed between those committed to values. One of the exciting developments in the abortion field is that foes are looking for the places they can work together in many parts of the country on issues such as the care of the young. This shows that we can make space for different views about how to apply honesty, responsibility, humility, love and a respect for mystery to real situations.

It is reasonable for people to reach varying conclusions starting from a spiritual base. Intolerance of others' deeply held beliefs is, therefore, the real sin today. We need to listen to those who care passionately about different sides of important issues because they are the people who can move us forward toward a deeper and more complete understanding. This commitment to listening must, however, be mutual. A vital part of any spiritual base is to know that one may be mistaken. Both sides must therefore be willing to be flexible.

We cannot dialogue successfully with those who claim that morality and spirituality are unimportant. We need to reject the views of people who believe that any activity that makes money is "OK" regardless of its effects on people and the society. We need to proclaim the need for people to live on a value base.

This is a truly difficult area to get straight for oneself let alone to explain to others. One does need to dialogue with those who do not agree with one's personal conclusions using their own value-base as a ground for their views. It is impossible for those who work from value-bases to find common ground with those who believe that their narrow self-interest must prevail whatever the consequences for others, or indeed for themselves.

Supporting positive directions

Survival requires that we learn to work with value-based people who disagree with us. Conflict is therefore inevitable. We must learn to make a clear distinction between conflict and violence. For example, President Bush often said during the Iraq crisis that he hoped to avoid conflict. But it would have been far healthier to accept the inevitability of conflict and to see how divergent views could be brought into alignment. Recognizing that there was a real conflict of views might have made it possible to discover fundamentally new approaches which would have satisfied the real needs of those involved.

One of the primary dangers today is that there is a tendency to force compromises rather than taking the time to understand why people and groups see the same situation so differently. Until we are willing to work through the real reasons for conflicts, the agreements we reach are likely to collapse once stresses develop. Our unwillingness to face the stress and strain of working through different attitudes prevents us getting to a point where all involved can be comfortable with the final resolution.

There will almost always be some virtue in the position of both, or all, people and groups involved in a disagreement. The leader needs to listen, and take account, of all the views and to help each side listen to the other. In addition, however, the leader needs to be aware that the behavior and goals of one group will usually be more supportive of compassionate-era directions than that of others. When there is a clear clash between supporting past dynamics or positive new directions, the right response from a leader is not to "compromise" equally between the various views but to push toward a more desirable set of values and institutional arrangements. Leaders cannot be "neutral" when there is a need for change.

If you have tried to walk this leadership tightrope in your own life, you do not need to be reminded of the difficulties of maintaining your balance. You are committed to honest listening; but you also want to help people look at the long-run good of the global culture while always remembering that their own perceptions, and yours, are inevitably limited and partial. The moment you, as leader, become absolutely sure of what is required at a particular moment, you also become willing to use power and violence to achieve it. You take this step because you feel you have the obligation to move in that one particular direction.

Leaders are choosing to use discussion and dialogue styles, rather than coercion, at the current time because there is growing evidence that they can achieve more positive changes through this style. The goal of leadership remains unchanged, however. It is to help people and the globe move in positive directions. Leadership is inspired by the saying of Lao Tzu: "When the leader leads well, the people say they did it themselves." We therefore need new tools for movement toward mutual understanding. True leaders go even further. They recognize that continued use of coercive power and violence is the greatest danger to the human race. Nevertheless, because each of us needs to stand for our personal understanding of our values, there will inevitably be times when being true to ourselves will force us toward mental violence. It is vital to remain constantly aware that choosing violence, rather than creative solutions, represents a major failure.

For many years into the future, there will certainly be times when this type of failure will be less costly than permitting people, groups or institutions to ride rough-shod over others. We are not yet at the point where all our swords can become plowshares. How simple the world would be if this were the case! Nevertheless the primary challenge of the nineties and the twenty-first century is to learn how to create a world in which disputes are increasingly settled by dialogue and creativity rather than by force.

The urgent need to move beyond violence requires a profound change in our definition of positive leadership. In the past the leader was the individual who had a clear, strong vision of what was needed and went all out to achieve it. It was accepted that those opposed to the change would be frustrated and angry—indeed these reactions were welcomed as evidence of the success of the effort.

Today effective leaders must adopt a profoundly different role. They need to bring together people who share a moral, value-based stance but have different views about appropriate directions. They need to create excitement about new visions enabling people with different views to think and act together. While there will still be opposition, the need is to seek common ground. Debate in the West tends to concentrate on disagreements rather than agreements. We should now reverse this style.

In the past, leaders were admired because of their powerful stands. In the future, leaders will be valued for their skills in bringing divergent people and groups together. This leads to a profoundly different definition of strength. Strength is the ability to remain aware of one's own core while valuing the reality that other people see the world differently. This type of individual has no need for violence, being able to remain centered without impinging on the rights of others.

Leadership styles

There are three primary steps leaders need to take when creating new patterns of thought and action. Deciding which one is necessary at a particular point in time depends on the nature of the interactions which are dominant in the family, institution or community to be supported. Having the skills to determined where the blocks to effectiveness are is one of the skills required of a leader at the end of the twentieth century. Organizations and communities which face new challenges will not normally be able to tell where they are blocked. This is the role of the outsider; to look at the realities and to help people to concentrate on the places where they are really in need of change.

One task is to build trust and a sense of interdependence. Most systems today are paralyzed by fear of others. This is true even of institutions—such as firms, schools, colleges and churches—which one would hope would be committed to pulling together. The problems involved in creating trust are even more acute when it is necessary to bring together people from different institutions, or even nations, who have very varied images of what they want. The essential virtue which goes into this development stage is love—a willingness to look beyond the flaws in each one of us and to support our common humanity.

The requirement for success in this task is the recognition that there are goals which unite all those who are meeting together and that these are more important than existing divisions. This is the fundamental challenge when one is dealing with clashes within existing institutions or communities. It is also the challenge when trying to unite groups or nations which have previously defined their interests in competitive ways. One way to achieve this goal is to "think" through the problem. It is, however, unlikely that this intellectual process will be successful unless the emotions are also effectively engaged.

One of the most creative approaches is to find ways to remind people of their common humanity and help them see that this is more important to them than differences in goals and ideologies. This was one of the first steps which was taken by citizen diplomats in the Soviet Union as they started their work in the mid-eighties. They aimed to relate to grand–fathers rather than to bureaucrats. As soon as bureaucrats took off their work hats, many of the apparently insoluble differences vanished. A sense of alignment began to develop: a belief that there were overarching agreements which lay beyond the differences.

We are searching for a global "story" which can unite all the inhabitants of the globe. It must be based on our common humanity—the fact that we share joys and griefs with those nearest to us. Our customs may be different but our need for family and community is a constant throughout the world.

One of the fascinating insights into the early nineties Mideast peace conferences came as NBC did a story on how the various countries were coping with the media. The public relations teams from the various nations found that they had been forced to cooperate to achieve a common task and that their attitudes were not very different. A sense of being colleagues, even if not friends, inevitably developed.

Trust building requires time. There is no way to rush the process. Effective leaders have learned that they need to go slowly at the beginning of a process. There must be opportunities for talk and play even though it often seems as though nothing is being learned or gained. Once people see that the others involved are human beings with all their complexities, stereotypes break down and rapid progress can then take place. The fear that always accompanies contacts with "strangers" changes into a fascination with difference.

The natural next step which follows after trust-building is to start visioning what should be done. However, because distrust has been so pervasive throughout the industrial era, some "New Age" organizations have got stuck at the trust-building stage, hoping for the development of "perfect" systems. They often fail to recognize that this goal is impossible and that the search for trust within a small group may cut them off from others who could work with them.

Building trust and interdependence is part of a complex cycle, not a goal in itself. People will be ready to talk about their visions, their dreams and what they think will make a difference once they lose their fear. At this point, people need to think creatively together. The goal is to get as many ideas as possible into the open. But this requires more than "brainstorming," which all too often means that people will throw ideas off the top of their heads rather than thinking about "break-the-mold" directions.

When people break out of current thinking, many of the ideas will be useless. But this creative phase enables people to begin to understand that alignment toward a specific goal does not mean agreement on all matters. People can work together even though they still have differences. This period of creativity provides the raw material out of which vision emerges. The overarching challenge at this time is to be willing to be honest about one's own understandings; to surface ideas even though one believes that others will disagree. This is the reason why trust is a precondition; otherwise people will limit themselves to what they feel is "acceptable."

Creativity will normally stretch the boundaries of trust. Each of us necessarily thinks in terms of our experience. There will be a tendency for this stage to bring stereotypes back into focus and to cast doubt on the progress which has been made in breaking down the barriers between groups. People can only imagine out of their past experience and they will therefore come up with ideas which may seem inappropriate, or even outrageous, when seen from a different viewpoint. All of those engaged in the process must be aware of the need for mutual support.

Once the new ideas have been scrutinized and culled, the natural step is toward action. Perceiving the possibility of enhancing their quality of life, people will want to do something. It is possible for the overall process to be blocked at this point. Our current emphasis on participation makes it difficult for us to freeze ideas so that action can take place. We are often willing to reopen discussion again and again to accommodate newcomers. We must move beyond this pattern because the creative process has a rhythm which must be honored. If it is lost, people will lose their energy and enthusiasm.

The action phase is the time when responsibility is at the center of our lives. We do what we have to do because as Martin Luther put it, "we can do no other." We have centered ourselves through our trust-building and shared creativity, now we have discovered action steps which we believe will make a difference. We therefore carry them out to the best of our ability.

But even if individuals, groups and organizations are willing to push toward action, our current culture does not possess appropriate action styles. While much has been done to help organizations learn to trust and to vision, action models for the compassionate era are scarce. The old patterns where an elite group forced changes are being rejected although it is all too easy to fall back into them. What is to take their place?

More and more people feel that total consensus should be achieved before action. But this denies the very nature of the change process. New ideas will always be controversial. Some people must be willing to step out in front—to take risks.

Action will often be divisive. Despite our best efforts, some people will see what we are doing as wrong. The effort, however, should be to minimize the differences rather than polarizing groups. Inevitably, however, action steps will also sometimes destroy patterns of trust. It is therefore essential that the cycle of trust-building, creativity and action is a continuous one—it cannot be done once and forgotten.

PART II

Socioeconomics in the Compassionate Era

Ensuring
Economic Freedom

As a UNIVERSITY STUDENT, I chose to concentrate on economics. I followed the advice of a career counselor who said the subject was suitable for me because I was interested in people. It was indeed an exciting area for learning, but not for the reason he gave. I discovered that academic economists are not concerned with human beings, or even with what actually happens. Instead they make predictions based on certain assumptions, regardless of whether or not they reflect real life.

My professor at Cambridge, Richard Goodwin, helped me understand the role of assumptions in economics, and indeed all the social sciences. It is quite possible to go through a university believing you are learning about the real world. Only the exceptional professor forces students to recognize that the basic issue is the validity of the assumptions they are studying, rather than the conclusions reached on the basis of the assumptions. Because I learned this lesson from him, my economics writing in the sixties and seventies always challenged traditional conclusions. I coined the word "socioeconomics" to remind people that economic issues cannot be kept separate from social impacts. In recent years, many writers have adopted similar views; an organization to study socioeconomic issues was created a few years ago.

Richard, a truly remarkable man, would not normally have been my tutor. At Cambridge, students relate to a single college and are restricted to working with a professor from that college. Dissatisfied with the teaching I was getting, I asked for the right to work with Richard. My request was considered unreasonable but I made a nuisance of myself until I received permission. This was the first time I grasped that behavior which seemed normal to me—in this case seeking better teaching—could be seen as odd by people who lived by the codes of the existing culture.

Richard's teaching eventually enabled me to perceive how

economics has dominated decision-making in Western cultures and, since the Second World War, most of the world. Raising productivity, ensuring full employment and avoiding recessions have been considered far more important than social and political issues such as poverty, health, education and crime. The human, and social, consequences of current socioeconomic structures has all too often been ignored. The current crime wave is one result of our failure to think more broadly about desirable directions. We fail to face up to the desperate alienation throughout the world which is caused by poverty and illness. When coupled with the drug plague, the consequent hopelessness threatens the viability of more and more communities.

Social issues are usually reduced to a consideration of their economic impact. For example, the economic fear of an insufficient number of workers in the nineties, because of the "baby bust," is the main force driving educational "reform." Throughout the twentieth century, we have accepted extraordinary changes in the goals and organization of society without fundamental thought, viewing them as secondary consequences of directions which seemed imperative from the economic point of view. This trend has gained force throughout the last fifty years, reaching its peak in the eighties when greed was proclaimed by many to be a virtue because it would help the economy work better.

One of the primary examples of social change is the unanticipated, and misunderstood, impacts which have resulted from the post-World War II goal of full employment and the later commitment to maximum labor force participation. Growing emphasis has been placed on increasing the number of people who hold jobs. Far more women are in the labor force than ever before in peace time.

The coming reversal of trends

Forces which drove people and the culture in one direction during the twentieth century will be reversed in the twenty-first. The pervasive emphasis on economics which has been acceptable to citizens throughout the twentieth century, largely because it succeeded in delivering extraordinary increases in the standard of living, will be reduced and eventually abandoned. The willingness to be dominated by economics is already waning. Economists and citizens alike are beginning to understand that the spurt in economic growth which took place in the twentieth century, particularly in the fifties and sixties, is now over. It was a one-time dynamic which cannot be repeated.

I have personally challenged the priority given to economics ever since my first job in the European Productivity Agency in Paris in the early fifties. The task of the agency, largely driven by American influence, was to increase production in Europe. I drove my bosses crazy because I continued to ask them why increased efficiency would necessarily improve the quality of life. This questioning attitude is now the norm.

People are putting other priorities ahead of their jobs and the creation of wealth. A growing number of people are looking for ways in which the work they do, and the lifestyle they develop, serves their own desires and wishes rather than supports economic growth. Another desire is for closer relationships. People are increasingly unwilling to subordinate their time with their children and their spouses to the demands of their jobs. Throughout Western cultures, there is a sense of overload. People feel that they are being asked to do too much and cannot cope with all their obligations. In a survey conducted in 1991 by the Hilton Corporation, two-thirds of Americans said they would take salary reductions in order to get more time off from their work.

This shift in priorities is partly driven by the fact that once a certain standard of living has been achieved, people are going to look for the time to enjoy it. In addition, environmental destruction is forcing reconsideration of priorities. The natural environments where many people go to relax and "recreate" are less and less available. This is partly because there are more people in any given space because of population pressure and partly because of damage to ecological systems by production processes.

One key challenge of the nineties is learning to live with less. The longer we put off facing this fact, the tougher it will be to come to grips with the realities of the twenty-first century. Increasing costs of energy, and growing damage to ecological systems, both require that current maximum growth strategies be abandoned. Each of us is therefore going to have to ask what "enough" means in our own lives. The nineties are seeing a movement away from the greed of the eighties toward a simpler lifestyle.

Thrift is coming back into favor. Pressures against conspicuous consumption are emerging. More and more people see movement away from frenetic purchasing as being in their self-interest. They are learning to measure success in terms of their quality of life rather than the quantity of goods they possess. Reducing purchases is not seen as a sacrifice, but rather as a way to maximize satisfactions. The next step is for all of us to recognize that these positive trends can only be effective after there are fundamental changes in economic structures.

Perceiving what these changes should be is not difficult. The real challenge is to muster the political will and citizen resolve to face up to the realities of the moment. This will only happen after citizens recognize that economists and politicians are committed to solving the wrong set of problems. No real improvement in our overall situation can be achieved until it is understood that more energy and resources are being used in the rich countries than are compatible with viable global balance. For the same reason, a commitment must be taken to reduce the rate of population growth as rapidly as possible throughout the world.

The need to change direction is urgent. Unless there is significant movement in the nineties, problems will become far more difficult. Before we can look ahead, however, we must recognize how the current situation evolved because proposals for new policies must fit into current dynamics. The purpose of this book is not to come up with exciting, but infeasible, ideas. It is to suggest proposals that can be absorbed into the society effectively at this time and thus alter the very dangerous dynamics in which the world is currently caught.

A brief historical survey

From the beginning of time, human beings have sought to decrease the effort they make and improve their conditions. Our imagination and creativity keep the world changing around us. Human beings are possessed by a discontent with things as they are. We are always looking for ways to make our lives "better," although definitions of "better" continue to evolve with new thinking. Some call this discontent divine. Others see it as the curse which is destroying the planet. In either case, it is a fundamental reality society must deal with as we think about how to set up systems appropriate for twenty-first century conditions.

Until now, much of human creative energy has gone toward increasing production. Since the beginning of agriculture, when humans domesticated animals and planted crops, a "surplus" above basic needs was increasingly available. Originally most of this surplus was seized by kings and priests. People were either rich or poor, with few in the middle. Similar conditions persisted through the Middle Ages.

Socioeconomic patterns have changed completely in the last two centuries as a result of the industrial era. Approaches designed to encourage and support innovation and invention are less than two hundred years old. Even more recent is the idea that human beings could be organized into systems which would support creativity and ensure rapid and fundamental change. Some of the implications of these new styles are spelled out in a remarkable book, *The Soul of a New Machine,* by Tracy Kidder.

The most critical socioeconomic consequence of the industrial era was the rise of the middle class. When looked at in the long sweep of history, this is a truly surprising development. The idea that most of the population would have a comfortable lifestyle would have been considered ridiculous in the nineteenth century. A few people aspired to be rich—much of the wealth was hereditary—while most knew they would be poor. The idea of upward mobility was still relatively unusual until the twentieth century. People expected, and were expected to, remain in the station to which they were born.

Early nineteenth century Britain looked down on economic upstarts. The novels of Georgette Heyer provide a delightful commentary on the Regency period when the aristocracy tried to keep itself pure and despised those in "trade"—the word for any form of business activity. By the end of the century, the pattern was profoundly different even in the United Kingdom. It was, however, the United States which led the fundamental change in social patterns. Industrialists became the center of power and prestige.

The opportunity for upward mobility, coupled with the availability of new technology through innovation and invention, led to dramatically increased levels of economic creativity. Production rose throughout the nineteenth century but growth was uneven. The pattern of the century was booms followed by busts.

Boom times developed and continued as long as the enthusiasm of manufacturers and purchasers was high because they believed that conditions were favorable and it made sense to build up their production and stocks to take advantage of the future. Sooner or later, production exceeded orders and the boom collapsed. Slumps developed. Firms went bankrupt and unemployment rates rose to high levels, with consequent great hardship because safety nets did not exist. Over time, the excess supply was worked off and the cycle started all over again.

By the beginning of the twentieth century, people could not afford to buy what was being produced and this created major economic swings. Henry Ford was the first to grasp that rich people would not be able to purchase all the motor vehicles that would come off the newly-invented assembly line. He also realized that if more people were able to acquire goods, then more could be manufactured on a continuing basis. He therefore created a major breakthrough in economic strategy by increasing the wages of his workers to $5 a day, so they could afford to obtain the cars they themselves produced. After initial strong opposition, other companies followed suit as they saw the benefits of this new strategy for selling goods.

Despite this extraordinary innovation, the level of demand still did not rise fast enough to keep up with supply. The 1920s saw a boom which created the belief that the good times would roll for ever. The bubble burst in 1929 followed by the deep depression of the 1930s. During this time the priorities of government policymakers lay in balancing the budget rather than dealing with the unemployment problem. As so often happens, an abstraction carried more power than the realities of the day. Policymakers were willing to subordinate the hardship of those without jobs and incomes to the supposed requirements of economic policy.

The impact of John Maynard Keynes

John Maynard Keynes, the great British economist, created the next fundamental change in thinking. He took Henry Ford's argument and made it respectable, proving to economists that lack of demand caused slumps and unemployment. He argued that it was the responsibility of governments to act in ways which would prevent unemployment and that deficits were therefore appropriate in recessions.

By the time the second World War was over, Keynes had convinced most economists that insufficient demand had been the cause of the misery in the thirties. Despite the pent-up demand for goods and services which had emerged during the war, the economics profession learned to fear a recession or slump similar to that of the thirties. Economists therefore convinced governments throughout the world that they had a responsibility to help demand rise in balance with supply so there would be enough jobs to go round.

I was at Cambridge University when this point of view was being advanced. As somebody who had been too young in the thirties to understand what had been going on, I simply did not understand how my teachers could be afraid that supply would get ahead of demand in the forties and fifties. People had money, they were having lots of children and they were more than willing to purchase. The idea that demand might fall behind supply seemed ridiculous to me—and it was. Once again, however, inappropriate parallels to the past were drawn and irrelevant policies were developed.

The most destructive patterns developed because government and advertisers joined together to encourage people to buy. Thrift was discouraged and credit became available for an ever-growing number of purposes. Over four decades, more and more people decided it made sense to buy before they had the required money. Individuals and families have chosen to meet their consumption needs through taking on various forms of debt in advance of receiving income. As Willis Harman, one of the pioneer futurists, puts it, most people moved from being citizens to consumers, with credit seen as the way to gain goods when we feel we need them even if we cannot currently afford them.

Most of us fail to recognize the enormous decrease in our future real income which we incur by paying the interest costs on credit purchases. Credit is seductive as I, like so many other people, have discovered. When you borrow money you do not pay taxes. When you try to repay the debt the difficulties begin because you have to earn enough to pay off not only the credit, but also the taxes on the money one earns. Indeed, while taxes were at their highest level, it became almost impossible to get out of debt once one had gotten into it.

Rising levels of personal debt have been accompanied by an ever growing national debt. Federal deficits started to increase when President Johnson used a "guns and butter" strategy at the time of the Vietnam war. Rather than cutting back on domestic demand to meet the cost of the war, he tried to meet both military and domestic needs. We are now at the point where interest payments are a rapidly growing part of the federal budget: past failures to control deficits has left governments with few options in the nineties.

If Keynes were alive today, he would be waging a vigorous fight against current economic policy. He aimed to show that governments were responsible for economic balance. He did not intend for them to embark on a crusade for ever-increasing wealth. Keynes clearly understood that his thinking would require citizens and governments to change the total structures of their economies and societies. Keynes made this clear in a much quoted essay entitled "Economic Possibilities for our Grandchildren." He wrote, "when the accumulation of wealth is no longer of high social importance, there will be great change in the code of morals. We shall be able to rid ourselves of the pseudo-moral principles by which we have exalted some of the most distasteful of human qualities into the position of the highest values."

The events of the seventies and eighties

The optimism of the fifties and sixties, and the high rates of growth in these decades, began to alter in the early seventies. One primary factor in this shift was the destabilization of the American economic systems as a result of oil shocks. More of the income and wealth of oil-importing countries was needed to pay for fossil fuels. Demand therefore began to move significantly ahead of supply in countries around the world. Inflation increased, along with interest rates.

By the end of the seventies, demand was so excessive that inflation in America was running at the rate of 13%. President Reagan broke the back of inflation at the beginning of his first term in office by creating a sharp recession. Increased anti-inflationary pressures also developed in many of the other rich countries. Higher rates of unemployment were accepted as tolerable by most economists, because they were thought to hold inflation down.

Starting in the seventies, the standard of living of most Americans began to decline: the average real wage in 1977 dollars, allowing for inflation, has declined from $189 to $168 over little more than a decade; this decline developed before the recession of the first Bush Presidency. Much controversy exists about what is really going on and why wage-earners are losing ground.

Several causes are obvious. One is that more money is being spent to buy raw materials overseas. A second is that America's growing debt leads to a transfer of funds from the U.S. to other nations. A third is that the change in tax structures caused the increase in income to go primarily to the top 1% of the population rather than being spread evenly. A fourth is that the number of high-wage production-line jobs available has decreased dramatically. More and more of the jobs created in the last decade have been low-paying, dead end activities which pull the average wage down. Although the United States has had a great deal of success in creating jobs, it has not been able to produce much well-paying work. One of the most dramatic consequences of these changes has been a major decrease in the standard of living for those under thirty.

The patterns which are emerging at the current time foreshadow the twenty-first century. Future activity will require imagination and creativity. Unfortunately far too many people do not know how to think for themselves. People who can only do what they are told will not have decent incomes in the future. Many of them will not be able to find jobs at all. One reason the poor are getting poorer is that fewer and fewer tasks can be accomplished simply by taking orders. These developments have been clearly reported in Robert Reich's book, *The Work of Nations.*

The situation of the middle class is changing rapidly. The continuing development of the computer is steadily eroding the type of work which is done by much of the middle class. The task of middle-level management is to take ideas developed at the top level and pass them down to workers. They also synthesize the results of activities within the organization and the feedback from workers and provide information to those at the top. Computers are continuously replacing this type of activity and will do so to a greater and greater extent in the future.

Whole levels of middle management are being eliminated and this process will continue, and even accelerate. The work of professionals is also being aided by computers. Computers, or machines guided by computers, can do any task where the exact conditions can be precisely stated in advance. The progressive replacement of human beings by machines controlled by computers is inevitable.

The good news is that more will be produced with less human effort. The bad news is that our economic system, as currently organized, turns this potential into disaster, creating unemployment rather than freeing time for creative activity. The fact that we can produce more using less time needs to be seen as the benefit it is. It can only be beneficial, however, after fundamental changes take place in socioeconomic systems.

The recent emphasis on free markets

The real-world developments of the last two decades have coincided with an enormous shift in dominant economic theories. Across the globe, the emphasis has moved away from ensuring full employment to control of inflation and away from intervention aimed at supporting desired social goals to setting markets free.

Free markets are currently touted as the answer to all problems throughout the world; for example in the Soviet Union, Eastern Europe and the Southern nations. In effect, "cowboy capitalism, based on greed," is being proposed without thought for its social or political consequences. It is true that free markets do ensure better resource allocation than communist or socialist bureaucratic models. They are not, however, the panacea which current dogma proclaims. Indeed, the fact that free markets produce efficiency is not enough of a recommendation. Various opposition parties in Britain have it right when they propose "social markets." Unfortunately, they seem unable to describe what this statement means.

They should not find this task so difficult. In the first half of the twentieth century Joan Robinson, a remarkable Britisher who recognized that economics had always advanced the interests of the ruling classes, showed what would happen if free markets were adopted in the absence of the conditions which made them appropriate. She proved that in capitalist economies, free markets would benefit the powerful and the rich against the poor and the weak.

This reality can be easily understood by taking an extreme case. A free market is often defined as one in which willing sellers and willing buyers can find a price which will "clear" the market: in other words where all available goods will be purchased. Suppose a famine develops and one merchant has grain because he has hoarded it. The food will certainly be bought at the price the merchant sets but it is ludicrous to argue that this is a free market. The possession of any sort of monopoly provides the opportunity to gain more than would be freely paid.

The same type of argument applies to free trade discussions. Suppose that the poor countries are selling their agricultural products in a free market. In these circumstances they have little, if any, control of prices. Suppose that the rich countries are primarily selling manufactured goods to the poor and are able to increase their prices above the level which would be set if buyers and sellers had equal clout. In this case the poor countries are obviously disadvantaged. Given that these are the current realities, a growing number of thinkers in poor countries, as well as many development experts, see free trade as being against the best interests of most developing countries.

In recent years, economists and politicians from the rich countries have tended to believe that the attitudes and the policies of less developed countries are obstructionist. In reality, the challenges from the developing countries to free trade doctrine are based on a more accurate understanding of economic theory than is used by rich-country economists.

Neo-classical economists, who developed the arguments for free markets, stated the conditions required if free markets were to ensure justice. Unfortunately, the people who currently promote free markets seem to have forgotten that these pre-conditions have not been realized and that current conditions therefore benefit the rich and powerful. Free markets produce equity, if and only if:

- no large firms exist to dominate prices and wages,
- information moves perfectly,
- labor unions cannot force up wages, and
- government does not intervene in the economy.

When these conditions are not in place, as they never can be completely, then free markets and free trade will benefit the rich and powerful over the poor and the weak.

A closer look at these four conditions shows that they are all related to the issue of power. Large firms often have power to set their own prices. Labor unions try to use power to increase the percentage of the resources flowing to organized workers. Information flows are often manipulated by those with power. Finally, governments use power to achieve the goals they have decided are desirable.

In the last decade, economists and politicians have recognized that fighting market forces results in inefficiencies. Unfortunately it has not, also, been recognized that the capitalist structure contains significant distortions as well. The challenge of the nineties is to dismantle the systems which benefit those with power and move toward a more level playing field.

REQUIREMENT 1. FIRMS SHOULD BE SMALL

Economists agree that if a single giant firm, or a small number of large firms, dominate the production or the purchasing of an item, they will inevitably have the power to control the price in ways which benefit them. They will also damage the interests of other firms and individuals. Similarly, if a country with large firms trades with a country with small firms and farmers, the country with large companies will inevitably gain an advantage. A true free market policy, therefore, would support the growth of small firms and remove incentives which support the continuance or growth of large ones.

Current trends favor the possibility of such a direction. In a world of rapid change, large, bureaucratic organizations are at a growing disadvantage compared with smaller, more flexible groups of people. Bigger organizations must move ideas through many layers of administration before they can be "heard" and then accepted or rejected. Large firms are therefore decentralizing.

The amount of control held at the center of effective large corporations continues to decline. Today decision-making frequently takes place in smaller structures, which can move far faster and more effectively. One of the dramatic examples of the decline of the "giants" has been the decrease in the power of the three major television networks. According to Nielsen Media Research 63% are watching the networks in 1991 as compared to 91% in 1979. People are watching other channels and are taking advantage of the VCR revolution.

A trend toward smaller organizations does not therefore need to be created. Governments simply need to get out of the way. But this is precisely what the U.S., and other, governments have been unwilling to do. They are willing to see small firms and banks fail but they get panicky when a large enterprise threatens to collapse. I was working in the Midwestern States during the agricultural depression of the mid-eighties where it was tragic to watch the effects of this bias. The collapse of a local bank in an agricultural area is inevitably devastating. The source of credit is gone. House and land values inevitably collapse. But federal bureaucrats who took over failed banks made matters even worse by calling in the credit which the bank had extended to companies which would have been viable if they had been able to maintain their loans.

Large organizations, on the other hand, have benefited from special treatment. Two primary examples are the bail-out of Chrysler and Continental Bank. Because Chrysler was thought to be too big to fail, the government put considerable money into the company. Despite this massive infusion of dollars, the company is again marginal. In a free market economy, failure must be allowed to happen. We are now beginning to realize that if individual failures are not permitted, whatever the size of the company, the risk of a system collapse is far greater.

Continental was the largest bank at risk in the first half of the 1980s. At a time when small banks were being permitted to go under, Continental was rescued by massive governmental intervention. The message sent was that small businesses and speculators who were stupid or imprudent would suffer the consequences, but those with larger bank balances would be bailed out. The Continental Bank bailout also sent a message to savings and loan executives, who adopted practices which they would have avoided if their money had been more directly at risk.

Large investors learned that the government was unwilling to tolerate the dangers involved in a major bank collapse and that they would therefore be safe, whatever their behavior. The current decline in the resources of the Federal Deposit Insurance Corporation, which insures banks, can be directly traced to this perception. Some who were involved in the original decision to save Continental now wish they had let it collapse; the long-run costs are turning out to be far more serious than acceptance of a bank failure would have been.

In addition, the government continues to support large depositors. While it is only obligated to pay out a total of $100,000 per account, it has often gone far beyond the legal requirements. It is charging the taxpayer with the costs of the failures rather than causing them to be paid, to the greatest possible extent, by the large speculators who gambled and should have lost. It is also rewarding the states where the greatest number of failures took place. Money is being transferred from geographical areas which behaved responsibly to those which did not.

The degree to which we are caught in old thinking is shown in our admiration for trends in Japan which are actually going in an undesirable direction, given this perspective. Japan has many of the largest firms and banks in the world. Up to now this has worked for them because they have been able to keep diversity out of their country. In the future, however, their current tactics will be ineffective. A growing number of Japanese know that they are not good at managing in the chaos which is so rapidly becoming the norm throughout the world. It is therefore ridiculous for the United States to try to follow outmoded norms.

The essential problem with corporations today is that they concentrate on short-run profits rather than long-run development. The basic criterion is whether sales are higher than immediate costs. At the extreme, this can even mean that legality is irrelevant. Indeed, some companies clearly see fines as a cost of doing business. This leads to the development of an extremely narrow line between legal and illegal businesses. So long as both legal and illegal businesses use power to make their decisions, the border between acceptable and unacceptable practices will often be unclear. Several years ago the *New York Times* summarized a report stating that "the qualities which lead to success in business are the same ones which lead to success in criminal behavior."

Companies should enlarge their sense of responsible behavior, looking at benefits and costs in a broader context. If companies do not learn to work with the overall dynamics of the culture and support it in constructive ways, they will find it more and more difficult to make a profit. In a paper written for the World Business Academy, Willis Harman asks "What are the tasks to which enlightened business is called?" He responds to his own question in the following way:

> If we are indeed approaching the point of "critical mass," where people suddenly realize (as in late-1989 Eastern Europe) that in some fundamental way the legitimacy of the present techno-economic system, and the values and beliefs that underlie it, has to be challenged, then the task shifts. If the transformation starts to happen with such rapidity that it generates a great deal of fear—fear of instability, of economic collapse, of mass unemployment, of an uncertain future, of the "crazies" in our midst—then the one thing people will crave most is stability. The overriding concern will be how the transition can be managed; how balance can be maintained; how we can keep the machine on the tracks. At that point the critical task changes. . . .
>
> This is the time the really critical role of business comes in. All the rest is preparation for the truly critical time in history when somebody has to reassure the fearful that the needed transformation can be accomplished without a lot of social disruption and attendant human misery. The experience of business leaders can be critical at that point—assuming that they are sensitive and aware enough to play a constructive rather than reactionary role.

REQUIREMENT 2. PERFECT MOVEMENT OF INFORMATION

Economic freedom depends on the availability of good information as does political freedom. Ideally everybody should be able to get correct information at the time they need it: differential flows of information inevitably give some people an advantage as compared to others. This is particularly obvious in the case of airline fares. In the current deregulated system, different passengers on the same flight may pay vastly different prices.

Some of the differences are dictated by the airlines, which have developed policies which force the business traveller, who has to make decisions at short notice and often cannot stay over a weekend, to pay higher fares. Some are simply the result of different levels of competitive pressures. For example, at the time I wrote this book, it was far cheaper to fly from one coast to another than from Chicago to Minneapolis. Patterns are often even more absurd. For example, it has been cheaper from time to time to buy a ticket from Spokane to Florida and disembark in Chicago, than to buy a ticket from Spokane to Chicago.

These patterns frustrate me because they cause me to waste time as I try to minimize the cost of my travels so that those who employ me spend as little as possible. They are far more damaging to people who fly only occasionally. Infrequent flyers often pay far more for a flight than the minimum fare. Airline and travel agents do not always tell people about the most attractive fares unless they are asked! It is only because I am aware of many of the quirks of the airline system that I pay as little as I do.

A lack of good information can be very costly in a very broad range of other fields. Today, almost every item is available at some sort of discount somewhere or another. This is the new version of the oriental bazaar. We no longer bargain with individual merchants on a face-to-face basis. Now we need to know where the best prices are available. Obviously many people do not have the time, or the skills, to search out the bargains and thus end up paying full price when they could have bought the same product for far less. Credit card issuers are now exploiting this pattern by offering guarantees but most busy people do not have the time to take advantage even of this simpler system. Knowing how to obtain good information therefore increases your standard of living. A systemic bias against the poor and the ill-educated inevitably exists in this area. If free markets are to be just, major efforts must be made to change this pattern. The children of the poor and the disadvantaged should be provided with opportunities to gain knowledge so they can break out of poverty.

If society commits itself to eliminating the information and knowledge biases against the poor and the ill-educated, many unexpected issues will arise. For example, fiber-optics, which are replacing copper cables for moving information, provide the potential of bringing a far wider range of information into the home. Given our existing economic system, fibre-optic systems will inevitably be installed first in rich and middle-class neighborhoods. One of the most effective uses of government money might be to reverse this priority and give the opportunities from fibre-optics to poor neighborhoods and schools first. This is, of course, a very different perspective from those which dominate efforts to help the poor at the current time.

There will never be totally accurate movement of information, of course, but if prices are to reflect real costs more accurately we must move toward this goal. One of the most important areas where rapid progress is needed is the inclusion in costs of what economists call "externalities." A company can sell goods at a lower price if it does not have to pay for damage to the environment. Information is needed to make it possible to charge companies for the ecological damage they do. A decision to tax pollution, which is suggested in the next chapter, is a step in this direction.

REQUIREMENT 3. LABOR UNIONS CANNOT FORCE UP
WAGES

Unions have lost much of their power in recent years. In part, the unions brought this reaction on themselves by abusing their position and causing widespread hardship to customers. There is therefore a growing tendency to assume that the free market system would work better if unions did not exist.

While the elimination of labor power is one of the conditions for fairness of free markets, undue concentration has been placed on this condition for realizing efficient free markets, while far less attention has been paid to the other three requirements. In a world where corporations are powerful, information movement is distorted and governments often serve the rich, unions are often required to act as a counterbalance. However, if they are to play this role effectively and also to be accepted as viable in the compassionate era, they are going to have to change their directions substantially.

Labor unions grew as a response to the overwhelming power of the nineteenth-century corporation. The position of workers in the nineteenth century was unattractive at best. They were hired when employers needed them, they received low wages when at work and they were let go at will. The individual worker had no opportunity to bargain on an equal basis with a far more powerful employer. Labor unions were supported because they were able to introduce some fairness into the process of setting wages. As a result of their efforts, a more reasonable share of the income of the firm went to the workers.

The strength of labor unions reached its peak in the 1950s and 1960s in the United States and many other parts of the world. During this time, labor unions and management in America essentially collaborated. They found it possible to raise prices and wages simultaneously, to the benefit of both management and labor. This approach worked until inflation began to increase as more players in the economic system adopted the same strategy. As a result, the United States became decreasingly competitive compared to many other parts of the world; its wages rose too high and its efficiency ceased to increase as rapidly as in other parts of the world.

In the last twenty years the unions have lost a great many members in most countries throughout the world. As a result behaviors are changing. This is true even in Britain where the unions have always been highly confrontative. It is being widely understood that unless management and labor learn to cooperate, jobs and markets will be lost. This result is inevitable in a world where the market is increasingly global and competition is not only internal but rather with all the world.

Is there still a place for unions or are they an anachronism? It is my belief that unions remain critically important when they commit to being part of a team with a significantly different perspective, rather than spending their primary efforts in fighting management. The perceptions of workers and management will always be at odds, and union/management discussions can provide a framework where differing ideas can be shared and worked through. In this way the inevitable conflicts can be creative rather than destructive and violent.

Where will tensions remain? One obvious area is around the proper levels of rewards within the new forms of organization which will inevitably have far less hierarchy than in the past. I like the idea of setting a maximum gap between the salary of the person at the top of an organization and the amount received by the worker who is paid least. A number of very effective organizations have set this ratio at 3:1 and I believe that something near this level is appropriate in many cases. I would suggest that the maximum appropriate multiple might be 10:1. This guarantees that there is no unbridgeable gap between the interests of those at the top of a corporation and those who are workers.

Unfortunately, trends have been in the opposite direction in the last decade. Benjamin Friedman, an economist at Harvard, has calculated that the ratio of the average salaries of the CEOs of the 300 largest companies in the U.S. to that of their average manufacturing employees was 20:1 in 1980 and 93:1 in 1990. The growing spread has led to much negative comment by business analysts and financial magazines in recent years.

Another unavoidable area of tension inevitably surrounds work structures and styles. People who look primarily at the overall directions of the organization, and those actually doing the work, will have different perceptions which will need to be mediated. Disagreements will inevitably arise. One of the most easily understood areas of tension exists in the airline industry. Issues look very different when seen from a pilot's seat rather than a manager's desk.

Management needs to keep as many flights moving as possible within their perception of safety requirements. Although pilots are interested in the same goal, the pressures to fly are stronger for management, which is committed to the bottom line. Pilots, by contrast, are primarily concerned with the safety of a particular flight. The pilot's absolute right to prevent a flight from taking off should be unassailable. A courageous union will be required to protect this right for as long into the future as I can see.

REQUIREMENT 4. NO GOVERNMENT INTERVENTION IN THE ECONOMY

The amount of government intervention required depends on two primary factors. The first is the degree to which the three conditions I have discussed above are realized. If there is a decrease in the number of large companies, an improvement in information flows and a decrease in union power, then government will have less to do. Equally critical, however, will be a revival of the moral code for social systems cannot function unless most people are committed to honesty, responsibility, humility and love.

Some governmental intervention will, of course, always be needed. The relevant questions are the points at which actions should take place, the goals which should be supported and the magnitude of the appropriate effort. The most critical, and difficult questions, revolve around social welfare issues.

Critics have suggested that the United States has a welfare system for the rich and a free market system for the poor. Unfortunately, this statement contains a great deal of truth. Why? Because the bills that benefit the middle-class and rich are easier to pass, while cuts in governmental activities which benefit the poor are simpler to make. Programs which benefit the underclass have less powerful constituencies than those which advance the interests of the powerful.

During the eighties, the burden on the poor has been greatly increased. Wealth has flowed to those at the upper end of the income ladder. The safety net is today not only tattered but torn. The tax system has become far less progressive. The census bureau recently did a study which compared income structures in 1969 and 1989—before any significant impact from the recession.

The study was based on the assumption that people with half the middle income are considered to have low relative incomes. Those with at least twice the middle income are considered to have high relative incomes. The proportion of people with middle-range incomes fell from 71 percent in 1969 to 63 percent in 1989. Half of the 8 percent moved into the higher income group and half into the lower. Another study showed that over 75% of the increase in income during the Reagan years went to those in the top 1% of the income distribution.

The challenge confronting us as we move into the nineties is complex. It is not a matter of rebuilding the liberal vision of the 1960s. The conservatives are right when they argue that the current welfare system encourages people to be lazy and cheat. Indeed many who are themselves on welfare share this understanding and see the system as a trap from which it is almost impossible to escape.

We must develop new socioeconomic systems which do provide equality of opportunity. A growing number of people are concentrating on the steps which can and must be taken to give the children of the disadvantaged a chance to escape the constraints which held their parents. The greatest positive impacts can be achieved from conception through the very young years, when patterns are often set for life.

The potential exists for positive directions if people are willing to look at the new dynamics and move with them. On the other hand, short-term horizons promote inertia in western societies. Margaret Mead, who was good at pithy sayings, once stated that: "In America the long-run is three months." In recent decades, the "long-run" has become even shorter! Most decision-making is today conducted with no sense either of the past which has shaped current realities nor the future to which people aspire. This failure to see the flow of events all too often means that issues are only taken up when they become crises and drop off the agenda as soon as some other question is "hotter." America seems extraordinarily crisis-oriented to Europeans like myself.

Problems are increased because government agencies are all too often dominated by bureaucrats who wait out political appointees. All Presidents have learned that controlling the decision-process as very difficult. President Kennedy once said, in effect, that he had to demand that something be done, ask why it hadn't been done and finally threaten dire punishment unless it took place. Then, and only then, was there a chance that action would occur.

Summing up, two conclusions must be stressed around the issue of free markets. The first is that free markets do ensure more efficient decisions than bureaucratically controlled systems. This has been proved by the collapse of controlled economic systems, such as in the Soviet Union. An estimated forty percent of Russian farm products, for example, never reach the consumer. Second, as long as there are differential levels of power, free markets and free trade will unfairly benefit some individuals, groups and countries as compared to others. One of the required commitments for the compassionate era is to move away from economic power and to permit free markets within social constraints. Fortunately, this trend is already established: all that is necessary is to release current dynamics rather than constrain them.

A new image

Herman Daly, an economist who challenges the growth ethic, has suggested that our present economic system is like a jet plane that must fly at high speed, because otherwise it will stall and crash. He suggested that we should start to think about a helicopter which could hover. However, a helicopter is both fuel-inefficient and noisy. I propose that we start thinking about a glider as our symbol for the future. I recognize the danger of pushing any analogy too far but there are some fascinating thoughts which emerge as one considers the operation of a glider.

First, the glider needs some initial energy input to get it airborne. Second, once aloft, the amount of time that the craft stays in the air depends on the skill of the pilot. Third, gliders are extraordinarily well designed to meet their purpose. Fourth, gliders eventually come to earth rather than continuing to fly for ever.

These are certainly useful images for thinking about economics in the compassionate era, where development and ecological balance must both be considered. First, any start-up activity will inevitably use up resources at the beginning. The appropriate questions are first, what is the minimum effective amount of resources needed to accomplish the purpose, and second, whether the gain will compensate for the expenditure of energy.

Second, just as an experienced pilot can find a thermal when the less skilled may miss it, an individual who knows how to carry through an activity has a far greater chance of succeeding than the uninformed. We can no longer justify a system that results in incredibly high failure rates for new enterprises of all types, both profit and non-profit. We need to educate and support local businesses rather than stand by and watch them fail. Communities should stop competing with each other for the limited number of firms which move each year and concentrate on supporting and developing the skills of local business and industry.

Third, the glider is brilliantly designed for its purpose. The post-industrial world will not have the resources to tolerate the overdesign and waste which is so common today. Overcoming problems by brute force, rather than by using imagination and knowledge, will not be acceptable in the future.

Finally, the image of the glider reminds us that nothing lasts forever: the craft eventually comes back to earth regardless of the skill of the pilot. We urgently need to relearn that just as we are afraid of personal death, we are also profoundly unwilling to recognize that institutions can totally outlive their usefulness. Huge amounts of waste are tolerated as we prop up obsolete profit, non-profit and governmental institutions.

I am not arguing that the glider is an ideal image. But it is true that people are going to have to learn to live with limitations on their power rather than believing that anything is feasible regardless of cost or waste. Current socioeconomic strategies stress human, computer and technological systems to the maximum. The goal is to work at 100% of capacity and possibly above! When crises come, there is little energy to cope with potentially disastrous consequences. We must put flexibility and redundancy back into human systems.

One key example of the dangers is the air controller system. Air controllers are asked to do more than is humanly feasible. The human costs to the controllers are very high. In addition, the risk of accidents is also increased. This is a recipe for disaster. Accidents are being caused by this strain, such as the collision between two craft on the runway in Los Angeles in 1991, and more will undoubtedly occur.

The alternative is to design human systems with "surplus capacity" so we work within the reasonable limits of human attention. In a few areas we have recognized this need for surplus capacity, expecting systems to be down some of the time. We do not expect fire fighters to fight fires continuously: our measurement of their effectiveness is in terms of response time in crises. In this case, society does recognize that efficiency and ability does decline beyond a certain point.

This type of thinking can now be applied throughout more and more of the society. People need the opportunity to be in peak form rather than be measured by the number of hours they work. Continuing toil and overload makes little sense when computers, and machines controlled by them, can take over more and more repetitive activity. Human beings can move back to more natural rhythms. Fortunately, there is growing evidence that they want to do so.

CHAPTER 5

Economics in the Service of Society and the Planet

MOST PEOPLE DO WHAT THEY ARE EXPECTED TO DO most of the time. Organizations and cultures could not function if individuals did what seemed best to them, without any attention to the overall system. Significant change cannot, therefore, be based only on individual shifts in behavior—institutions and societies must alter if any significant change in direction is to be possible.

Behaviors and directions will change only when we set new goals and reward different activities. This is true of all sorts of organizations: families, firms, schools, churches. An estimated 85% of behavior is controlled by the organization of a system and only 15% by the choices individuals make.

We can ask teachers, lawyers and others to function differently, but as long as the systems that control them remain unchanged, only a few people will alter their behaviors significantly. When those in charge of systems see the failure to make the desired changes they conclude that their initiative has failed and abandon it. They then launch a new approach without changing the system and fail again. This series of breakdowns is often called "moving the deck chairs around on the Titanic."

Cultures operate in the same way. Industrial-era behaviors are based on a particular set of assumptions and goals. For example, the incentives built into the welfare system are widely recognized as perverse because they encourage people to live off the state rather than develop their own skills. Under these circumstances, blaming poor people for their behavior is unfair. They are doing what we require of them. If we want to encourage different behavior, we must first change the system.

Real change requires putting in place a different set of reward structures that support truly different forms of behavior. Specifically, we must abandon the goal of maximum economic growth and discover ways to reduce the rate of increase in population. To do this we must rethink all the incentives built into industrial-era approaches. The approaches adopted must also help to reduce the power that people currently have to distort market forces for their own benefit.

As you read this chapter, remember that the steps necessary to achieve system shifts sound "shocking" because they go against the conventional wisdom. They will only seem credible as long as you remember the need for fundamental change.

The material in this chapter primarily examines rich country dynamics. This is where economics has become most dominant and where the change in directions needs to occur first. This does not mean that my arguments do not apply in the Soviet Union, Eastern Europe and the poor countries, but this is not my primary focus.

Taxes

Presidents Reagan and his successor George Bush have argued vigorously for a decrease in federal taxation but the percentage paid in taxes has actually increased rather than decreased, at the same time as the federal deficit has increased dramatically. The goal of reducing federal taxes is nevertheless feasible in a world where we must develop ecological balance, reduce violence and decentralize decision-making.

First, as decision-making moves back to communities, the amount of money raised at the national level should decline as federal entitlement programs are replaced by local action. This factor alone should reduce the need for federal taxation.

The amount of money needed for the military should also diminish dramatically as levels of armament throughout the world are lowered. Achieving maximum savings depends on whether the influence of the military/industrial complex, so named by President Eisenhower, can be sufficiently rapidly curbed.

The interest cost of the debt load, which rose rapidly throughout the eighties, can be decreased by cutting rates of growth and inflation: both of these will help decrease interest rates. Rates have been high for two reasons in recent years. One is to offset permanently rising costs. The other is the growing shortage of capital throughout the world as the amount that people want to do outruns available resources. When maximum economic growth strategies are abandoned, this will free up capital and therefore lower its cost.

Not only can tax levels be lowered, the ways taxes are levied should be significantly changed. Tax systems are never neutral. They impact various groups more or less harshly, depending on how they are set up. In the early post-World War II years, the United States tax system exempted almost all the personal income required for necessities from income tax. Inflation has reduced the value of exemptions drastically. As a result a far higher percentage of the population pays income taxes than forty years ago.

The impact of the social security system has also changed dramatically. Social security taxes were always levied on the first dollar of income earned since the program's inception, but the rates were very low in the 1930s and 1940s. Now the rates are over 7% for contributions from both the employer and the employee. The statistics are startling. Social security revenues now bring in 37% of federal revenues as compared to 20% as recently as 1970.

Current taxation policy is the result of a conflict between two fundamentally different ways of thinking. The first model is based on the assumption that benefits of growth will be broadly shared and that the best way to improve the economic situation of most people is to ensure maximum rates of economic growth. A phrase that is often used to explain this set of beliefs is that "a rising tide lifts all boats."

People who think in this way argue that tax rates should be low even on large incomes because they discourage effort by the most competent and therefore damage the interests of the poor. This view has been predominant for the last decade, not only in the United States, but in many of the rich countries. It is being challenged these days both on grounds of equity and, also, the ecological need to limit rates of economic growth in the rich countries.

The second model of taxation proposes that the rich should pay a larger percentage of their incomes because the deprivation which results from taking a dollar in taxes away from a poor person is more significant than the pain of taking a dollar away from the rich. The implication of this view is that taxes should be progressive with more taxes levied as people get richer.

So long as economic growth was the primary goal of economic systems there was a case for the first set of proposals. However, today, when the rich countries need to concentrate on equity and the quality of life, the argument for adopting the second approach is overwhelming. The same logic applies in the countries which are striving for development. Large disparities of wealth get in the way of the development process rather than supporting it. The traditional large gap between the rich and the poor needs to be narrowed by socioeconomic, particularly tax, policy.

What goals should, therefore, be adopted for taxation systems in the rich countries given the arguments I have made about required future directions? I believe that tax systems should:

■ Be designed to level the playing field so that the pain from taxation is as equal as possible. This means that the tax system would be progressive, taking more resources from the rich than from the poor. This compensates for the fact that our current economic system concentrates power, and resources, at the top of the economic ladder and unfairly discriminates against the poor.

■ Be easy to collect and hard to escape. Tax systems are honored when people feel they are making their fair contribution: they break down when people believe they are paying too much either in absolute terms or because some people are cheating.

■ Be used to encourage highly desirable behavior patterns and to discourage dangerous ones. This latter goal may cut across the others. For example, cigarette and liquor taxation is regressive because the poor smoke and drink more than the well-off. Indeed, higher rates of taxation on gasoline are also regressive. But these taxes move the culture in desirable directions and the regressive impacts can be offset by other types of taxes, particularly income taxes.

The adoption of these goals would change taxation policies profoundly. Although there is a myth of progressive taxation in the rich countries, the rate of taxation is usually remarkably similar throughout the tax brackets, with both the poor and the rich paying a little more in percentage terms than those in the middle class.

A taxation system based on the principles described above would curtail the tax breaks of special interest groups and move us toward radical simplification of the tax code. I am, of course, aware that movements toward simplicity have been subverted repeatedly and determining the amount of taxes one owes has become progressively more complex. However, taxpayers could demand real simplification of the tax code and impose this goal on Congress if a plan which gathered broad support could be found. Governor Brown placed this issue on the agenda in the residential election of 1992 although his plan was deeply flawed.

No one likes paying taxes. Democracies have nevertheless been able to preserve an essentially voluntary system with tax avoidance kept to a tolerable level. In recent years, this system has been breaking down. It can only be restored if everyone believes tax rates are reasonable and they are levied fairly.

CONSUMPTION TAXES

A large part of the tax burden should be raised through consumption taxes rather than income taxes. Consumption taxes tend to discourage demand and encourage savings. Consumption taxes should be low on food and pharmaceutical drugs, higher on most other goods and highest on liquor, cigarettes and gasoline. Consumption taxes should normally be included in the purchase price rather than added on at the point of sale. Gasoline taxes are, of course, already levied in this way.

Consumption taxes are often seen as attractive by economists who promote growth, because they believe this will increase the pool of savings and therefore the amount of investment. If they are introduced into a society which is still committed to maximum growth and labor force participation, this result may well occur. If, on the contrary, they are set up as part of a move to reduce growth, they will tend to reduce demand and permit a decrease in the amount of time that people have to spend working. The number of people in the labor force can then decline and people who want to do so can choose to stay home.

Energy taxes are a special type of consumption tax. Almost all countries in the world have high taxes on energy products, particularly oil and gasoline, with prices at the pump three or four times as high as those in the United States. The United States can solve much of its overseas deficit problem, and also decrease its dependence on overseas oil dramatically, by moving toward the energy tax rates which apply in the rest of the world. Such a move will, inevitably, require significant changes in behavior patterns and force cuts in local and long-distance travel but this shift is already long overdue.

We must make a long-run commitment to increased energy taxes. The shift must not be too abrupt because the impact would be very disruptive. On the other hand, the decision must be irrevocable because increased prices for energy will fundamentally shift the direction of the economy and the culture. For example, assumptions about future levels of road and air travel will change dramatically and necessary infrastructure costs will be significantly decreased.

I propose that the increases be phased in over five to eight years and be fully in place no later than the end of the nineties. Moving faster than this would probably be more disruptive than it is worth. Taxation would increase by about 25 cents a year which would bring the cost per gallon up to the approximately $3.50 already paid by the British—with similar rates in other European countries. Some of this money should go to the States and some to the Federal government. However, it now seems possible that Europe will increase its prices still further: and the 25 cent annual increase may therefore have to continue for even more years. As gas taxes rise, more and more people will decide to work at home. The potential for telecommuting increases all the time.

I am aware that this proposal is often seen as almost "treasonous." The goal of raising gas taxes by even 5 cents a gallon was one of the nails which destroyed Tsongas's Presidential bid. The right to cheap travel is taken for granted in the United States. It is only as people mesh their understandings of the ecological and resource needs of the future with their economic and personal understandings that the political support for such a measure will develop.

SOCIAL SECURITY TAXES

Whatever the tax rates used for consumption, sin and energy taxes, the poor will inevitably pay a larger percentage of their income than the rich and thus be worse off than at the current time. Despite the fact that social security is normally presented as a government insurance policy, this has never been the case. Payments for retirement are only loosely related to the amounts people contribute.

President Roosevelt "sold" social security as a way of providing pensions to everybody on a pay-as-you-go basis. It was a narrow system designed to force savings so that people would have a pension when they retired. In recent decades it has been broadened drastically and now covers all sorts of other benefits which should be met be general taxation. Social security taxes should now be eliminated and the tax cost transferred partly to consumption taxes, partly to income taxes and partly to corporate taxes.

If you are under 40, you should be well aware that the social security system will not survive to give you the benefits for which you are paying. Around 2030, there is going to be one retired worker for every two people in the labor force. This means that a huge percentage of earnings would be transferred to retired workers. I cannot imagine any circumstances in which such a model of generational equity will be acceptable.

It is time for social security to be abandoned, with guarantees that those who have paid funds into the system will be adequately compensated when they are old. We need to develop new approaches which will fit into the lifecycle patterns of the compassionate era when work cycles will be far more complex and people will "retire" at a far later date.

Current policies around social security are one of the most shocking governmental scams of our time. In the eighties, social security rates were raised to provide a surplus which would pay for the increasing number of retirees in the twenty-first century. This decision never made sense because the problem for the future is the transfer of real goods and services from workers to non-workers rather than financial exchanges. The later decision to use the social security surplus to keep down the apparent level of the federal deficit makes a total mockery of the rationale for raising social security rates. Senator Moynihan has tried to force the Senate to deal with this issue without success.

INCOME TAXES

Consumption taxes should be the basic tax in the future. Income tax would then only be levied on incomes above the level required for basic needs and should be adjusted each year to take inflation into account. This approach was used throughout the history of the income tax, until persistent inflation reduced the value of deductions in the last half of the twentieth century.

Three levels of tax might be considered. The first would apply for those earning above the average income. All income below this would be free of income tax. The second tier would apply when people had more than ten times the average income. And the final level, which would be heavy, would be paid when people received twenty times the average income. All income would be included; there would be no deductions or exemptions. The possibility of a postcard return would be real.

Capital gains taxes would be levied at the same rate as taxes on ordinary income. But they would be adjusted for inflation so that people do not pay for gains which occur because of rising prices. The trend toward a close relationship between state and federal income taxes would be encouraged so as to limit the amount of time individuals spend preparing their tax returns.

CORPORATE TAXES

Corporate taxes have dropped dramatically in recent decades. This change was based on the justification that corporate taxes are inevitably passed through to customers, workers or employees and this is undesirable. Corporate taxes do indeed tend to increase the cost to the consumer. They are therefore appropriate in the changed context I am proposing, because they do tend to reduce the drive toward maximum economic growth. The percentage of total taxes paid by corporations should rise again to the level paid in 1950. This will not be as onerous as it might appear because the employer's part of the social security tax would be absorbed into the corporate tax system, lessening the burden on the marginal firm.

Another consequence of this shift would be to decrease dividends because net profits would fall. As dividends go overwhelmingly to the rich, this would also tend to reduce the degree of income disparity.

INHERITANCE TAXES

In the long-run, inheritance taxes and gift taxes should be abandoned. Income should be taxed when it is received for the first time at rates which seem fair to the people in the culture. However, given the concentration of wealth at the current time, it seems appropriate that really large estates should continue to pay significant tax.

ADVERTISING TAXES

Institutions should pay a significant tax on advertising above a minimum figure which would exclude most non-profits and mom and pop operations—say $20,000 annually. Such a step would dramatically reduce pressures to consume. I am aware that it will be difficult to define advertising appropriately, and to distinguish it from information movement, but the need to reduce consumption makes the challenge worth the problems. Indeed, if the advertising tax exempts information hot-lines and other similar activities, this can shift corporate resources away from promotion and towards customer support.

Taxing advertising will have significant secondary consequences. The first would be to reduce the amount of money flowing to professional sports and popular artists who rely heavily on sponsorship and advertising revenues. The second result would be a massive shake-out in the information and entertainment industries. This is already beginning to happen with decreasing funds available to support the current array of papers, magazines, television programs, etc.

Since "infoglut" is one of the most serious problems of our time, the long-run results can only be desirable, but there will be negative consequences as some information outlets are lost. It will therefore be critically important for each of us, in our personal and institutional decisions, to weigh where we are putting our information dollars. We should use them to support those efforts which seem most in line with our vision of the future.

POLLUTION TAXES

All activities inevitably create unneeded by-products, but we can make choices about how these by-products will be handled. We can either carelessly discard them, with consequent damage to air, land and water or develop careful policies that limit negative consequences. Only recently have we recognized the danger of continuing the first pattern.

Many years ago I coined the phrase, "Nothing is ever wasted; everything is always wasted" to draw attention to the fact that a product's value is dependent on the situation. Waste occurs because something is in the wrong place at the wrong time. On the other hand, waste can often be made valuable by processing or other means. As companies and communities understand this, more and more recycling is taking place.

Any significant review of the total waste problem must recognize the relative amount of waste from households and from business and government. While cutting down on municipal waste is useful, as is already happening is a number of communities, it is by far the smaller part of the total problem. The real issue is to begin to reduce substantially the amount of waste in industrial, government and military activities.

Pollution and waste can be curbed in several ways. One choice is law and regulation. This is the route that is normally chosen today. Fines can be levied when regulations are not followed. Fines are so small, however, compared to the resources of firms, that they are unlikely to affect the policy decisions of those companies which are willing to cut corners. The recent movement toward jail sentences for executives may make them more careful, but this increases the jail population, which is hardly a desirable result when overcrowding and costs are already major problems. In addition, the distinction between "country-club" jails and those that most inmates have to endure raises major equity questions.

The alternative choice is to "sell" licenses to pollute. This type of approach is based on making decisions about the speed at which pollution can reasonably be reduced. Once this choice has been made, pollution rights are allocated by auctions. This is only a rough measure of need but it is often preferable to bureaucratic choices so long as power has been more or less equalized. Selling pollution rights also has the benefit of raising resources which can be used to reduce the tax burden on others. In the real world, there will need to be a mix between coercion to prevent certain types of pollution and the use of the free market.

STOCK AND COMMODITY TRANSFER TAXES

Stock and commodity markets provide the best available way to set prices and values despite their major imperfections. For these markets to operate effectively, enough people must be involved and transactions made, so that all points of view about present and future realities are represented.

This valid rationale for stock and commodity markets should not be extended to a belief that society benefits from large-scale speculation, which takes advantage of very short-term market or indices shifts. On the contrary, such speculation draws energy away from other more useful types of activity. This type of trading could be substantially reduced by the introduction of a more significant transaction tax on securities and commodities sales. If the rate were the same in all national markets, investors would not move business from one national exchange to another. Such a tax would bring in significant money even at a very low rate: part of the proceeds might be used for global needs.

Changing lifecycles

Our economic system is built around a work week which typically ranges from 35 to 40 hours, five days a week. Societies will only come to grips with the appropriate directions for the future after we recognize how little time people actually spend on the job in the modern world. If one relates the total number of hours in a person's life to the amount of time they spend on their jobs, it only amounts to some 15%. This is down from about 35% in the nineteenth century.

When I cite these figures people look at me disbelievingly. I point out that even on a "working" day, people work only about 33% of the day. They do not work on weekends, they get vacations and public holidays. They do not start work till 16, 18, 22 or even later. Most people are now retired by the age of 65, many leave or are forced out of their jobs even in their fifties, and the average lifespan continues to rise.

The potential for fundamental changes in the way to structure work is therefore obvious. If only one hour in seven is spent at work during one's life, the possibility of dramatic changes in lifecycles is obvious. It is time we moved beyond thinking about decreasing the hours of work each week to imagining totally new patternings for life. For example, it might be beneficial for most people to take a year off every five or seven years to relearn and to recharge their psychic batteries.

This decrease in job-related activity does not mean people necessarily have vast amounts of spare time, indeed there appears to have been a decrease in leisure. The evidence also suggests people are more stressed than in earlier periods. They are spending a great deal of time commuting, for example. The amount of paper work required to keep track of everything from medicare to tax returns, from product guarantees to insurance, is numbing. And when one adds the airline and hotel travel plans, and everything else that a consumption-conscious culture pushes on us, we never seem able to catch up.

One of the extraordinary developments of the last forty years has been the change in thinking about leisure. In the sixties and seventies people believed they would have more time to themselves. In the eighties and nineties people find themselves increasingly overstressed and overloaded. We have created a "reverse leisure society," where those who have the most responsibility also have the least time to enjoy life.

An even more complex issue is emerging as the relationship between organizations and their workers shifts dramatically. People no longer expect to stay with a single institution all their working life. Nor do they believe that their basic loyalty belongs to the organization for which they work: they place importance on their family, their community, their church and other relationships which impinge on their lives.

In reality, only a small number of people were willing to give up their whole existence to their organizations even in the past. But enough people chose this lifestyle that it became the norm for those who wanted to get ahead rapidly. Today, however, institutions are being forced to develop a wide range of options if they are to hold onto their best workers. They are finding that this does not raise nearly as many problems as they originally thought.

There is no longer a single track from the bottom of an organization to the top. You will no longer automatically be sidelined if you are not totally committed to the success of the firm, but have priorities of your own. A growing number of firms, over 4,000 by one count in 1990, are actively encouraging part-time, flex-time, shared jobs and other creative options. They recognize people are more creative when they are happy, and that overloading employees is a recipe for failure.

In 1991, IBM introduced a program which will permit people to work part-time indefinitely. It also expanded programs for allowing employees to work from their homes. Christine A. Scordato, director of research for Catalyst, an organization which fosters leadership development for women, recently conducted a study on flexible programs. She said: "The vast majority of the companies in our study were overwhelmingly pleased, sometimes much to their surprise. They've become advocates. It's a good way to retain qualified, experienced employees. One manager said, 'I'd rather have half of that person than none.' "

People will change their activities continuously even if they remain in a single profession all their lives. The skills needed by plumbers and doctors, electricians and astronomers alter as new technologies are learned. Life is also becoming a mix of work and education. Those who do not keep up are going to lose their chance at a fulfilling life. Lifecycles therefore need to be restructured so that learning can be more effectively integrated into them. The patterns of integration between work and education must be significantly altered.

We can anticipate great changes in the way life is structured in the future. The current division of life into three periods; education to prepare for a job, doing the job and being retired is a uniquely industrial-era pattern. Retirement did not exist in hunting and gathering or agricultural societies; people were expected to do their part until they died. The idea that there needed to be a long preparation for usefulness in the work world also first emerged in the industrial society. These industrial-era patterns will not persist into the compassionate era.

It is therefore critically important that we consider how lifecycles are likely to change. First, the idea that education should be concentrated in the first 15 to 25 years of life must be abandoned. This will be a pragmatic decision driven by the speed of change and the absolute necessity for people to continue learning throughout their lives. In addition, work will start earlier. It will be recognized that adolescence should not be spent in the classroom because people in their teen years are full of energy and need to use it. Much of the discipline required for life can be learned in these years. Activities enabling people to meet others from all classes and races has much to recommend it at this time of life.

At the other end of the life span, the current concept of retirement will be abandoned. This too will be a pragmatic necessity. Because of far longer lifetimes than in the past, personally-challenging and societally-supportive activity will need to continue into the seventies and even the eighties. Although people will want to decrease the intensity of their activities as they grow older, most will stay involved. While many individuals are today fleeing their jobs as soon as they can afford to do so, there is also a growing search to find activities which contribute to the society and provide personal satisfaction.

A third major shift will take place in family life. As is well known, the number of women in the labor force has increased steadily during the second half of the twentieth century. Too many of them have so far been confronted with an effective ultimatum; give your full life to the company or be relegated to the "mommy" track where there is little chance of developing your skills to the full.

The Western commitment to maximum labor force participation has produced a growing number of families where both parents hold jobs. It has also made it necessary for almost all single-parents to find paid activity. This has created enormous pressures on schools which have to carry out tasks which were previously the responsibility of parents. It has also produced an ever-growing demand for child care.

In the future, new structures must be set up which permit both males and females to take time off for parenting. Time spent in this way should be seen as opportunities for self-development by both parents and employers. The skills required for successful parenting are high-level ones; taking time out to raise children should therefore not be seen as disqualifying people from a successful career.

Two profound shifts are required in parenting strategies. First, people should not choose to have children unless this is truly important to them. At present, many couples decide to have children when they realize their fertile years are almost over; they are traumatized by the ticking of the biological clock. This is no longer an adequate reason for child-bearing unless it is accompanied by a passionate commitment to raising the next generation of children so they can develop their potential to the full.

The second need is to break out of the belief that all families should be small. Some people who find their satisfaction in raising kids may well choose to have several children. Those concerned with population growth should not abuse them. Parents who can raise competent and compassionate kids are highly valuable. The increase they cause in the population can be offset by others choosing to remain childless, putting their energy into being real, or fictive, aunts and uncles. Each of us needs to commit to raising the next generation in ways which gives them the maximum chance.

Rethinking income distribution

Our attitudes toward income distribution are obscured by an extraordinary level of misinformation. At the end of the nineteenth century, economists developed a remarkable theory which "proved" that the amount each person got paid was equal to the value of their contribution. Unfortunately this theory only applies in a simple agricultural world and has little relevance in today's complex societies, where we are all dependent on the efforts of others for our success.

In today's conditions, income distribution depends largely on social norms. The amount teachers get paid relative to plumbers is not primarily a result of supply and demand but of accepted patterns of thinking. The wealth paid to people who manage the society does not result from hard data that a CEO is worth a given amount. It often arises from a cozy relationship between those who set salaries and those who receive them. The relationship between the payment to a nation's leader and that paid to sports stars is evidence of warped priorities, not of relative worth.

Given that income levels are largely set by social norms and not by economic imperatives, we must begin to ask ourselves what is the appropriate gap between the rich and the poor in a society. I have already argued that the amount of power in the society should be reduced, and that the progressiveness of taxes should be increased. This will result in a decrease in the size and number of high incomes.

I want to examine at this point how we should deal with the problem of the underclass. Almost everybody agrees that this issue is becoming increasingly intractable. People who do not have the ability to learn throughout their lives are doomed to exclusion from any chance of an effective life. Two factors must be dealt with here. One, which is taken up in the next part, is the need to design a society where learning is at the center of life.

The other is to ask whether a society can afford to develop a permanent underclass or whether the costs are too high. The evidence about the dangers of a permanent underclass is increasing every day. Cities are disintegrating as the number of poor increases. Crime rates are rising. The percentage of the population which is not being educated continues to grow. Something different obviously has to be done.

The answer I developed to this problem in the sixties was Basic Economic Security (BES.) This was later called a "guaranteed income" or a "negative income tax." BES provides all citizens with a basic standard of living because they are in a rich country. There were two primary rationales for this proposal. One was that we were already guaranteeing incomes. Nobody was permitted to starve but the approaches used were messy, untidy and costly. Second, the idea of income as a right would help to destroy both the psychic and practical aspects of the current welfare trap.

President Nixon adopted this idea when be proposed the Family Assistance Plan. If it had been passed at the time when it was initially proposed, I have no doubt it would have been successful. It would have given everybody a basic income, which would have provided a sense of self-respect and an opportunity for self-development. At the end of the sixties most people hoped for better things and believed that the government was benign. It would also have stopped the development of many middle-class support programs whose rationale would have been undercut if appropriate mechanisms to deal with poverty had been available.

Today, the balance is harder to draw. There are many potential negatives which could sabotage a guaranteed income plan in today's world. One of the greatest dangers is the one expressed in *Player Piano* by Kurt Vonnegut and by many other science-fiction writers. These writers fear that if the underclass is provided with an income, they would then be ignored and deprived of any possibility of purposeful activity. As a result, this group would be marginalized to an even greater extent.

The difficulties of introducing a BES system are increased by the fact that more people feel justified in abusing government systems than in the past. The degree of disaffection with the establishment has grown. A properly developed plan could have provided many people with a sense of pride if it had been introduced 20 years ago. Now a larger percentage would simply waste the funds rather than use them effectively.

Even so, I am convinced that the benefits of BES exceed the costs. BES provides resources to everybody without being dependent on bureaucratic regulations and whim. It signals that a rich society can afford an income for all citizens based on the wealth accumulated over time. It simplifies the maze of regulations which have grown up and will help to eliminate many middle-class support measures which should not exist. It encourages society to remember that the justification for providing resources from government is primarily financial need.

Nevertheless, BES proposals are still a stopgap. We need to move forward to a time when support to individuals is primarily carried out at the community level. We shall do better when there are fewer federal taxes and services. More money should be left in the community so that it can make its own decisions about how help should be organized and the amount of help that should be given.

One desirable step in this direction would be to continue the currently developing dynamic which provides communities with waivers that permit them to organize economic support systems in ways which seem good to them. As communities take more responsibility, the amount of money their inhabitants send to state and federal governments should be decreased.

Social service agencies throughout the country are already being challenged to rethink the way they operate. The present welfare model demands a set of clear rules for allocating benefits. The employee working with the client is responsible for understanding the rules and applying them exactly. When an employee fails, that person is called to account for her errors. The federal government requires the error rate to be kept as low as possible and has penalties for states and organizations which cannot get the error rate down below the required minimum.

People are unique, however, and no set of rules covers all the possibilities. The greater the number of rules and regulations, and the larger the number of possible loopholes, the harder fairness becomes. If, on the other hand, there is a very tight framework, many people will not fit within the rules.

What is the alternative to current models? Society ought to help people in terms of their individual requirements. It should enable them to find the type of help they require when they need it. One first step toward developing this model would be the availability of an information line to inform people where to apply for help through a single phone call. Such a system should be staffed by individuals who are competent enough to discover real needs in a complex human situation. This sort of system exists everywhere in Britain and also in a growing number of communities across the United States.

If helping systems are set up for this purpose, workers cannot be supervised in the traditional way. They cannot be evaluated on the basis of whether rules and regulations were correctly applied. Instead, judgments must be in terms of whether the available resources were used as effectively as possible to help those in need. We must therefore learn to distinguish between those who are deserving of help from the community and those who are not. Some people who have had a run of bad luck genuinely need support, while others are willing to take advantage of any available programs.

I have come to believe that the ability to make this type of judgment about commitment and effort is central to life itself. All our relationships are in a very real sense governed by the need to make this choice. When do you push children harder, when do you give them love and caring, when do you push for creativity? When do you help a co-worker over a rough patch and when do you demand performance? When do you help a family and when do you demand they help themselves?

If we were all fully adult, this problem would not arise but many of us are not mature now and are unlikely to be at any time in the foreseeable future. Choosing between those who need support and those who abusing systems is always a judgment call. It depends on hunch and instinct and guts. It is one of society's primary responsibilities.

CHAPTER 6

Positive Actions as Consumers and Workers

You AND I CAN DIRECTLY AFFECT OUR LIVES through consumption, work-style and work-place decisions. The individual choices we make alter the perceptions of producers and decision-makers. Choices in these areas often have far more impact than our votes, where all too often we find little difference between the candidates of the various parties.

Why do so many of us fail to recognize the impact of our own personal choices? Part of the reason is the current belief that only those in power can create changes in a culture. In reality, the impact of a change in tastes and styles is far more pervasive than that of orders given by those at the top. Each of us needs to think about the things we buy, the ways we spend our time, our use of resources and the possibilities we have for influencing patterns in our place of work.

Our consumption decisions are "votes" about the future of ourselves and our society. If we perceived our purchases in this way, we would be far more careful about our choices. One dramatic shift in consumption patterns is the movement toward healthier prepared foods. More and more packaged foods have low fat and sodium. The demand of people for better nutrition has led manufacturers to invent new lines. These have increasingly taken over the available display space from less healthy dishes. Similarly, the fast food restaurants have reduced the amount of fat in their dishes.

It can be argued that this is not enough. Because of the amount of packaging involved in prepared foods, their environmental costs are high. It would be better if people were willing and able to buy in bulk and prepare more foods for themselves. But this option is not realistic for many today and we must take comfort in the progress we are making, while realizing much remains to be done.

I recently heard about a further result of this change in nutrition preferences from a woman who is responsible for a school food service. She had just been to a convention where suppliers were making their pitches to school districts. When she initially walked into the display area she was startled to find that instead of the air being filled with grease and fat from fryers, as had been the case in the past, only about three companies were preparing food in this way.

Another area of significant change has been around alcoholic drinks. More companies are reformulating their products so they are less alcoholic. Non-alcoholic wine and beer are also more widely available. Similarly, decaffeinated coffee and tea are now easy to find on supermarket shelves.

Huge changes have taken place in the way we live. We often fail to recognize them because we concentrate on the alterations that are not yet complete rather than on the gains we have already accomplished. As a result, we often conclude that our situation is hopeless instead of recognizing significant progress. Certainly the shifts are slower than would be desirable but a better awareness of our accomplishments would encourage each of us to go further. Feeling that nothing is happening hampers our ability to be creative and take risks.

Another indicator of our positive directions is the growing availability of recycled products. Recycling aluminum cans was one of the first significant efforts. This happened because the economics were easy. Recycling aluminum is much cheaper than getting it from bauxite. More recently, great progress has been made in the field of paper. Recycled paper damages the environment less than cutting down additional trees, but the economic benefits are smaller, and recycled paper may still cost more than virgin.

The block to greater levels of recycling often results from a failure to develop the demand for the recycled product. In most cases, the commitment to recycling has grown faster than the creation of uses for the recycled product. Each time this happens it slows the development of a viable system because the amount of money which a recycling process can earn is inadequate to support businesses. Becoming ardent recylers is not enough. We must also support those who create and sell recycled goods, buying them whenever we can.

As we begin to think about what we should buy, all sorts of complexities emerge. For example, the answer to the argument about whether cloth or throw-away diapers are more damaging to the environment is not clear cut. At first sight, the resources used to produce disposable diapers, and the environmental costs when they are thrown away, seem clearly higher than for those made of cloth. Once all the costs associated with the transportation and washing of cloth diapers have been taken into account, the equation is not nearly as obvious.

We have to increase our judgment skills. We must be careful about accepting all the claims of the companies adopting environmental themes. We need to ask whether their ads are a public relations ploy or whether they have actually shifted to styles of production less damaging to the environment

In addition to changing our shopping habits, we can be proactive by asking the managers of stores to stock more desirable products. They pay an amazing amount of attention to the few people who speak up. For each person who makes requests, a dozen or a hundred keep silent. By changing the purchasing patterns of stores, we break through another of the problems innovators face. While they can commit to better products, they will only stay in business if they can sell them.

How we spend our entertainment and information dollars also has strong impacts. If we support violence in the movies, there will be more violent movies. If we support pornography, there will be more pornography. If we support family values, they will appear more often in our entertainment. If we are willing to support local drama and the arts, our community is more likely to have a vibrant cultural life.

Another critical question is our choices about where we spend our information dollars. Many groups are trying to put out information about the compassionate era. Most of them are struggling. Some of their problems result from competing groups doing the same things. But much of their difficulties stem from the fact that too many of us are spending our money on industrial-era information systems rather than supporting those who are thinking and acting to move us in new directions.

I know many change-oriented people who take *Time, Newsweek, Business Week, Atlantic* and *Harpers.* They do not take *In Context* and *The Sun,* not to speak of periodicals with even smaller circulations which are providing critically important information. And yet these magazines give us a better grasp of where our culture is moving and thus enable each of us to make better decisions. Subscriptions to the leading-edge publications will also reduce the financial stress on those who have chosen to devote their lives to producing this sort of material.

Another way we can make a major difference is to move away from consumption and toward saving. We can decide we don't need many of the things we are buying. Many impulse purchases languish on our shelves and stuff our closets. How often have you heard people lament, when they are moving, about the amount of junk they have accumulated over the years?

Resources for Creative Change

To receive your copy of *Guidebook for the '90s: Resources for Effecting Personal and Social Change* please complete and mail this card. We screen hundreds of publishers and networks for books, tapes and organizations to assist you in...

✔ coping with overload
✔ engaging in sacred play
✔ creating sacred time & space
✔ making sense of the times

✔ discovering high vocational adventure
✔ catalyzing creativity in organizations
✔ exploring the new consciousness
✔ and much, much more!

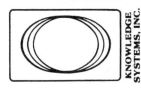

KNOWLEDGE SYSTEMS, INC.

Name _____

Address _____

City & State/Prov. _____

Zip/Postal Code _____

Knowledge Systems, Inc.
7777 West Morris Street
Indianapolis, IN 46231

Buying less decreases the damage we do to the earth. Fortunately, thrift is becoming a "growth industry." A growing number of people are wondering how they got caught up in the desire for possessions and forgot about having time for themselves and their citizenship obligations. They also see thrift as a way to live more lightly on the earth. Being thrifty and savings-oriented is a challenge in a culture that bombards us with consumption opportunities. Buying on credit cards is particularly hazardous to our ability to balance our finances. Thrift must become an initial priority, with savings a first step. We must learn to match expenditures to the amount we have available, keeping savings sacrosanct.

Savings impact our own lives, of course. But a significant move toward additional saving would also dramatically change the functioning of the economic system. Demand would drop below supply and a recession or slump would develop. At this point, unemployment becomes a problem. Given today's thinking the only response that seems appropriate to most people is increasing demand again. In effect, then, economists and politicians will try to neutralize and reverse the decisions which are being made by citizens. As long as industrial-era thinking persists, this is indeed the only option.

An obvious alternative does exist. We could reduce supply. One of the most viable ways to achieve this goal would be to reduce the number of hours that people spend working during their lives. People could be released from job structures they find unattractive and freed to do more of the things they like. This move would be popular because recent polls have shown that people would like more time for themselves even if this reduced their income. This opens up the whole question of the work we each do, and should do, in the future.

Right livelihood

As we think about the work we want, we need a sense of historical perspective. Slavery, bondservice and serfdom were once the most common forms of master-worker relationships. The Civil War was the watershed that changed these patterns for ever. The only acceptable mode after this time was the wage-contract. The employer was responsible for paying a wage whenever the worker was present at the job.

The new pattern had very different consequences from the old. People had increased freedom to move upwards in the society. But conditions for most wage-earners in the late-nineteenth century remained terrible. They could be laid off whenever the employer wished and no security existed for the unemployed. The stories about the sweat shops of the late nineteenth and early twentieth century make this point vividly.

Only at the end of the 19th century did social safety nets begin to prevent the starvation and early death of those who were unable to find work and had no kin to look after them. The twentieth-century saw an ever-growing commitment to support those who were unfortunate.

One of the results of our changing structures is that the commitment to a day's work for a day's pay is a declining ethic. More people see their jobs as a necessary evil which enables them to do what they really want. Work is not seen as worthy of commitment but as a way of getting money. High quality standards and good decision-making are, of course, impossible so long as these patterns continue. In addition, those who are willing to be creative often find themselves blocked by rules and regulations. Most people are now so busy doing their "jobs" that they don't have any time to do their work.

The proposals now being made for "right livelihood" must be understood in the light of this historical evolution. Right livelihood is the most common term used to express the desire people have to make a living in ways which satisfy themselves and support the planet. It expresses the desire to find work for which individuals are competent and where their skills contribute to something worthwhile. We therefore need to reform our educational systems so they will help people discover their strengths and weaknesses and enable them to choose where they can be most effective.

Another aspect of the necessary evolution of work structures, at the end of the twentieth century, is helping people reevaluate whether they want to continue to hold a job. The trend in the last thirty years has been for more and more people to enter the labor force. The first major wave was made up of women who wanted careers. The second wave has primarily consisted of people, largely female, who feel they must work in order to make ends meet.

Many people, however, earn less from their job than they pay in additional expenses. After deducting social security, taxes, child-care, increased costs of food, clothing and transportation, as well as money spent on weekends to make up for the frustration of the excessively busy work weeks, net income is often negative. I made this point recently in an Iowa community: a person I talked to afterwards provided a specific example. He told me that his secretary, who earned about $15,000, was quitting because a debt-counsellor had shown her and her husband that they would have a better chance of balancing their income and expenditure if they abandoned one salary than if both of them continued to hold their jobs.

People can earn a living while spending less of their lifetimes working for financial compensation than in the past. This goal can be achieved in several ways. One of them is for one income-earner in a multiple job-holding family to quit. A second is to decide how many hours to work; this may involve part-time work or job-sharing. A third is to make fundamental lifecycle changes so that the rights of people to income and services are structured in very different ways.

Here are some examples. Imagine a society where the right to go to college at reduced fees, or none at all, could be secured by community service work in the teenage years. Those who chose not to take this option would be required to pay for their education. Another option would be for retraining and reeducation credits to be part of workplace benefit packages. If people took advantage of them, they would accumulate credits over several years which would enable them to spend significant time catching up with changes in their own career area—or to move to a new one if they wanted to do so.

The philosophy of right livelihood does not imply that all of life will be enjoyable. No form of work is pure pleasure. All activities are boring and frustrating at times. The goal, however, should be to ensure that round pegs are placed in round holes and that people learn, as they are growing up, not to expect Utopia. This goal also implies that no group or class should be freed from doing the toil of the culture. One of our current problems is that there are too many people who simply have no idea how much unpleasant, tedious and repetitive work is required to support their "high-level" activities.

I recognize that the goal of right livelihood will appear unrealistic to many. Skeptics will doubt that people could manage this much responsibility for themselves. This cynicism about the capacity of individuals emerges from the same set of beliefs that has denied the validity of all the past movements toward greater freedom in human cultures—from the abolition of slavery to giving women the vote. The current economic crisis will, however, only be solved if we move beyond the control models which prevent imagination and enthusiasm.

The relationship between work, income and prestige has already changed dramatically and will continue to alter as we move toward the twenty-first century. Industrial-era systems wrapped these three aspects of life into a single package. People's jobs determined not only their income but also their status. In addition, work either provided the ability to grow or forced people into dead end job, and life, situations.

In the compassionate era, lifestyles and lifecycles are going to be radically different. More and more wealth is going to be created by machines, continuing a trend which started at the beginning of the twentieth century. It has been possible to manage this trend up to the current time by raising wages, shortening hours and extending social safety nets.

The ability of past solutions to manage the impact of computers is weakening fast. The problems of poverty are becoming more severe in the United States and most of the rich countries. Welfare systems are increasingly recognized to be counterproductive. We now know that the rich-poor split is creating increasingly dangerous conditions for all of society. Only a radical shift in the way we manage the problem of poverty and class will make a difference to current dynamics.

Creating change in organizations

ORGANIZATIONAL CULTURE

I have dealt so far with the ways in which people can affect their own lives. I now want to take up a more complex issue: how can individuals be effective in changing the nature and direction of the organizations in which they work? A growing number of approaches are being used. I set out below one set of guidelines you can choose to start the process of change.

We now know that each organization has its own unique culture and that change must grow out of the success criteria which are already in place. Each organization defines certain types of activity as acceptable and denies validity to others. Most people tend to go along with what has been defined as the norm and to shun those patterns which are perceived as undesirable. Those who choose to challenge the institution often find themselves shunned or even fired.

When conditions were stable, perpetuating past patterns made sense. Today, when all of us live in the rapids of change, stasis is fatal. How can each of us be involved in helping organizations discover their success criteria for the future? People must learn to recognize that their existing organizational culture really does dominates thought and action.

So long as people remain blind to the ways current structures control behavior, suggesting alternatives is ineffective because they will be essentially "invisible." The first step, then, is to get people to think about how the organizational systems within which they work and live constrains the way they look at the world. One person who works to shift perceptions has gone so far as to organize "funerals" for the old organizational culture in an attempt to free up space for new ways of looking at the world.

The second step is to help people see the difference between the stated and the actual culture. Even if a shared understanding exists about how an organization operates, it will almost certainly be inaccurate. Beliefs about the ways things are done within an organization, and what actually occurs, are always widely divergent. This is not only true for organizations. Long ago, anthropologists discovered that there is always a significant difference in societies between the "stated" culture and the "actual" culture. People assume that life is carried on in a particular way, but the actual patterns are usually very different.

Changing dominant patterns of thought is far more difficult than might be expected. People can hold remarkably divergent views without being aware that their positions differ from those of others. In addition, there are usually major latent clashes within organizations which emerge from varying perceptions of past history. These are typically hidden from view because nobody wants to deal with them.

A process of dialogue must move through many levels of mistrust and miscommunication before new, shared understandings start to emerge. This effort is normally slow, painful, and time-consuming, regardless of the skills and sophistication of the group. There are few shortcuts. The process has to be experienced rather than learned.

GUIDELINES ON INSTITUTIONAL RENEWAL

Following my work on institutional renewal at Eastfield Community College, where I spent considerable time in the 1970s, I developed a set of guidelines which seem appropriate for effective institutional change work:

■ All existing and emerging leaders should have the opportunity to be involved. This attitude has two primary consequences. On the one hand, everybody who is willing to lead needs to be given the chance to do so. On the other, expecting everybody to be involved is neither possible nor desirable. Starting with 1 to 5% of an institution is enough. Any more may overwhelm the process. Once the process gets moving, others will join. At the end of the first year of our Eastfield effort, many of those who had been believed to oppose change adamantly were helping the process along.

■ The people at the top of the institution must be "on board" and willing to be highly supportive. The head of an organization cannot renew an institution. Indeed too much involvement by top management can be counterproductive. But those who are actually doing the work must believe they are supported by those at the top, otherwise they will feel they are going out on a limb which may be sawn off at any time.

■ The people at the top of the organization must be sophisticated in managing "boundary conditions." Many programs fall apart because what goes on in one institution challenges others. There can also be failures because those who govern or fund institutions fear the loss of control inherent in a participatory mode and therefore want to maintain their control. It is essential that Boards and funders be kept aware of what is going on in ways that prevent them from feeling threatened.

■ Coordination must be by "people-persons" and not "program-people. Dozens, even hundreds, of models are available which would improve systems if people were willing to adopt them. The basic problem is not a lack of programs but rather the inertia which persists because people feel they cannot make a difference. Those involved in facilitating change need to motivate and inspire. They need to help people alter their self-images and encourage those who are dubious about their capacity to make a difference. This type of process will develop the next generation of leadership.

■ People must be encouraged to participate in dialogue with one another, without taboos about stating personal perceptions. They must learn to listen to views which they do not like. One of the hardest tasks is getting people to talk about their own views rather than stereotypes. They need to move beyond statements like: "Managers feel . . ." or "Teachers believe . . ." to "I" statements where they state their personal feelings. Generalizations can follow after people are in touch with their own patterns of thought and belief.

■ Information about the rapidly changing world must be introduced. Some new ideas will develop as people talk more honestly about their perceptions and the wide range of understandings which exist in all groups thus become visible. Typically, however, outside influences, such as lecturers, reading materials and video tapes, should be introduced to make people aware of how different the future is going to be from the past. The need to bring people up to date with emerging realities grows more urgent with every year as the certainties of the post-war world are swept away and new possibilities and dangers develop.

■ It is essential that the people in the organization become aligned with one another. This is the precondition for giving people more freedom to make decisions for themselves. Until alignment occurs, top-down decision-making remains inevitable and cannot be avoided. The Soviet Union is a very large-scale example of what happens in the absence of alignment. The first step in achieving alignment is the development of trust and a sense of interdependence. The second step is encouraging a process of creativity where people become aware of the options and alternatives. The third step is providing guidelines which permit people to make decisions for themselves within broad limits.

■ Finally, the involvement of outsiders is usually necessary. The outsider is purposeful neutral rather than supporting any individual or group in the change process. The outsider supports the program. When things go wrong, the blame can be placed on the outsider so that the internal process can go forward with as little disruption as possible. Those who want to be a consultant to change processes should not need to be "loved:" rather they should be willing to carry the burden of doing the best they can while not worrying about whether this will lead to recognition or permanent activity. (Nobody can think only at this level but being primarily concerned with one's own personal success and rewards almost guarantees the failure of renewal efforts.)

Institutional renewal should not be started unless the key players are willing to carry it through. Once people gain a sense that they may have more control over their lives and organizational decision-making, you cannot remove this empowerment without the high probability that the last state of the organization will be worse than the first.

Change processes can get sabotaged in two primary ways. One danger is that existing leaders often authorize, and seem excited about, fundamental reorganizations but do not recognize that they have strong personal needs to control others. Because they state their goal as "more responsive organizations," they often fail to perceive that the directions and solutions others will propose as they gain influence, will not be the same as those they would have chosen themselves. The consequent clash of priorities then becomes unacceptable to them. Programs are therefore often killed just when they are becoming effective. People who step out of line become pariahs, deprived of influence.

The other difficulty is that movements toward greater initiative may threaten other related systems or those "higher" in the organization. The President of an organization might be comfortable moving toward flatter management but the Board might not. A unit of an organization might want to change toward more freedom and autonomy but the head office might not be willing to have its control lessened in this way. My work in the Dallas Community College District fell apart for this reason. We showed that one of the community colleges within the District could be more creative and responsive. This threatened the control of the District Office. The key staff person was hired away. Control was reestablished.

The guidelines I have suggested above are, of course, counsels of perfection. Very often, efforts will have to go ahead with less than fully satisfactory situations. Keeping these optimum conditions in mind, however, will help minimize the problems that inevitably arise in any change process.

New dynamics emerging in organizational change
LINKING DECISION-MAKING AND ACTION THROUGH
COMMITMENT-BASED SYSTEMS.

The computer is increasingly taking the place of middle management. People at the top of systems can often discover the detailed results of different possible approaches through using simulations. In order to evaluate potentials, however, they need to be in close touch with those who are the actors. This allows them to get an accurate picture of what conditions actually are inside and outside the organization.

The need for closer contact between the top and the bottom of organizations results from the fact that accurate movement of information within organizations is essential. SAS, the Scandinavian airline system, has pioneered efforts in this direction. Recognizing that flight attendants largely determine the image of the company, SAS has developed direct links between top management and those who work with customers, providing the latter group with a great deal more authority to make decisions. Similarly, some American hotel chains have given their managers far greater latitude to make cash payments to customers who have been badly treated.

This type of approach can also transform internal attitudes. If workers feel that management cares about them and their ideas, they will almost certainly be more productive. In addition, the chance of thefts and sabotage decreases dramatically because workers have a feeling of "belonging" to the organization. Profit-sharing can reinforce these desirable directions.

Two major trends are therefore developing. First, closer coordination is developing between those at the top and those who know what is actually going on in the system. Second, the ranks of middle management are decreasing with extreme rapidity. Gervase Bushe, one of the most exciting of management thinkers, suggests that top management, the shapers of the overall effort, should be in close contact with those who are actually doing the work. He also cites the need for people he calls "integrators," who ensure that work can be effectively carried out. These integrators play a very different role from existing middle managers.

There is a fourth group, who are the leaders, but they will often be invisible. Lao Tzu stated many centuries ago that "when the leader leads well, the people will say they did it themselves." The purpose of the leader is to create situations where visionaries, actors and integrators can get on with their tasks in ways that combine to create an effective whole.

I believe that this fourfold split is going to be critical to effective organizations in the future. One group will be the visionaries who enjoy thinking about a future which they want to realize. A second group will be the actors who like to "get on with it" but also know how to tell the visionaries when their ideas don't work or how they can be improved. The third "integrating" group will consist of those who keep the system moving forward smoothly—these are the people who support both visionaries and actors. This group includes personnel people and accountants for both of them make the operation of the company possible. The fourth group will be the leaders who understand when to concentrate on action, vision and integration.

This shifts the discussion about desirable forms of organization for the future. At the current time, most people who are concerned about people getting greater satisfaction from their work concentrate on changing legal structures so that work places are controlled by workers or are structured as cooperatives. The implication of the argument I have made above is that it is far more important to ensure that people are placed in positions which suit their preferred style. The next challenge is to rethink remuneration structures so that the contribution of all four groups is equitably recognized.

We shall need all our skills to prevent breakdowns resulting from the effects on morale which will inevitably follow from the rapid decline in the numbers of middle managers. Keeping organizations operating effectively during the shift from a hierarchical to a communications-based structure is difficult.

Those who do still have roles to perform may become less productive because they worry about being fired. The process of downsizing middle management is costly not only in terms of paying for early retirement but also because of the inevitable damage to morale. Every time that a RIF (reduction in force) takes place, people are less willing to place their trust in the organization and do their best work.

Constant reorganizations also take their toll. Compassionate-era structures only work effectively when people come to know each other and are able to anticipate what behavior will be acceptable and what is not. Individuals need to know each other's styles so they can play to strengths and avoid weaknesses. If turnover is constant, relationship building does not occur and effectiveness declines.

The difficulties increase with each reorganization. People begin to realize that the time spent on rebuilding trust after each shift is wasted, because as soon as relationships begin to develop they are torn apart once again. The problems are increased when organizations commit to a "lean and mean" philosophy. The rhetoric is meant to apply to the outside world but all too often it also impacts internal behavior.

The trend toward reductions in the number of middle managers has been most dramatic in business where whole levels have already been wiped out in many corporations. Governmental systems, on the other hand, have been less impacted by the new understandings and normally still have the same number of management levels. One of the trends in schools and colleges has been an actual increase in the numbers of managers as compared to those actually doing the work. Significant reform will not start to develop in government and education until many of the structural layers are removed.

USING DIVERSITY

It would be difficult enough to make the required changes in organizational structures if everything else were stable. The task is made much more difficult because the labor force of most organizations is increasingly diverse. The percentage of minorities in the labor force is growing fast and it will continue to rise in the future. Some estimates suggest that as much as 80 to 90% of the increase in the labor force will be minorities in the nineties. The percentage of women has also been increasing although it may be reaching a plateau and some forces may lead to a reversal of the past growth.

This movement toward increased diversity is irreversible. The campaigns of both David Duke and Patrick Buchanan gained much of their strength from the feeling of whites that they were losing ground in their own country. The issue, however, is not whether we want diversity or not, but whether we shall make it America's prime strength or, on the other hand, permit it to destroy her potential.

Diversity provides a source of strength for those organizations and cultures which are willing to work with it. Given the pace of change, it is essential for organizations to have as good a grasp as possible of what is going on in the world. The more different viewpoints they can access, the better off they will be. There are today, for example, very strong black and female feelings about a number of marketing techniques which are being employed to exploit them.

This is particularly true for cigarette marketing. The very heavily male, white management of tobacco companies is clearly underestimating the long-run dangers of the approaches they are taking. These assume that the decline in smoking by the middle-class can be made up by attracting the poor, women and the young. They would do well to listen to those who can inform them about the backlash which is already developing.

Fortunately a growing number of firms are realizing how much they can gain from listening. Many approaches are being developed to learn more about internal and external attitudes. They are not only used to ensure more commitment to existing goals but also to permit discussion about directions which will benefit all the stakeholders in organizations.

An effectively pluralistic society will challenge all the current prejudices about the relative competence of women, minorities, the young and the old. These patterns continue to affect judgments to a far greater extent than most people are willing to admit. One can discover how little has been achieved by watching dynamics in groups. It is far rarer for men to interrupt each other than for them to interrupt women. Young people of either sex, however bright they are, tend to be ignored by those in power as do the old. Stereotypes about minorities are still very strong, despite thirty years of attempted integration.

Few institutions really use the strengths which minorities and women can bring to a system. If females and non-whites want to get on, they are normally required to adopt the styles which are currently predominantly used by white males rather than bringing their own strengths into the organizational system. Most institutions are willing to promote women who adopt male styles and minorities who adopt white styles. Those who persist in acting "differently" will typically find it far harder to be successful.

Even those organizations which recognize how difficult this issue of diversity really is, and make major efforts to accommodate different styles within the organization, typically do not manage all the problems well. I know of one non-profit group which is strongly committed to compassionate-era style activities; interestingly most of the staff are females who seem more comfortable with process and cooperation than men. This organization makes efforts to honor people whose style falls outside the mainstream. Despite their very real commitment to diversity, they sometimes find that the differences are too large to bridge and the person chooses to leave or has to be fired.

In addition, of course, there are many institutions which are still largely unaware of the need for sensitivity and continue to perpetuate the patterns which lead to continued frustration from women and minorities. I recently heard about a board meeting where the vast majority of those present were male. At one point the chairman announced that it was time to go to the men's room. He stated that everybody should come with him so that the meeting could continue, thus isolating the females in the meeting room. It would be pleasant to believe that this is a limited pattern. However, while this example is particularly outrageous, it does reflect the attitude which still exists in all too many organizations.

The changes which are needed to support and benefit from diversity will disadvantage those who only know power approaches. There will be two levels of struggle. One of them will be more or less out in the open with people consciously challenging any diminution in their ability to use coercive power. An encouraging trend in the last twenty years has been the number of people who have learned, in the course of discussions about power, that more effective styles can be adopted.

More serious problems occur at the subconscious and unconscious levels. It is difficult enough to get people to change even when they have the skills and the willingness to discuss effective decision-making rationally. It is far harder to break through the blinders which prevent people from recognizing that current management and organizational styles advantage the white male and make it difficult for women and non-whites to make real progress. One cannot discuss an issue of which an individual or a group remains unaware. The process of chipping away at blindness is always slow and painful and often seems impossible.

I have been learning skills to make this process easier throughout my work life. The key reality, of course, is that there are no slick formulas. There is a need for much patience and empathy with others. Above all, we must have a major commitment to staying open personally and recognizing that our own blindness to certain issues, of which we are definitionally unaware, is as irritating to others as their blindness on other issues is to us. Mutual tolerance of the inevitable frustration which exists when people of different views get together permits continued struggle and keeps the learning process moving forward. So long as nobody believes they have the whole truth and others do not, there is a possibility of mutual growth.

One of the hardest lessons I have had to learn is that any possibility of positive movement vanishes as soon as I, or anyone else, is convinced of their superiority. All those involved in discussions must agree to the search for new understandings. When this commitment does not exist, the dialogue efforts of one group will be lost in the self-righteousness of the other. Real progress toward more effective styles depends on discussion among the people at all levels of organizations.

The leadership styles required for compassionate-era institutions are profoundly different from those which were effective in the industrial era. The question is how we can learn the new skills which will work in the future. Women and men, whites and minorities have much to learn about this transition. All of us need to be as open to each other as we possibly can, recognizing that we exploring profoundly new territory.

SUPPORT OF CUSTOMERS

More and more organizations are recognizing that it makes sense to satisfy existing customers than to have to "buy" new ones through advertising and public relations. I am using the word customer in the broadest sense of an individual who benefits from the services of an institution. An ever-wider range of techniques is being adopted to satisfy people. Once again, businesses are in the vanguard.

In the fall of 1990, the *Wall Street Journal* ran a story on the ways in which companies reacted to complaints. It found that most responded rapidly and were willing not only to make amends for bad products and services but also to provide extra coupons and even monetary repayments for frustration. More and more hot lines have been created to inform callers how to use, assemble and repair products. Guarantees are typically longer lasting than in the past and have fewer exclusions.

When I was the keynote speaker at the Interactive Industry Video Conference in December 1989, I sat down with an executive of one of the major computer companies. He told me that starting from the spring of 1990, their salesmen would be told to pitch the products of rival companies for specific purposes if this would keep their customers happy.

In this new context, it is also going to make increasing sense to ensure that products have optimum lives. Even if people are able to keep an item longer without repurchasing, thus decreasing sales, satisfied customers are likely to inform their friends and this will increase the overall market for the product.

The advantages of keeping customers happy may seem obvious. But until recently there was little interest in the customer after a sale. Once the product had been purchased, it was often felt that the transaction had been completed. Those stores or businesses which took a different attitude were the exception rather than the rule.

Businesses often have an easier time seeing the importance of a shift toward service than government and non-profits. The consequences of changes are visible both in terms of the bottom line and also because customer satisfaction is an effective marketing and public relations tool. The advantages for non-profits and government agencies are often more at the interpersonal level, and therefore more difficult to perceive.

In addition, attitudes that still dominate many non-profits, church groups and government agencies may make it difficult to achieve the necessary changes in directions. Non-profits often assume that people ought to be "grateful" for the services they are receiving. So long as this remains true, there will be little perceived need to serve clients well:

rather the primary effort will be to satisfy the employees and the volunteers who are seen as doing unpleasant jobs. When employees and volunteers do believe their work is worthwhile, they will have the psychic energy, enthusiasm and joy which makes serving others a pleasure.

Most government agencies are so caught up in making sure that they don't get into trouble that they have little time, or space, to worry about the personal needs of human beings. Indeed, meeting real needs is not really the defined goal of bureaucratic systems. Rather they are set up to carry out a task defined by others and the fact that the task may not mesh well with the needs of the population being "served" may well be seen as irrelevant. In addition, the feedback loop from the government worker to the politician who sets tasks, or even the political appointee who determines how the task will be carried out, is in almost all cases weak and sometimes non-existent.

"Success" is therefore measured in terms of whether the rules and regulations are observed, not whether actions help people. I remember talking one time with people at the Arizona State Department of Economic Security. We spent a good deal of time considering how workers could be given the freedom to address real needs rather than those defined by state or federal authorities. In the end we decided that there were few areas where significant progress could be made so long as current systems and expectations remained intact.

MINIMIZING WASTE

A final area where each of us can have impact is in finding ways to limit waste. There have been two major sources of waste in the production process up to the current time. First, a large number of companies have had ineffective quality controls and have had to reject a significant amount of their production. The drive to satisfy customers will reduce the amount of waste from this source. The costs of having to scrap or recall products, or redo services, are increasingly recognized as intolerable because of the impact they have on costs and marketing. More and more organizations are therefore putting their emphasis on creating conditions so that things can be done right the first time.

The second source of difficulties is even more pervasive. There has been a tendency to assume that it is cheaper to throw wastes away than to recycle them. There is today a growing recognition that "waste" can be a profit-center rather than a cost. More and more companies are seeing that it does not make sense to junk products which can either be useful to them or can be sold to others. This movement toward a cost-effectiveness approach will usually be more effective than legal prohibition.

I recently received a newsletter from a printing company which showed the potential from recycling. Written by the manager, it said, "I had no idea that the economics of recycling could be so dramatic for a company our size." Some of the details cited are:

> Thomson-Shore recycles film, plates and paper (we actually sort waste paper into seven separate categories) to the extent that we recover over $1500 per week from these recycling efforts. Now following an employee suggestion, we have added significantly to that savings.
>
> For years, we have used a rubbish hauler to pick up the material we could not recycle. This was office waste, trimmings with glue in them, cardboard, etc. We filled up six dumpsters per week and paid roughly $2700 per month to have it hauled away.
>
> Now, with adding the recycling of about two-thirds of our office waste and all our cardboard, we switched from using dumpsters to renting two trash compactors, which we have emptied once each in six weeks versus six times in six weeks for our dumpsters. This has cut back our waste disposal cost to about $850 a month. In addition, our income from recycling is going up a bit.

The overall message of this chapter is that all of us, regardless of our role or our position, can play a role in the movement toward more sustainable patterns. Some of the activities can be personal. More of them require us to work with our peers and colleagues to change the way we think and work together.

PART III

Society in the Compassionate Era

CHAPTER 7 ─────────────────────────────────────

The Learning Society

THE DEVELOPMENT OF LEARNING SOCIETIES IS THE KEY challenge of the nineties and the twenty-first century. This new goal should replace the drive for economic growth which has dominated Western society during the last hundred years. We shall therefore need totally different yardsticks to measure the success of human cultures in the future.

Learning societies will not emerge automatically from our so-called age of information. Indeed, most people are today aware that we are living in an age of misinformation. This is, indeed, one of the primary causes of dissatisfaction. The gap between what we are told is going on and our personal observations of reality is now too wide to be bridged without trauma.

The underlying requirement for a learning society is that we develop high levels of communication skills. This will permit us both to filter out misinformation and also to create our own more accurate knowledge sources. Sir Geoffrey Vickers, a remarkable Englishman, made this point clearly in a highly provocative speech at a seminar in Spokane in 1974. He said:

> 1. The world we live in demands and depends on skill in communication and in knowledge relevant to communication to an extent far beyond anything previously known. . . .
> 2. Communication also depends on trust . . . and imposes on communicators a duty to sustain the level of communication, not only by their skill and knowledge but by being trustworthy communicators.
> 3. This is the more important because there is a "law" of communication similar to "Gresham's Law" in economics. Bad communication drives out good communication. A small minority with a few bombs and a lot of self-righteousness can soon reduce the level of communication in a whole society to the basic level of mutual threat.

4. Thus the duty I have described assumes an importance, as well as a difficulty, which can hardly be exaggerated. It seems to me a trans-cultural human duty to sustain the level of communication, to resist its debasement and to cooperate in raising it.

5. The direction in which this duty points seems to me the direction of the more human, rather than the less human; a vector which we can recognize as trans-cultural and which claims the allegiance of the whole species. It may be the only dimension in which any kind of progress is possible. It is surely a precondition for progress of any other kind.

The challenge is, of course, immense. In today's society there are a great many people who make their living by saying anything, however ridiculously false. Indeed, gossip of the worst kind has been raised to an art form in the day-time expose show which is popular because it is salacious, while still sounding familiar.

Communication within cultures is therefore being degraded. Communication across cultural barriers is, of course, far more difficult. The Japanese film *Rashomon* was perhaps the first to enable us to see the same story from very different points of view. A story of violence by a Samurai warrior toward a woman was shown in several ways. The viewer was left to decide where the truth lay.

This movie showed body language and styles to help us understand what was really going on. It introduced us to the difficulties of discovering when people are telling the truth and when are they shading it or deliberately lying.

The quality of messages also changes with the medium used to send them. Text, art, games, video, audio, computers and telephones all have their own quirks and implications. Some people learn best from one medium and some from another. Meshing the message to be sent with the best way to send it is one of the biggest challenges in communication.

Another way to gain additional insights about how communication really takes place is to learn various languages. Perfect translations from one language to another are impossible because a language carries a worldview with it. I speak French well: it therefore compels me to be a different person than when I think and conceptualize in English. Unfortunately, languages are taught in school at the wrong time in children's lives. There is clear evidence that learning a language is fun before the age of 10. In teen-age years and at college it is a chore, if not worse. As a result, far fewer people benefit from knowing other languages than should be the case.

There are many other "languages" besides those we normally

consider, such as French, Spanish, Hopi, English. For example, physics is a language which provides a unique way of looking at the world. I first fully understood this when I was being driven back from a speaking date. A high-school physicist explained to me that, when working with students who were only taking a single course in his subject, he did not primarily require students to perform experiments. Instead he concentrated on why he personally found it interesting to look at the world as a physicist.

Similarly, astronomers and engineers, artists and physicians, plumbers and golfers all have unique views which are worth understanding. This is the reason why I find it easy to talk with other people and to learn from them. The world they have chosen to live in is fascinating even if I do not have the time to enter it for myself—and in some cases would not want to have anything to do with it.

Beyond nineteenth-century schooling

The need for effective communication, as Vickers presents it, goes well beyond current understandings. Indeed, we all too often act as though information, communication, learning and schooling are the same concepts. We seem to believe that if we improve the schools, we shall ensure communication and guarantee learning. This simplistic thinking conceals the urgent issues which face us today.

We all too often forget that existing patterns of schooling only go back as far as the middle of the nineteenth century and that they were bitterly fought when they were introduced. John Taylor Gatto, New York City Teacher of the Year in 1990, made the point this way in his acceptance speech before the New York State Senate.

> Our form of compulsory schooling is an invention of the State of Massachusetts around 1850. It was resisted, sometimes with guns, by an estimated 80 percent of the Massachusetts population, the last outpost in Barnstable not surrendering its children until the 1880s, when the area was seized by the militia, and children marched to school under guard.
>
> Now here is a curious idea to ponder. Senator Ted Kennedy's office released a paper not too long ago claiming that prior to compulsory education the state literacy rate was 98 percent, and after it the figure never again reached above 91 percent, where it stands in 1990. I hope that interests you.
>
> Here is another curiosity to think about. The home-schooling movement has quietly grown to a size where one-and-one-half million people are being entirely educated entirely by their own parents; last month the education press reported the amazing news

that children schooled at home seem to be five or even ten years ahead of their formally trained peers in the ability to think.

Traditional schooling patterns work against the imagination and relationships we shall increasingly need as we enter the twenty-first century. The profound, underlying messages of traditional schools are to:

■ obey those in charge without question,

■ put excessive emphasis on specialization,

■ erect rigid boundaries between courses, particularly those in the arts, sciences and humanities and between academic and practical subjects,

■ expect certainty and stability,

■ understand that the world is divided into superiors and inferiors and therefore learn to struggle to be on top.

How are these lessons taught? The teacher and the principal are authority figures with the right to reward and punish. Children and young adults are expected to obey rules, largely without question. Margaret Mead made a wry comment on this pattern. She pointed out that children who left school for the real world at the age of 16 or 18 were expected to make decisions for themselves while the high-school and university student continues to be protected within an artificial world.

Traditional teachers also lead their students to believe that there are answers to all questions. Most students still see no necessity, or even possibility, to be creative because they are brought up to believe that the teacher knows the proper response. This pattern also leads them to expect certainty and stability. One of the most difficult steps in my own career came when I discovered that there was nobody who would, or could, do my thinking for me and that I had to work through realities for myself.

The acceptance of traditional educational patterns is ingrained in students over time. In the sixties I managed, after great effort, to convince a college teacher that he ought to consider working with students in a dialogue mode. I didn't know whether to laugh or cry when he came back after one hour in the classroom saying: "Well, I tried to get the students involved but they weren't interested. I always knew you were wrong when you talked about the potential of kids." Reversing twelve or more years of using one style is not achieved in a single hour!

Industrial-era patterns of grading impose a model of superiority and inferiority. They force people to see themselves as "good" or "bad" students. Good students are usually defined as those who feedback to teachers what they have previously been taught. Bad students are often people who rebel against the system, some of them are very bright while others find the whole process of schooling irrelevant to their needs and potentials. The ideas of "bad" students are frequently the most novel, but they tend to be silent because they have been squashed in the past.

The imposition of a single method of evaluating people also prevents us from recognizing various types of skills. The model which used to exist in the one-room school, where teachers typically found a valid reason to give a prize to all students for something they did well, should be emulated today. Current patterns of grading reinforce the failures of existing educational systems.

Passing and failing grades are based in large part on the relationship of the teacher to the student. Good students are nurtured and therefore do better; weak students are often ignored and do worse. Grades are therefore, in large part, a self-fulfilling prophecy. There is a classic story about this pattern. On one occasion, a teacher was provided with a list which reversed the grades of students. At the end of the year most of the young people had met the expectations which were thus generated. Weak students blossomed under the increased attention they received. Those who had previously done well withered, because they were ignored.

Another example of the power of expectations developed when a teacher went into a classroom at the beginning of the school year and gave all her students A's. She also made it clear that she expected them to learn to live up to this standard. By the end of the year, parents were besieging her to find out what she had done for their child because grades had improved so greatly. The change was not so much in the teaching; it was the context which had been altered to demand excellence.

Our grading patterns introduce an even more serious problem. So long as the only options a student knows are being on the top or at the bottom, most people will find it more attractive to be among the successful with power and money than to be without. Indeed, once people have experienced superiority, even equality with others begins to sour. This is the viewpoint which Gilbert announced in one of his comic operas claiming that "when everybody's somebody, then no-one's anybody."

On the other hand, current patterns of schooling are providing many people with such a poor self-image that an increasing proportion of the population are resigning themselves to being on the bottom. They downgrade their very real skills and come to feel that they have no significant contribution to make. The waste of human potential which occurs in this way is huge and chilling. We have all met many people who could have done far more with their lives if they had been challenged.

Perhaps the worst consequence of traditional schooling is the way it isolates students from reality. The better the school, and the teaching, the more complete the isolation. When working with Oakland Community College, I had an opportunity to meet with students from one of the "worst" schools and one of the "best." The drop-out rates in the bad school were horrendous but those who remained were aware of dynamics in the real world and able to resonate to the real issues I raised. They knew the way human beings interrelate and the dynamics of the culture; they had street-smarts.

Those in the rich school had the academic learning but no ability to understand reality. They were informed about the Amazon Rain Forest but had no idea why people in Brazil acted the way they did. They assumed that all behavior could be changed by laws. They lived in a narrow context with a single set of patterns and had no idea that others saw the world in profoundly different ways.

New educational directions

The amount of ink spilled around issues of educational reform shows no signs of abating, Regrettably, the real questions remain illusive. We can only understand the debate if we recognize that the educational world is locked in a major struggle at the current time. Some want to maintain current schooling patterns while improving their efficiency. People who advance this view argue that there is nothing seriously wrong with what is currently taught by industrial-era schools and colleges. They want to recommit to their traditional goals of providing the best current answers to questions and testing people on their ability to regurgitate them.

While testing approaches are becoming more complex (the latest buzzword is "authentic assessment," using portfolios, essays, and some-times even critical thinking) the emphasis is still on learning a core body of information which is the same for all students and can be measured by national tests. Unfortunately, the greater the emphasis on tests, the more teachers concentrate on helping students pass them to the exclusion of other needs.

Those on the other side of the argument believe that students need to learn to learn if they are to enjoy, and be competent in, the compassionate era. They propose that people should be evaluated on their ability to continually develop themselves. They recognize that each student has unique potentials and that it is the purpose of education to unlock the drive to develop, believing that great teachers connect with the unfolding child. This group recognizes that once students have been challenged, they can be given their heads for they will find their own way.

It was Richard Goodwin, my British economics professor, who started my commitment to learning. He forced me to look at theories in more imaginative ways. He kept after me when I accepted, at face value, ideas developed by earlier economists. He expected me to use my brains, not to adopt arguments made by others. He was one of the primary people, besides my wife, who started me on my learning to learn journey.

Understanding the nature of the educational debate and its direction is increasingly difficult today. Despite their very different goals, people who support fundamental change, and those who deny its necessity, use the same rhetoric to support their profoundly different proposals. There are, however, major surprises as one evaluates the arguments used to support various positions. Many of those who reject the need for radical reform support their case by quoting the "success" of the Japanese educational system. They fail to recognize that Japanese educators are dubious about the long-run consequences of the rigid Japanese system which emphasizes data and logic.

There are at least five major areas of disagreement between those who believe that fundamental change is necessary and those who are convinced that limited reform of current systems will be enough. First, the current system concentrates on what happens in schools and colleges while those who want change argue that education must be broadened to include parents, churches, the media and indeed all the forces that can help people see the world in a new way. Second, the current system concentrates on the period from 5 to 16, 18, 22 or 30, while those who want change look at the whole of life from conception to death. Third, the current system uses a very limited number of styles of learning, while those who want change believe that people learn in a wide variety of ways. Fourth, those who want to preserve the current system opt for a broadened core curriculum while those who want change believe learning can only be achieved by treating everybody as an individual. Fifth, traditionalists opt for teaching answers while those who want change believe that the best learning comes as one struggles with questions.

Widening the learning process

There are many forms of competence. Bruce Campbell described the issues involved for *In Context* magazine.

> In recent years, new definitions of intelligence have gained acceptance and have dramatically enhanced the appraisal of human competence. Howard Gardner of Harvard University in his book, *Frames of Mind, the Theory of Multiple Intelligences*, suggests that

there at least seven human intelligences, two of which, verbal/linguistic intelligence and logical/mathematical intelligence, have dominated the traditional pedagogy of western societies.

The five non-traditional intelligences, spatial, musical, kinesthetic, interpersonal and intrapersonal, have generally been overlooked in education. However, if we can develop ways to teach and learn by engaging all seven intelligences, we will increase the opportunities for student success and create the opportunity to, in Margaret Mead's words, "weave a social fabric in which each diverse human gift will find a fitting place."

I would personally add an eighth intelligence, the ability to discern patterns and contexts.

The traditional norm has been that every student should learn a core curriculum; if they are failing at one subject in this curriculum they should spend more time on it. This approach is designed to assure that there are no major gaps in an individual's knowledge. A basic problem with this approach is that it forces students and teachers to concentrate on palliating weakness rather than developing strengths.

The second flaw in the core curriculum model is that there is too much "central" material today for anybody to learn all of it. The validity of the concept of "core" can only be preserved by assuming that the political, social and cultural history of one's own group and area is critically important and that of all other cultural groups is marginal. This pattern of thinking is one of the primary causes of current violence because individuals do not develop the ability to empathize with profoundly different cultural visions.

Human survival now requires the development of a planetary consciousness, and a sense of the cultural contributions made by people around the world. This must be woven into a recognition of the need to live within a value-based culture which recognizes the ecological limitations of the world. This is the "story" which can permit us to live in peace and to ensure the well-being of our descendants.

Students need to grasp this understanding at the same time as they are encouraged to do well in their best subjects. One primary advantage with this new approach is that students find out where their commitments are and can move with them. Future learning systems should provide people with opportunities which fit their developing skills; they should also measure abilities in terms of how close people are to fulfilling their personal capacities rather than against an average for the culture. There will be continued opportunities to learn later in life if something important has been missed.

One of the primary problems at the current time is that learning is normally defined in academic terms. As a result we fail to recognize how much people know about their chosen subject—whether it be automobiles, gardening, the raising of children or computers. Indeed, there is a particular block around computers. Because the younger generation is so much better with computers than those who are older, adults tend to grossly underestimate both the skills of students and the importance of competence in this area for the future. A few schools let teenagers teach computers because they have the best skills—I wish more would do so for this makes it clear that competence determines whether one teaches rather than a degree.

One critical lesson we must understand is that people learn remarkably rapidly when they have a reason to do so—they seem "dumb" when the subject does not interest them. The consequence of teaching to peoples' strengths will therefore be most dramatic for those whose competencies lie outside the academic arena. At the current time, the American pattern is that students are typically taught using the same basic track until they get into middle or high school. Then those who are not "good" enough to go on to college suddenly get shunted onto a vocational or general education track which usually seems like failure to them and to their parents.

Alternatives should be provided for students who do not fit the verbal/linguistic and logical/mathematical styles starting from their early years. Societies must recognize the need for many different types of skills. Indeed, there is more danger that the world will come apart because of a lack of plumbers than from a shortage of thinkers! I am also more worried about the limited number of people who have empathy as compared to the huge number who concentrate on logical analysis.

Many American educators fear any form of "tracking" system because it excludes some students from academic success and the ability to attend college. Once we accept that academic studies are not the only valuable type of learning, this criticism becomes invalid. Society today sacrifices much of the potential of most of those who have non-academic skills. In the future, it is essential to give everybody their best chance; errors will inevitably be made but if the system is open enough, nobody will be forced to continue along the wrong lines.

A growing number of tests have been developed which enable parents and children to learn what activities are most appropriate for each young person. These tests are not foolproof, of course, and they should not be used to force a child to take a route which does not seem desirable to him or her. But there will be fewer problems in education if we teach people using the styles which come naturally to them and support them in achieving their desired directions than if we set societal goals and force everybody to meet them.

To support those who are likely to carry out physical work, new connections between schools and the work place should be developed. John Hoerr, writing in *Business Week*, showed that there was "no link between school and work in the U.S." He proposed that "To bridge the gap between school and industry, the U.S. should establish a national system that combines worksite and classroom learning and prepares students for identifiable jobs." This is a common pattern in Europe and has been successful in providing students with a sense of purpose in life.

A full commitment to providing relevant education for each individual will require society to face a further very difficult issue. Children who are cut off from positive experiences in their first five years are unlikely to become learners when they enter school. There is also clear-cut evidence that abused children very often turn into abusing parents, and also frequently into criminals.

To break the cycle of poverty and abuse, disadvantaged young children will need far more support than they currently receive from conception to their entry into school. Because bureaucracies are unable to work with the required sensitivity, tactics and strategy to achieve this goal will have to be developed at the community level, using skills created by community and family education.

Learning results from challenge. There will be few positive changes so long as schooling remains homogeneous, bland and boring. Education, like life, should be exciting, surprising and fun. Positive development occurs as people have experiences with the unexpected. The vital skill is to stretch students and to challenge them to do a little more than they feel capable of managing, not only intellectually, but in many other ways.

John Dewey caught this point in *The School and Society* published almost 100 years age. He argued the importance of "close and intimate acquaintance . . . with nature at first hand, with real things and materials, with the actual processes of their manipulation. . . . The School has been so set apart, so isolated from the ordinary conditions and motives of life that the place where people are sent for discipline is the one place in the world where it is most difficult to get experience—the mother of all discipline worth the name."

Learning societies will be designed to prepare people to live in a radically changing world. They will encourage students to understand that change can be exciting rather than threatening. They will provide each of us with the skills to manage our lives. Teachers will enable people to grasp the thrill of living for personal growth and development rather than dull security.

Some critics argue that most people cannot understand broader horizons. I am personally certain that the essential reason for so many of our failures with young people, and indeed older ones, is that we underestimate their competence. They are far more capable than we give them credit for being. If we treated students, and citizens, as if they were twice as bright as we think they are, I know that half of our educational problems would vanish.

Readiness for change

There is a general assumption today that educators want to continue current patterns and would reject a move toward a person-centered life-long learning curriculum. My experience is exactly the opposite. In meeting after meeting across the U.S., the hunger to support children and learners is present. Administrators, teachers, boardmembers and parents are looking for ways to move but feel hog-tied by current rules and regulations.

I recently worked with a group drawn from all parts of Lewis and Clark Community College in the River Bend area of Illinois, just north of St. Louis. After a good deal of struggle, we managed to reach conclusions which stressed very different educational challenges from those of the past. The statement we produced argued:

> We believe that education empowers individuals by giving them choices. Education enables them to develop their personal potential by eliminating or bridging obstacles. Education allows citizens to participate in the political, economic, scientific, technological and aesthetic progress of their culture to the greatest possible extent. Formal education is not an end in itself, it supports a learning process which continues throughout life.
>
> Lewis and Clark Community College is a community of learners, mutually committed to the pursuit of excellence in the learning process and to providing open access to education. This is the vision which has inspired the community college movement from the beginning and it has resulted in a system of education which is significantly different from the traditional one.
>
> We are committed to creating an environment in which creativity can flourish. We believe that progress is the result of purposeful, systemic, rational and compassionate decision-making. The most effective learning occurs when conscious and consistent efforts are made to integrate theory and practice.
>
> Members of this learning community are characterized by:

—a sense of the responsibilities of global citizenship and environmental stewardship

—an ability to work with others and to share skills to achieve goals

—a flexible mind able to adapt quickly to change

—a wide range of communication skills, including reading, writing, listening and speaking

—an ability to make ethical and moral decisions

—an ability to analyze problems and think critically

—a mastery of independent learning

—a mastery of appropriate content.

This statement has now been adopted as the credo of the college and hangs in the office of almost every member of the college administration, teachers and staff.

Education should be based on a belief that every healthy human being, and indeed every organism, has a desire to develop. If this commitment did not exist, life would never have emerged and would not continue. People do not need to be forced to learn. Rather they need to be provided with a context in which their natural drive to learn is set free.

Positive education starts from a belief that children are whole. Marillee Masters, founder of Childlight, puts it this way:

> Children are connected to their inner self in a rather magical way which allows for delightful creativity, spontaneity, and freedom to be who they are. As adults, we seem to be searching out paths to this very end—this sense of ourselves as whole and wonderful, capable and lovable, creative and healthy. Is it possible to continue to nurture this innate way that children begin life here as human beings, so that they stay connected to their inner self—whole, healthy and positive about the individual they are? Could this be the missing link in education today? Many educators and professional child-care givers are answering "yes" to these questions.

Current schooling destroys spontaneity and creativity. This is often done physically as well as mentally. Fortunately, the compassionate era we are entering requires the enthusiasm and drive of all human beings and education must therefore be restructured so it will support these skills. A New Orleans ghetto school has proved that this is possible. Based on the vision of a nun, students were taught in ways which supported a positive self-image and worldview. At the end of one year of this type of schooling, existing students told new ones that "fighting" was not acceptable behavior.

New knowledge structures

We are all continuously knocked off center by events but we need to come back quickly. You may have seen the dolls which rest on a circular base but have weights which cause them to recover their upright stance when they are pushed to one side or the other. This is the balance model toward which we must strive throughout our lives. Balance permits us to live in the question, to face the issues with which we are struggling rather than endlessly escape them. In order to be able to live in this way, knowledge will have to be structured in new styles. It must be available to everybody so they can learn what they need to know at the time they want to learn.

It is often stated that information doubles every three or five or seven years! The figure used depends on the method of calculation employed by the individual making the announcement. When I hear this type of statement, I reply that while information may be doubling, there is ample evidence that knowledge is halving and wisdom is being even further reduced. People maintain power by monopolizing and distorting information. If they know something that other individuals and groups do not, they can run rings around them. If they can get their preferred statistics used, rather than those of another group, they are far ahead of the game.

The level and standard of discussion has declined drastically in the second half of the twentieth century. Statistics developed on different bases are used as clubs to convince rather than as sources of illumination. The support of ideologies is more important than respect for others. Elections are fought using distorting images: positive for one's own side and negative for the "enemy." Truth, and the search for truth, have been primary casualties of the last four decades.

Even those who want to handle information honestly have major difficulties in doing so. One central problem with current information techniques is that they are still largely geared to the time when the world was more or less stable. Students are therefore taught using text books which were written as much as five, or even ten years ago. This is disastrous because, in today's conditions, the speed of change makes material written as little as a year ago obsolete. Any world affairs text book written before the break-up of the communist empire and the invasion of Kuwait is wildly misleading. Indeed, it sometimes seems as though even magazines are out of date by the time they are published.

There is a fascinating parallel here to the problem that "tech prep" has already had to master. Teaching people how to work with a particular machine or technique was proving counterproductive. Profoundly new approaches had to be developed which encouraged students to learn to learn so they could keep up with new developments. Automobile mechanics, for example, cannot only understand a particular model; they have to develop the skills to keep up with constant change.

It is deeply depressing that academic fields have lagged behind in making this shift: students are still taught the conclusions derived from assumptions which were valid in the past rather than being challenged to develop the skills to change their assumption patterns with events. Given the progressive breakdown of current information systems, there is an urgent need to develop a process which will provide an continuously updated overview of primary issues.

My proposal is that teams be established to do this work; they would have the responsibility of stating the various credible views on a particular topic. I have described this approach as a possibility/problem focuser. The group addressing an issue would listen to those on all sides. They would push and probe in order to discover the extent to which the positions advanced were coherent and consistent.

They would then state the arguments made by the proponents of the various positions stressing, in particular, the areas of agreement and disagreement as well as the causes and consequences of different positions when these could be understood. The viewpoints would then be presented to decision-makers and the public so that the clash between various attitudes and proposals could be worked out in an intelligent and creative dialogue. These groups would not search for a single, objectively correct statement but rather for a way to bring together divergent perceptual views.

For these documents to be useful, the debate cannot be defined simplistically or academically. Most people are not "tidy" thinkers. The wide range of opinions that exist around each issue must be stated so that people will feel comfortable about surfacing their own ideas. A colleague of mine, Eugene Martin, has developed this technique to the level of an art form using audiotapes.

Why is it necessary to create a balanced picture of various debates which are currently occurring within our culture? If our views are not supported by reality, then it is important we change our positions rather than continue to push them. Commitment should be to the truth and not to one's own current view. I am personally delighted when I find somebody who can show me why my views are incorrect and thus enable me to gain a more accurate picture of reality. Anybody who takes this stance will inevitably support a p/p focuser approach.

On the other hand, those who are primarily interested in

manipulating people, will disapprove of broadening the debate to look at all relevant viewpoints. I went to Washington DC, soon after I had developed this approach, expecting to find support because it seemed to me that the p/p focuser approach would improve policy. An individual, who was far more realistic than I, pointed out how this approach would make it far harder to exercise power and would therefore be unacceptable to most politicians and special interest groups.

My hope is that p/p focusers will become available on every critical topic at a number of levels of difficulty and in various media. P/p focusers will, of course, be available on line through computers and also in print, video, audio and interactive formats. Another critical requirement is that the arguments in p/p focusers be kept constantly up to date. These documents cannot be written and forgotten. They must reflect the current state of ideas in the light of changing realities.

The teams responsible for these documents must therefore stay together and revise as frequently as is necessary. P/p focusers also need to be written for people at various decision-making scales. For example, individuals need to consider different issues when thinking about how to continue their own education as compared to those which should be examined by those who have the opportunity to change educational systems.

Two primary questions have to be considered before we can be sure that the p/p focuser system of ordering knowledge will move us forward. First, how will it be decided what are the most important questions which need to be considered? Fortunately this question does not have to be decided centrally. If this form of knowledge structuring becomes accepted, competing p/p focusers on the most important topics will be issued by various groups. Colleges and universities will come to concentrate their efforts on subject areas rather than disciplines.

The second question which has to be examined is how to determine what viewpoints are "credible" and therefore deserve to be included in a p/p focuser. Fortunately, this issue will also be resolved idiosyncratically by the many groups which are engaged in the production of p/p focusers. The logic of the p/p focuser approach, however, is to push forward to an ever-more inclusive vision.

The p/p focuser approach will help recreate the center in politics. Political decision-makers will gain the knowledge and support which will make it easier for them to support positive directions rather than going along with the special interest groups which so often harass them. Once a p/p focuser which covers all the issues is available, it will be easier to place the ideas of a fringe group in perspective because their place in the total debate about a topic will seem less compelling. The p/p focuser, and other similar techniques, are the best potentials we have for breaking through the patterns of the past and discussing the potentials of the future.

This brings us full circle. Geoffrey Vickers demanded that society commit itself to ensuring that accurate information be available. This requires profound change in our social and educational systems so that institutions no longer have the right to distort information to achieve their goals. The p/p focuser is one of the tools which will move us in this direction.

CHAPTER 8

Redesigning Social Policy

PEOPLE WILL DEVELOP POSITIVE DIRECTIONS FOR THEMSELVES if they can find challenging images, understandings and models in storytelling, art, their families and real life. Today these necessary supports are in scarce supply, particularly for minority communities. Our culture concentrates on the depressing and the negative rather than seeking out the developments which will create a higher quality of life.

We need to learn a lesson from businesses. They are beginning to understand that concentrating on their possibilities, rather than their problems, leads to far more dynamic results. They are therefore moving toward approaches which support positive directions and creative individuals, rather than spending most of their time concentrating on what is wrong. Communities will become more effective when they adopt similar strategies.

Supporting people in change processes, rather than being negative about them, will be one of the key elements in moving us from the industrial era to the compassionate era. Learning to see individuals as having potential rather than being weak, shiftless and negative is a key need of our current time. Most people respond positively when they are given the chance to develop themselves. On the other hand, they behave ineffectively, or even destructively, when the culture makes it clear that it expects nothing from them.

There are many reasons for failures to change behavior as outside conditions alter. The first is that it is easier to live with certainty than uncertainty. If one is absolutely sure what is moral and what is not, thinking becomes unnecessary. Second, as the pace of change gets faster, people get frightened and tend to cling to the past to avoid being overwhelmed by the future. Current destructive levels of fear cause individuals to cling onto moral and social codes even after they have obviously become irrelevant.

Finally, people find it difficult to distinguish between the continuing need for moral values and the specific codes which are appropriate for particular moments of history. Honesty, responsibility, humility and love are as important today as in the past. The way these values can be realized in today's conditions is inevitably profoundly different from what was appropriate in previous centuries. The challenge today is to develop policies and directions which will encourage as many people as possible to achieve their hopes and their goals, within the context of a viable, long-run ecological system.

In the remainder of this chapter I shall look at a number of issues where directions must be dramatically changed. I have aimed to discuss those issues where the most fundamental changes are required, and are feasible, at the current time.

Health

The health issue has been forced into the forefront of political activity by the frustration of citizens. About 34 million Americans have no health care insurance; those who are not poor enough to qualify for government support and not well enough off to purchase insurance have the most serious problems. Costs for those who do have insurance protection continue to spiral out of control. Unfortunately, most of the responses to the current crisis are based on a simpler, long-vanished world. They do not face up to the increasingly esoteric, and painful, questions which have developed along with advanced medical technologies.

We are faced with the need to develop profoundly new health systems. Market approaches are clashing with personal and social taboos around life and death issues. The growing ability of doctors to diagnose and treat patients forces us to reconsider our economic limits and our moral beliefs. What sorts of interventions in reproductive technology are appropriate and which should be prevented?

Does it make a difference if the mother paying for surrogate pregnancies is unable to have a child or simply wants to avoid the frustrations of pregnancy or the pain of giving birth? What happens if a child born to a surrogate mother is handicapped? Should people go overseas and buy organs which increase the risk of ill-health, or even death, of the organ donor?

These are no longer esoteric questions; they are becoming mainstream issues. We are no longer sure who should make the most critical decisions. Much of the discussion of health issues is currently being dominated by finances: we need to bring it back to the central question of who will make the tough decisions and what will they be.

In addition, the rights of patients, and parents, to make choices is denied in a surprisingly large number of cases. Doctors, and law courts, are claiming that they should make decisions for patients. Many hard choices have been pushed into the law courts in recent years. It is all too obvious, however, that judges have no more skills in making these hard choices than anybody else. Indeed, the law's commitment to objectivity is not helpful here. Tragedy cannot always be avoided. We need systems which support those who have to make tough decisions and to honor them with compassion and dignity.

The most difficult issue is around the right to death. The number and percentage of people throughout the world who are being kept alive solely by modern medicine is rising. The cost of delaying death is a high percentage of total medical care. It has been estimated that well over 50% of all medical expenditures are incurred within a year of death. Most of us have faced the challenge of how to support a loved one at the final stages of their life, and death, with all too little guidance from either our doctors or our pastors.

When should people be allowed to die? The early-nineties interest in the book *Final Exit*, which provides information on painless ways to commit suicide, shows the growing concern about this topic. The close vote on the "right to die" initiative in Washington state proved that the issue is here to stay. People are finding ways around the commitment of the medical profession to keep them alive. Society must now develop new approaches which prevent people from choosing suicide when they have the potential of a good life ahead while supporting them, and their loved ones, when death makes sense. Hospice is a wonderful institution which has found new ways to support patients, their relatives and friends in these transitions.

Lying behind these medical issues is a far broader question. Should the ability to obtain health care be determined by command of resources or based on some other set of criteria? We are learning so much about how to keep people alive that hard choices are going to have to be made about who gets the health care which will preserve their health and maximize their lifespans. Do we want to value youth or skills or brains or money? Once we look honestly at the current directions of the medical system, it is clear that fundamental choices are already being made without really facing up to their implications. Oregon, which has made an honest attempt to prioritize the care that can be afforded, has often been vilified for its efforts.

One of the most obvious questions revolves about when heroic efforts should be made to save premature babies. Technically, it is now sometimes possible to keep a child alive when its birth weight is around 8 ounces. Should society pay the costs of such a procedure, which are often in the hundreds of thousands of dollars? Given that the amount of money available for health care is limited, is this the appropriate way to use resources or do higher priorities exist such as routine care for the poor? Should the rapidly growing evidence that severely premature babies will be far less healthy and more at risk than children born close to term make any difference to our decisions?

This question has further ramifications. It is now broadly agreed that providing pre-natal support for all is far more cost-effective than intensive care for preemies because mothers who do not get pre-natal care are most likely to have early, and small, babies. Why don't we provide money so that everybody gets the help they need to bear babies near, or at, term rather than have to provide major funding for dealing with premature children? Should our priorities be rearranged so as to support pre-natal care?

On one of my recent speaking trips I discovered a county in Oregon, Deschutes, which has committed to supporting all pregnant mothers and has decided that "no one will be refused service based on inability to pay." This commitment should spread rapidly across the country.

The same wasteful patterns exist when children have continuing health problems. School-based clinics can provide care at a relatively low cost. They can also increase the opportunities for students; for example, by improving the chances of asthmatics graduating. We know that if people with this disease do not get timely help, they are often forced to enter hospital and large amounts of money are wasted.

We need to spend far more money on promotion of health than we do at the current time. This can save resources and limit total spending. It will not, however, avoid the need for rationing medical care. Most of the current discussion about the future of health care repeats the pious hope that the goal should be to provide all the quality care required for all citizens throughout their lives. This goal is infeasible because of continuing advances in medical knowledge; society cannot afford to deliver all possible care to everybody.

Medical care is already being rationed; the amount of knowledge now available makes this pattern inevitable. The real question is what principles, and processes, should underlie this rationing. Should it be by age, money, skills, or contacts? There are elements of all of these approaches in the current mix: what is the right pattern for the future?

The medical issue is difficult enough when we look only at the rich countries. Once we consider the gross disparities between the rich and the poor, the issues become far more difficult. For example, AIDS is treatable in the rich countries, although it is hardly ever survivable. In the poor countries, it is an early death sentence because the money is not available to use existing medical knowledge.

In the poor countries, gains in primary health indicators such as length of life and infant mortality are more effectively achieved by improving water supplies and sanitation rather than by better individual access to medical care. Limited funds must therefore be concentrated on public health for many decades into the future.

Equality of opportunity

The sixties saw two major developments which aimed to help the poor. One was designed to support the poor through a variety of programs pulled together in the War on Poverty. The programs were designed to produce a social safety net so nobody would starve, and most people could avoid severe hardship. President Kennedy's policies, which were built on by President Johnson, revolutionized our perception of the problem of poverty.

Moving in parallel with the War on Poverty, the federal government recognized its obligations to blacks. It broke through the segregation barriers in the South and began to develop programs to compensate for the continuous pattern of neglect which had kept blacks, and other minorities, from being able to compete fairly for available opportunities. At a later date, women forced the recognition that they too had been unfairly disadvantaged. They were therefore included as beneficiaries of several government programs which aimed to level the playing field.

Both of these sixties developments are under challenge today. Anecdotal stories of gross abuse of government programs have led to a growing backlash. More and more candidates for political office are calling for "workfare" which requires able-bodied welfare recipients to hold jobs if they are to be paid money. One of the reasons there is so much pressure for workfare is that parents, who do work for a living, are frustrated when others are supported although they do not hold jobs.

Is it desirable for everybody to hold a job? For example, is it more valuable for a person to work at a minimum wage rather than to stay home and look after their children? The growing costs of absent parents and broken homes are increasingly obvious in the ghettoes of this country. We shall inevitably gather extremely bitter fruit from the violence which has become endemic in so many slum areas. Raising children well is, in my opinion, more important than forcing people into meaningless, dead end jobs.

Governments are too often unconscious of the need for people to regain a sense of self-esteem. A job is certainly better than the deadening sense of despair which welfare fosters. But supportive parents are critically important in today's culture and if people are willing to play this role they should be honored, rather than denigrated.

Workfare is often sold to the public on the grounds that it will reduce taxes substantially. But even if every able-bodied person on welfare is found a job, it will only eliminate a small proportion of the total welfare bill. Even the most optimistic estimates of savings promise little relief from taxation. Welfare abuse and cheating is not the cause of the great bulk of payments: it is the growing number of people who are old, sick, disabled and ill-educated which is forcing up costs.

The drive to promote workfare has become, in many parts of the United States, an opportunity to promote racial prejudice with an acceptable face. Despite the evidence that the poor of all races are caught in the welfare trap, whites find it convenient to blame minorities, particularly blacks, for excessive welfare rolls. Similarly, drug problems are usually presented in ways which emphasize black and minority offenders and exclude whites.

Confronted with this relentless drumbeat of criticism about their behavior, blacks are increasingly angry. Figures show that well over 50% of them believe that the white race is engaged in genocide. They see the decimation of young black adults, particularly male, as the best evidence for their thesis. (Homicide is now the leading cause of death for black males up to the age of 35.)

The increasingly bitter clash around affirmative action emerges from this clash of perceptions. Whites believe they are excluded from jobs because blacks get preferential treatment. Blacks, on the other hand, feel that little progress has been made in equalizing opportunities. Those who continue to demand affirmative action programs point out that the average wage for minorities and women is still well below the national level, even when corrected for educational levels. They also stress the abundant evidence which proves the existence of a glass ceiling (a term used to describe the inability of women and minorities to reach the very top of organizations).

While there is still clear evidence of needed support for minorities and women, it is also obvious that massive opposition to affirmative action programs is developing. These programs will almost certainly be withdrawn, or gutted, unless they can be restructured in a way which will be seen as fair by the majority of the population. Can strategies be developed which will maintain our commitment to those who need help?

I believe we can, and must, find ways to care for the underprivileged. The critical step is to decide to help all the disadvantaged, regardless of sex or color. It is time we moved beyond helping all minorities and all women, regardless of their current skills and income. Rather we need to support people who have few resources and whose children will be even worse off unless we develop new policies.

How can we define the disadvantaged effectively? Two approaches might work. One would be to ensure that all individuals and families who fall below a certain level of income and resources would receive help: this would be an extension of the BES approach described in Chapter 5. It would use the income statistics which are already available.

An alternative would be to provide support for all the people who live within geographical areas which are significantly poorer than the average. This approach has already been used for certain educational and economic development programs. The court cases which have led to greater equalization of school costs per pupil across states are an example of an approach which targets poorer geographical areas. Providing resources to everybody within a given area can have positive consequences; better-off people may be prepared to stay in the area so as to receive benefits. If they did so, this would break one of today's primary problems where poor areas remain disadvantaged because those who succeed move out of them as soon as they can afford to do so.

Once selection criteria have been defined, the most effective styles of programs would have to be determined. At one level, it is easy to see what is needed. Most of us now recognize that it is more effective to "teach people to fish, rather than to give them a fish." In other words, we need to move people toward self-esteem and self-support rather than to develop programs which give resources which are immediately used up and leave no significant consequences behind. Indeed, they may even further reduce the level of commitment in the community.

Up to the current time, self-support and a job have normally been seen as synonymous. Given the revolution in production technologies, the range of activities which communities support must inevitably widen. Raising kids, caring for parents, enhancing neighborhood solidarity, solving societal problems, supporting fundamental change are all roles which will be needed and should be supported in the future.

We now know that the critical period to break the cycle of poverty is from conception to age five. Children who have not gained a sense of the excitement of learning and life by this age have little chance of being successful adults. Some parents will welcome help which gives young children a better chance than they had themselves. Others will resist. One of the hardest choices in the future is when we should force opportunities on poverty-stricken families. The rights of the individual and the community can clash dramatically at this point.

Justice systems

Western justice systems are out of balance. Our current patterns emerged from previous centuries where power was all on the side of the prosecutors. An accused person had little chance of going free even if they were innocent; a truth that pervades the folk-songs of the seventeenth and eighteenth century. As a consequence, the drive for the last two hundred years has been to prevent the excessive power of the state from overwhelming criminal defendants.

Today the pendulum has swung; the rich and the powerful have found ways to manage the current legal system so as to avoid punishment while the poor are far more likely to go to prison. And when the poor do go to prison they spend their time in far more unpleasant jails than the "country clubs" usually chosen for those who commit white-collar crime. I find it shocking that we excuse the privileged with the statement that "they have suffered enough" while the poor, who may steal because of the needs of their children, are attacked with the full weight of the law.

American and British legal systems are based on adversarial strategies. The idea that the truth might be discovered in any other way seems incredible in countries where this model prevails. The law courts can be compared to a medieval jousting ring where the strongest prevail: all too often it is the person with the best lawyer who gains the verdict rather than the person with right on their side.

A growing number of lawyers are moving toward alternative forms of dispute resolution. One of the reasons for this move is the clogging of the courts which make it impossible to schedule timely trials. But there is also a growing sense that a more advantageous settlement to both sides can be found through dialogue than by using the court system.

What changes must be made? We must face up to the fact that we have a class-based system of justice where the rich can afford to hire those who know how to work the system while the poor use court-appointed lawyers. The resulting mess is only kept from collapsing by inequitable plea-bargaining where the powerful cut good deals and the poor often go to prison. The search for a just society must therefore inevitably precede any hope for a fair legal system.

Some positive steps could, however, be taken even without systemic change. The law could learn to distinguish between the one-time offender and the repeat criminal. The object of the justice system should be to keep people out of jails unless they are hardened offenders. Everybody can make a single slip: it is the repetitive pattern which must be avoided. People who go to jail all too often emerge as committed criminals. It has sometimes been argued that jails are the only really successful educational system, producing criminals with an 80% success rate!

There is also a continuing clash between those who want to use the justice system to reform and those who want it to punish. We must recognize that the goal must be to improve the future of the individual, if possible, and to protect the society, when necessary. Criminals who can be redeemed should be so they can benefit themselves and their society.

We are now discovering that we cannot afford a large military; hopefully the next step will be to realize that America cannot afford to have a larger proportion of its population incarcerated than any other country. This does not mean that there will be no jails. Some people are incorrigible. They need to be locked away, if necessary for life. The fact that the failure resulted from their parents' behavior, or from the patterns of the society in which they were brought up, does not change the fact that they are too dangerous to be free. The cost of incarceration should not, however, exceed the amount charged for attending Harvard. This is evidence of misplaced priorities.

One of the real problems in moving forward to a more intelligent system is that criminology cannot be an exact science. Some people will inevitably be released and then commit further crimes. Some are going to be held who have renounced the criminal mind-set. Parole systems have to be run by fallible human beings—expecting zero errors is an unreasonable assumption. The Willie Horton tape, exploited so mercilessly by the Bush campaign in 1988, was therefore a cheap shot, which made it even more difficult for parole boards and governors to make hard choices in an uncertain world. The commercial was particularly destructive because it appealed to racial prejudice.

Crime will continue to increase until there is a broad and deep recognition in the dominant society of the violence which current social patterns do to the lives of the poor and minorities. Violence goes both ways in societies. There is the visible violence of the criminal. There is also the systemic violence of the society against certain classes and races. Denial of the feedback loop between these two patterns is naive. The Archbishop of Canterbury, in England, got into a great deal of trouble when he stated this inconvenient truth.

Underlying all these issues is the loss of our moral codes. They must be regained. Religion, spirituality and system theory all confirm that societies will not work without honesty, responsibility, humility and love.

One of the all-too possible scenarios for the future is that society will be split between the rich and the poor and that more and more people, but particularly the disadvantaged and minorities, will go in fear of their lives because of the level of violence.

The drugs issue

Justice questions are today closely related to drug strategies. Well over 50% of the current crime problem results from the purchase, sale and use of illegal drugs. Despite this agreed reality, the official rhetoric is that we must continue the same policies. There is, however, an alternative. Drug use could be decriminalized. Even considering such a possibility is often seen as totally unacceptable. Those who raise the subject are often accused of being addicts themselves. I should therefore state, for the record, that I have never used illegal drugs and, indeed, aim to avoid any form of medication to the greatest possible extent.

When the War on Drugs is discussed, the parallel with prohibition is rarely cited. America tried to stop drinking through a constitutional amendment and failed. When prohibition was repealed, liquor sales were increasingly heavily regulated and taxed. Over time there has been a sharp decrease in the sales of hard liquor, and a movement toward less alcoholic drinks. Given the success of this strategy, why are we unwilling even to consider the same approach for currently illegal drugs? Both alcohol and illegal drugs alter human consciousness, the costs of abuse of alcohol have been estimated to be ten times as high as those of drugs.

Indeed, if one broadens the picture and also looks at the issue of cigarette smoking, the issue becomes even more clouded. Smoking has been estimated to do ten times as much damage as alcohol and one hundred times as much as that of drugs and yet smoking is not only legal but tobacco growing is subsidized. Indeed as we look even further, we are forced to recognize that prescribed medical drugs are also routinely overused and abused. This aspect of the drug issue is rarely discussed although there is plenty of evidence of how "respectable" people use both uppers and downers to control their moods.

There is no rational reason to treat harmful and addictive substances so differently. It is time we faced the fact that they are all dangerous and damaging. I can understand why people try to prevent their children using drugs. I remain shocked by the fact that many parents are willing to encourage their children to drink alcohol in order to keep them off illegal drugs; this was the accepted pattern in many parts of Arizona when we were living there.

What would be the benefits of decriminalizing drugs? One primary gain would be to eliminate the obscene profits which are the direct result of drug prohibition. Limiting supply through police control keeps prices and profits high and makes the drug business financially attractive. If drugs were decriminalized, fewer people would find it worthwhile to sell them. Law enforcement would not be corrupted to the same extent. Whole countries would not be at risk of being governed by drug cartels. The profitability of attracting addicts would decrease.

Another gain would be the reduction of crime and the overload in the criminal system. The number of drug-related murders which may be as high as 50% of the total in many cities would fall dramatically because drug profits would be far lower. Decriminalizing drugs would also reduce one of the primary dangers to civil liberties at the current time. The fear of drugs has led to visible, and invisible, attacks on civil rights.

One of the most serious of the dangers comes from mandatory sentencing guidelines which leave no opportunity for judges to consider individual situations or circumstances. Judges should be able to consider all the circumstances of a case when sentencing. Relying on individual judgment is, of course, also inequitable with some judges being "too strict" and others "too lenient." But the injustices which come from differing sentencing patterns by various judges are less serious than decisions made without looking at all the realities in a case, particularly when the penalties are excessively severe.

What would be the primary dangers of decriminalization? It is usually argued that young people would be at still greater risk. This is frankly nonsense. Just as alcohol and cigarette sales to minors are controlled, drug sales could be far better limited if decriminalized. Minors would actually be safer because the number of pushers would be significantly decreased by the lessening of profits. Some young people would, of course, continue to use drugs. However, tobacco and alcohol continue to be used and abused among the young despite our best efforts. Total control of harmful products is therefore obviously infeasible.

Would drug use among adults increase or decrease? There is no way of forecasting. The future would depend on whether a major societal effort was made to reduce the use of all drugs, including those currently illegal, as well as prescription drugs. The current campaign against illegal drug use loses much of its effectiveness because it does not seem logical. Why are drugs illegal and alcohol legal? Why is it acceptable for a mother to damage her functioning with prescription drugs but marijuana is illegal? Why do we make a joke of Dad coming home drunk ? Only a coherent message will help people, especially children, avoid addiction.

Decriminalizing drugs will not be enough by itself, of course. The whole issue of drugs is bound up with the growth of the underclass in Western societies. A fundamental change is required in the way we support children from conception through their schooling years if the cycle of dependency and abuse is to be broken. You may believe that people would never stand for decriminalization. My admittedly unscientific polls have shown that there is already substantial support for this step even before many "respectable" academic and political voices have had the courage to speak out for it. I am convinced that the results would be very surprising if one of the polling organizations asked the public how it felt about this issue.

You may feel that drug decriminalization is wrong. If you couple this stance with a belief that you should prohibit smoking and the use of alcoholic beverages and also control the abuse of prescription drugs, I admire your logic but will dispute the practicality of your ideas. If you want to continue the ban on illegal drugs alone, then it will be obvious by now that I do not understand your position.

If drugs were decriminalized, then we could apply the same sorts of controls to the sale of illegal drugs as we do to alcohol and to prescription drugs. Some people would get around the rules as is always the case. But most people would work within the system which had been developed. Truly dangerous drugs could be placed on prescription which is also the case for legal drugs. While there will still be abuse, it can be more easily limited once the chance of obscene profits is removed.

Some of my colleagues have argued that the chances of this book being influential will be weakened by treating such a controversial issue. I have decided there is no point in stating my views unless I pursue their logic fully. The drug issue threatens to destroy the civil order, both internally and internationally. It must be faced and dealt with if the other questions I raise throughout this book are to have any chance of a positive solution. Failing to examine a primary cancer which is currently destroying the viability of city life, and which can be treated, would be irresponsible. This book aims to show that it is possible to develop a coherent model for the future. I cannot make this case convincingly if I pussyfoot around the problems of the day.

The drive to self-destruction has deeper roots than can be reached by the criminal code. The need is for a more loving and caring society where children are given the chance to develop their potential. We need better parents not more laws. We need more caring helpers not more regulation. This is the real choice of the nineties. Shall we commit to rebuilding a loving and caring society? Shall we recognize the rage that our current systems are creating in people at all levels of society? Shall we face what happens when middle-class children are given all the consumption goodies they want but are deprived of loving support to discover who they really are?

Provide birth control to anybody who wants it

The issues I have raised so far in this chapter have dealt predominantly with rich country issues. The next two sections deal primarily with global and third world questions. The basic long-run threat to personal freedom throughout the world results from overpopulation. In a growing number of geographical areas, serious shortages of land, water and breathable air are inevitable. This is not a long-run extrapolation where unexpected developments may change the final outcome. It is a short-run certainty. Indeed, the problem is likely to be even worse than currently understood because the rate of increase in world population is still faster than had been expected, despite the consequences of famine, diseases and wars.

There are two primary requirements for economic and political stability in the twenty-first century. One is that people in the rich countries stabilize, and eventually reduce, the amount of resources each of them see as basic to a decent standard of living. Some population experts have come to see this reduction in consumption in the rich countries as the only critical issue. They argue that the degree of population pressure can be best determined by multiplying the number of people by the standard of living. It is indeed important to recognize the validity of this approach. All too often, people from the rich countries prefer to concentrate on the rapid increase in numbers as this appears to lessen their responsibility.

Nevertheless, this approach oversimplifies the population question. It is possible for the absolute numbers of people to be so large that they stress natural systems even if there is only a very low standard of living. This danger is already emerging in many of the poor countries. There must therefore be a very rapid and substantial decline in birth rates. Fortunately, there is plenty of evidence that there is an unsatisfied demand for effective birth control technologies in most of the developing countries. The need is not to create it but to satisfy it.

Reproductive rights are still perceived by most people as the most personal of all the freedoms, despite the fact that the overall impact of individual choices has enormous impact on societal issues. It is inevitable that once the state begins to control this aspect of life, it will intervene in many others. China has already been forced to restrict births dramatically as there is simply not enough land for the population to continue to expand. The country has therefore developed, and fairly successfully enforced, a policy of only permitting a family to have one child.

It is tempting to spend considerable time looking at the implications of such a policy for the long haul. The Chinese have always lavished a great deal of love on their children. What happens when all of this love is concentrated on single children? What does this imply for the culture of China in the twenty-first century? How does one prevent infanticide of female children so that a male child, who is much more valued within the Chinese culture, can be born? What would be the implications of combining a single child policy with a growing capacity to determine the sex of children? Regardless of such fascinating issues and byways, we need to recognize that maintaining the policing structure required for the compulsory limitation of births will prevent the Chinese government from moving in the directions required for more responsible freedom. The level of coercion required to control births almost inevitably requires the maintenance of a police state.

If compulsory birth control is to be avoided in the future, then voluntary contraception must be encouraged now. A total, and immediate, global cultural commitment should be taken to ensure that anybody who wants to prevent conception have the information, the means and, if essential, the financial support to do so. The means chosen for this purpose should be appropriate to the culture. The value judgments of other societies and religions should not be permitted to impinge on such choices. If birth rates are not reduced soon, death rates will rise again dramatically through famine, plague, infanticide and warfare.

Why has the subject of high birth rates failed to be placed at the top of the world agenda? Many have hoped that birth-rates in the poor countries will fall without government intervention. They have based their beliefs on a parallel with the countries now rich. As standards of living rose in the Western world, many families chose to have less children. The belief was that a similar pattern could develop in the poor countries. In a few countries, it will contribute to desirable directions but it will seldom be enough to produce the needed changes by itself.

What are the fundamental causes of high birth rates? They are in part traditional: children are evidence of male potency, and female fertility, both of which are highly valued in traditional cultures. These attitudes change slowly, of course. While many women would be delighted to decrease their number of births, men are often unwilling to accept such a change in values.

Another critical factor is that children in traditional societies are the primary method of providing social security to the old; young people are the guarantee that parents will not be in want. The United Nations, particularly UNICEF, now hopes that parents will come to believe that the first two or three children will live long enough to support them in their old age, therefore leading to a willingness to cut back on the size of desired families. While this approach could be effective if people do believe the argument, the AIDS epidemic will inevitably make it far more difficult to convince parents that their children will survive. In Uganda, for example, some 8% of the country's population already have HIV symptoms and whole generations are being decimated. The crisis is even worse in other parts of Africa.

There is a final issue that still confuses discussions. Power was based on numbers in the past for people provided "cannon fodder." In today's world, numbers still translate into clout at the ballot box. These factors still lead some leaders of minority and ethnic groups, as well as countries, to fear a low birth rate and support pro-natal policies. A 1980s book by Ben Wattenberg, deploring the birth dearth in the United States, got an enormous amount of attention for these reasons. Our thinking must be profoundly changed. The danger in the future is overcrowding. In almost all areas of the world today, increases in population decrease the quality of life rather than increase it.

The need to limit births as effectively as possible raises several critical issues. First, experience shows that female birth control risks significant side-effects for many women whether the intervention is chemical or invasive. In this light of this reality, it is highly unfortunate that modern birth control technology has been biased toward controlling the female capacity to conceive rather than limiting male capacity to inseminate. I am personally convinced that the primary reason for this bias is that most birth control researchers have been male and that most men are still terrified of any form of intervention that might interfere with their potency.

This pattern is fortunately already changing. An enormous number of vasectomies have taken place. This shows that men are willing to take risks with their own reproductive systems in order to create secure, effective birth-control. It would, however, be highly desirable to develop long-run chemical inhibitors of the fertility of sperm which had no impact on sexual desire or potency without the largely irreversible character of vasectomies. There has already been progress along this line and it is highly probable it could be accelerated.

Rapid progress in any birth control technology is however unlikely at the current time because of a second central problem. Many pharmaceutical companies, particularly in the United States, are not currently willing to take the risk of developing birth control methods. They fear they are going to be sued in the inevitable cases where something goes wrong; there can never be totally safe interventions in the human body. Even where effective research is going on, as is the case in France which has developed a substance which acts immediately after conception to prevent the development of a viable fetus, no United States company has been willing to take the risk of making it available in America. The legal system has to be changed if the necessary rapid development of birth control technologies is to take place.

This raises an extraordinary issue. Cigarette and alcohol companies can sell a product, which is agreed to be dangerous, and the law courts have so far held that they are not normally liable for damages. On the other hand, it is possible to win suits when birth control technologies, which are designed to meet a major need, fail. The argument appears to be that because cigarette companies label their products as dangerous, they are therefore exempt from suit. Does this mean that it is enough to label prominently all the possible dangers from a product to be free from liability? Can you imagine the "pill" being covered with large-print warnings from the surgeon general about the dangers? Would this be worthwhile if it exempted birth control technologies from legal liability?

The third problem is even trickier. What can be done to shift the views of religious groups, and particularly the Roman Catholics? What is it going to take to get the hierarchy of several churches to understand that their concern for the preservation of the fetus in poor, crowded countries increases levels of suffering and death? How can caring people encourage births in countries where the death rates of infants and children are already so high?

I see the Catholic stance as a classic case of developing rules for a particular time and forcing their continuance long after they have become totally inappropriate. In a world where life was short and infant mortality was high, it made sense for families to be large even at great risk to the mother's life. This goal started as a secular imperative which eventually, and perhaps inevitably, came to be stated in religious terms. To buttress this view in today's radically new circumstances, and even to reinforce it, is tragic and unacceptable.

The necessary support for the Catholic position is that the soul comes into existence at the moment of conception. It is argued that from the moment that the sperm and the egg join, a different quality of life exists. It is difficult for most outsiders to understand this stance. Indeed, most Catholics in the United States have already rejected church doctrine in the area of sexuality. Unfortunately, most of them seem content to restrict their thinking to local situations without accepting their responsibility to support people in other parts of the world where old doctrines continue to be enforced.

The resistance of the Catholic church to changes in sexual mores and patterns cannot be discussed without also challenging the policies of the American government. Many attempts to limit births in the poor countries have been sabotaged by the United States which insists that no support be given for abortions. It is surely the height of arrogance to force nations to base their policies on the biases of less than 50% of Americans. The unwillingness to accord validity to the behavior patterns of other cultures is one of the primary factors which leads to such cynicism about the openness of the United States to a pluralistic world order.

People have been struggling to draw public attention to the problems caused by rapid population growth ever since World War II. But this issue has never managed to get the attention it so urgently deserves. Continued rapid population growth will certainly destroy any potential for resolving the crises of our time. This issue has to be moved off the back burner and made central. The population bomb may not be as immediately dramatic as environmental concerns. There are certainly deeper and higher emotional barriers to facing its dangers. Nevertheless, the long-run consequences of population growth at current levels will inevitably be disastrous, both to human freedom and ecological balance.

Maintain an urban-rural balance

What settlement patterns will be most appropriate to provide a high quality of life to current and foreseeable populations? The answers to this question are complex. Relatively few people realize that the largest cities in the world are no longer in the developed world but in the poor countries. Migration to cities occurs for a number of reasons. Many of them are essentially uncontrollable. The first was well expressed in an old popular song from the First World War: "How are you going to keep them down on the farm after they've seen Paree?"

The bright lights are attractive to young and ambitious people and they seem far more exciting than rural life. Knowledge of the bright lights is of course far more pervasive than it used to be. It is spread by television where satellite broadcasts bring glitz and glitter into the slums and favelas of the third world. The flickering light of a television set is now one of the constants wherever electricity is available.

The realities of the big cities have, of course, often been a disappointment to those who go there with exaggerated hopes. The streets of New York were not paved with gold! The unhappy aspiring film star who moves to Los Angeles is still a staple literary and movie plot. Conditions in the large cities of the poor countries today are, however, infinitely worse than most people who live in the developed world can imagine. Polluted water, food scavenged from garbage dumps, disease, high infant mortality, violence and living as squatters are all part of the basic conditions for many urban dwellers in the poor countries.

Why then does migration continue? There is a well-known tendency among migrants to exaggerate the benefits and to minimize the costs of any move they make. They do this partly to bolster their own self-image and partly to look good to those they left behind. The consequence, however, is that people in the rural areas gain a far more positive picture of the benefits of moving to cities than is warranted by the facts. Migration is also supported because relatives who have already moved into the city are expected to give support to others who come later.

How can the balance of advantage be shifted? It would help if a fairer picture of the advantages and disadvantages of city life was available and there has, in fact, been a little progress in this direction as the glitter days of the eighties fade. Most communicators nevertheless see the city as exciting and the rural areas as "dullsville." This attitude inevitably affects habitation patterns and will continue to encourage movement to the cities until it changes.

It is important to recognize, however, that part of the perception which causes people to move to the city is based on a bedrock of reality. Duncan Goheen, who has done a great deal of work in the Philippines, made this point well in a letter to me.

> I interviewed migrants who moved from the countryside into Manila. I asked them why they traded fresh air and open space for the squalor and seemingly unbearable conditions of street living in Manila. Their answer was that when the rice bowl is empty, it's empty. Starvation is at the door. In the city, there is always a way to earn a few pesos. A few pesos a day will put enough rice on the table to ward off starvation.

There are several very substantial steps which could be taken to cut down on migration out of the rural areas. First, governmental policies still tend to advantage city-dwellers over those in rural areas, often by providing cheap food and cheap gasoline to reduce the prospect of riots. Mexico City, despite its overwhelming problems, still provides incentives for people to move there. There needs to be a rigorous reexamination of all current policies to equalize conditions or maybe even to give advantages to the rural areas.

The second step is to look at how rural life can be made more attractive and more exciting. The potential of video and computers to change the balance of advantage is very great. Far more attention should be paid to wiring rural areas with telecommunications and electricity than to improving transportation, which demands non-replaceable oil products. There should also be a major effort to teach people using audio and video, which are natural to them, rather than by insisting that information be primarily gained through reading. The Yavapai Apache describe their library as primarily designed to support "paper-reading:" they recognize that there are other forms of communication such as sand-paintings, rugs, dances and conversation which can be "read."

One primary challenge of the nineties and the twenty-first century is to make rural life more attractive throughout the world. This will be achieved in part as people come to see the costs as well as the advantages of city living. More importantly, with the true coming of telecommunications, people will be just as much in touch when they live in a rural area as in the cities.

The recovery of rural life also depends on a profound shift in economic thinking. The economies of the poor countries will be damaged so long as food aid is sent to them on a continuing basis. (Famine relief in times of bad weather is, of course, a totally different matter.) The availability of cheap food from other countries destroys the viability of the rural areas. It makes it impossible for communities in the countryside to sell their goods at reasonable prices or maintain social cohesion. The agricultural areas of the poor countries need to be strengthened rather than undermined.

Raising the economic issue leads, of course, into some of the trickiest questions of all. There is a need for land reform to support peasant farming in many countries. The future seems to lie with locally controlled development initiatives which are labor intensive. Aid should be given out in small amounts which support small-scale activity. A number of approaches have already been created to hand out micro-loans: the default rate is unbelievably low.

Twentieth-century development models have failed. There has been a significant decline in living standards in many poor countries over the last decade. There are several reasons for current trends. One is that the poor countries are facing heavy interest costs on their past borrowings. In many cases, they are actually paying out more in interest than they are receiving in new loans. In effect, the rich countries are today receiving money from the poor countries rather than sending it to them.

A second reason for the worsening conditions in the poor countries is that they are often paying more for their imports and getting less for their exports. A growing number of specialists in third-world issues believe that the continuing integration of the poor countries into the world production and trade net is worsening their situation rather than improving it. They are challenging the belief that freer trade will benefit the developing world.

We can no longer base our planning on the belief that people around the world can reach rich-country standards of living. Until now, world development theory has been driven by the belief that every area could eventually come to enjoy the wealth available in Europe, Japan, North America and Australasia. The fact that very few of the poor countries were actually moving in this direction was largely ignored. Similarly, poor people within the rich countries assumed that their children, or at least their grandchildren, could eventually be rich. We have to recognize at this time the ecological limitations to growth which will prevent rapid world-wide economic growth.

So long as we could hope for an endless increase in income and wealth, gaps between the rich and the poor seemed acceptable, whether within or between countries. There was always the hope that you, or somebody you knew, would get to the top. Today the recognition of limits makes great differentials in wealth increasingly unacceptable. Energy and ecological restraints have transformed the debate around income distribution. In the future, we shall have to accept "enoughness" rather than struggle for an ever-rising standard of living.

Choices

What then are the options for the future? The first is to hope that the gap between the rich and poor can persist for an unlimited amount of time into the future without causing unbearable tensions and violence. The second is to assume that the violence between the rich and poor will become increasingly dangerous because the gap between rich and poor persists and the deprived are no longer willing to tolerate it. The third is to develop directions so that the gap between the rich and the poor begins to close.

At first sight, the first scenario may seem the most probable. The tragedy of poverty has continued, and even deepened, in the second half of the twentieth century. Despite many efforts and much frustration, the poor nations have failed to develop effective mechanisms to challenge the socioeconomic structures which tend to advantage the rich as compared to the poor.

The harsh fact, however, is that the steady increase in population in most parts of the world is bringing more and more areas to the brink of crisis. In 1990 I heard an expert on Mexico City talk who believed that there were only five years left before a catastrophic breakdown unless priorities were dramatically shifted.

In the rich countries, there is increasing rage and violence among the poor. This is still largely directed at people who also live within poor communities, with those outside them being relatively safe. The failure of the educational system to provide real opportunities to the underclass threatens, however, a rapid worsening of the situation. Violence may then move outside the poverty areas and affect the middle-class and the rich to such an extent that their quality of life declines precipitously.

People might put up with misery if they were they still isolated and unaware of alternatives. But today the gap between the standards of living of the rich and poor countries, and the rich and the poor within countries, is increasingly broadly known. Indeed, people living in slums and favellas in many countries of Latin America can receive Western television programs, such as *Dynasty*, which inevitably create envy. Frustration is increased because those who watch in the poor countries think that the standards shown in these programs represent the norm in the rich nations. The viewers do not know that they reflect the patterns of a tiny group of people engaged in conspicuous consumption.

Each of us has a choice. We can support the process of creating a just society and increase our own chances of having a reasonable quality of life. Or we can watch current trends continue and condemn ourselves and our children to patterns of breakdown which we cannot even imagine.

CHAPTER 9

Rebuilding Communities

COMMUNITIES ARE HEALTHY WHEN LEADERS GRASP OPPORTUNITIES as they become available and tackle problems before they become crises. Each of us need to be a leader in this sense, sharing the responsibility to help shape the future.

Effective community is dynamic and even, at times, chaotic. Much disagreement and conflict take place in functioning communities. Order, however exists below the surface. People are willing to make decisions based on the overall interests of those involved. They understand that their perceptions will necessarily differ from those of others, but this does not prevent them from seeking common ground. They work to achieve their perceived self-interest, but define it in very broad terms.

The traditional image of the way to manage cultural affairs in the United States has been a melting pot. We believed that we should submerge all differences between traditions and develop a single pattern. We saw it as the only way to bring together the immense range of traditions of America's overwhelming flood of immigrants.

While melting pot models have been a major theme of American thinkers, they were always more image than reality. Today, ethnic groups are increasingly unwilling to submerge their past histories and cultures into a dull uniformity. Each group wants to draw on its traditions for sustenance in the rapids of change. If they do not already have their own traditions, they create patterns which distinguish them.

We need a new image. My favorite one is a tapestry. The colors of each of the wools is unique. Together they produce a picture. Suggesting that the colors of the wools be toned down is neither wise nor desirable. The various strands should be used where they will add rather than subtract from the overall design. An effective community will honor and enjoy the many traditions of the individuals and families within it. In return, it will ask everybody to support the larger whole.

The compassionate era is based on the belief that security comes from mutual understanding, support and partnerships. The basic step we must all take is to learn to enjoy diversity and to live within pluralistic systems. Strong people are fascinated by differences and realize that they can learn from others who do not share the same worldview. Only as we change our images of strong leaders can communities flourish and fulfil the urgent tasks of the nineties.

People need to find differences fascinating rather than frightening. Most of us are still afraid of others who are different because of their cultures or the color of their skins. As we move toward learning societies, we shall recognize that we can benefit most from people who see the world in significantly different ways.

In the future, we must not only cope with different sexes, ages and races, but we must also cease to marginalize the handicapped by seeing them as totally different. All of us are handicapped; we have areas where we are incompetent. I have, for example, no spatial sense and rely on my wife to compensate for this failure. We need to recognize that those we single out as handicapped have specific areas where they do not function well, such as being deaf or blind, but may more than compensate for these limitations by their other strengths.

What tasks will vibrant communities undertake? Communities must support and guide children as they grow up. Communities must provide educational opportunities throughout life. Communities must honor the old. Communities must provide economic opportunities. Communities must help people stay healthy and ensure protection for their members. Communities must prevent violence and provide social justice. Communities must be fun.

Communities have many faces and each member will see his or her community somewhat differently. In addition, communities are complex and ever changing. They can never be utopian because their members inevitably have their own unique quirks and patterns. This chapter is primarily centered around local geographical community.

The word community also has a broader meaning. Many of the ideas in this chapter can be extended to cover other community patterns. Community can develop in work and professional groups, in social service organizations, in churches, in bioregions and among those with the same hobbies. Community is, in many ways, a state of mind. It exists whenever people are committed to each other and willing to work to achieve desirable goals. It is, however, still the exception rather than the rule, because community requires people to be open and honest with each other rather than hiding their motives and commitments.

We must not confuse family and community. Families are small enough that people feel a profound and immediate sense of commitment to each other and have deep empathy for the joys and sorrows of those within their family. Community is also built on personal relationships, but the larger number of people involved makes having the same depth of feeling impossible. We cannot have the same depth of emotion for most friends as we do for our spouses, or parents or children, because our lives would be an unmanageable rollercoaster.

Deciding whether a group of people should aim to relate like a family or a community is one of the crucial decisions in human relationships. Some firms and organizations call themselves "families;" determining whether this is an appropriate image for them is very important to their eventual success or failure. I challenged one organization in this area recently; a number of its members found it freeing to be permitted to break out of this way of looking at those they worked with because they felt the required "togetherness" was phony.

Community cannot be achieved once and for all; it requires continuing effort. Like all human patterns, community tends to break down over time unless we nurture it. The sense of community has been weak in the second half of the twentieth century because of the consumption emphasis of the culture and because of general overload. People are rebuilding community in a variety of ways as we enter the nineties. Each of us has the ability to be a part of this process of renewal.

The pressure to cooperate

The most visible challenge today is maintaining and restructuring relationships between the diverse parts of communities. The need to keep up with the pace of change makes this continuing task more difficult. Old assumptions and ties are being shattered. All too often new ones are not replacing them because of the lack of trust between groups and organizations. People and groups feel abandoned; they believe their contributions are being ignored or dishonored. Walls of mistrust increasingly divide communities.

Mistrust between groups is dangerous at any time. It is particularly destructive at the current time because communities are facing ever-growing pressures to economize resources. They will only be able to provide even basic services if they deliver them in the most cost-effective way. Fortunately, potentials for major savings do exist. One approach is to eliminate duplication between programs. In most larger communities, several organizations deliver similar services with little or no coordination. This is particularly true with addiction-related services.

Too many municipalities and overlapping service districts hamper the effective delivery of services. Rearranging boundaries is not enough, however, because they themselves are becoming "fuzzy." The industrial-era belief that each area and activity was separate is being subverted by the growing knowledge that everything is related. Little progress has, however, so far been made in recognizing what this new approach means for decision making.

Another reason for high costs and waste is that many facilities are idle much of the time. For example, churches intensively use a large proportion of their buildings only once a week. Most office buildings are empty on the weekends. Greater collaboration would make it possible to use existing buildings more effectively. Building additional structures would then be unnecessary.

Looking further into the future, we may need to change the way we organize our calenders. Major shifts are already taking place as children move to year-round schooling and the summer vacation ceases to control scheduling. Education is being provided at the times when people can take advantage of it and when they find they learn best.

Even the weekend may be abandoned in the twenty-first century. Work facilities would then no longer be used intensively for five days while recreation facilities have light loads with the opposite pattern holding true at the weekend. We will still need times of rest, but they would be staggered. Indeed, as one looks at the reality of our societies, rather than their formal structures, far more moves have taken place in this direction than we normally recognize. Retailing is already a seven-day-a-week operation and a growing number of meetings take place on weekends to take advantage of the cheap fares airlines provide if the passenger stays over a Saturday.

Even when the potentials for reducing resource use are highly visible, groups are still often unwilling to collaborate. Many people prefer to control their own organization rather than work with others. Each one of us needs to learn to move toward collaboration, recognizing the barriers our attitudes and organizational structure create. Even with the best of good will, collaboration is difficult. One of the primary problems results from current legal structures. Getting coverage for legal liability is increasingly costly, and any proposal for joint or unconventional use is first checked with lawyers, who are always cautious. It is particularly difficult to gain acceptance of joint work among private, public and non-profit organizations.

A first step to break through the barriers is to help individuals and groups communicate openly. The typical community is divided into cliques which distrust, and even fear, others. Few "safe and open spaces" exist where people can say what they believe without fear that it will affect them personally or damage their careers.

We can use many models to encourage communication. I recently worked as a consultant for a year in the River Bend area of Illinois which contains ten industrial communities just north of the Mississippi River from St. Louis. People were challenged to work together to create a better future. An intelligently developed program broke down barriers and led to more creative decision making. One of the most exciting aspects of the project was watching an evolution in relationships. People started off "knowing" that their own position was right and those of all others were wrong. As the year progressed, there emerged far greater respect for, and understanding of, the views and positions of others.

People began to recognize they were seeing different realities and, for this reason, supporting different goals. This sense of diversity evolved from two strategies. First, we encouraged everybody to listen to the views of others. Second, we placed the clash between visions in the context of the nineties and the twenty-first century. We made the distinction between dying and emerging systems as clear as possible. Over time, people came to see that continuing to support past success criteria was impossible. We came to see new directions as essential.

Supporting greater openness was not, of course, easy. Two steps were taken. One was to bring new ideas in from the outside. Creative and dynamic speakers were invited. The most exciting and forward looking materials in book, audio and video form were recommended and made available in libraries. The effect of this approach was limited, however. Most people do not integrate new ideas rapidly; they continue to work with their existing models despite new input.

We therefore encouraged local people to surface thoughts and ideas normally considered too controversial or too far-out for discussion. Other participants then began to broaden the scope of discussions and to transform the nature of possible solutions. We used a number of techniques to encourage movement in this direction. One of the most useful was to help people see that ideas they considered "far-out" were, in fact, credible. As people realized they were not alone in their views, they were more willing to talk honestly about what they really wanted.

One of the more interesting River Bend groups brought together several of the businessmen in the community with those in charge of school systems. Initially, the business people were sure easy ways to economize must exist. They were shaken when they discovered that the educators had already taken the most obvious steps and that few easy economies remained. At the end of the first year, they had made significant progress in setting up a continuing dialogue. Many other River Bend groups developed similar patterns.

Paradoxically, an increase in cooperation within and between communities can also lead to problems. Too many "coordinating" groups may spring up. Each of them then feels it has the right, and possibly the power, to make decisions. I first saw this problem clearly when I was working in Spokane, Washington. A relatively small number of people met in a large number of different organizational settings. Each group developed ideas without considering the impact on others. I created an image which has illuminated this reality for others. I suggested that there are a number of trains in a station. People move from one stationary train to another. But they never manage to get any of the trains moving out of the station.

My first instinct to resolve this problem was that an effort should be made to create a single coordinating group to make decisions. As I thought further, it became clear that this approach was not going to work. Each organizing group saw itself as critically important and was therefore unwilling to subordinate itself to others. Indeed, a significant number of groups felt they should have primary control.

The political system is naturally led by the City Council and believes that it should make the basic decisions. The business community looks to a new organization called Momentum. Other groups in the non-profit sector also try to influence directions, particularly through the Community Foundation. I therefore decided that the only way to achieve progress would be to develop far higher levels of communication between the various groups.

New decision-making structures

Communities will only be effective if they accept the responsibility for dealing with tough issues. A primary reason why so much power moved to the national level in the twentieth century was that many critical questions were allowed to fester. Only the President and the Congress had the courage to make tough choices in the forties, fifties and sixties—a pattern now being reversed. Imagination is most visible at the local, and sometimes at the state, level. On the national scene, on the contrary, old ideologies are clashing with little contact to current realities.

The power which has been progressively concentrated at the nation-state level during the twentieth century must now be diffused. I am well aware that moving in this direction requires a reversal of trends. The risk in providing communities with freedom to make their own decisions is, however, less than that which exists when a centralized system is asked to come up with answers to cover a wide range of different realities.

The mark of the well-informed citizen in the past has been an understanding of world affairs. Today we need to spend more time learning about our own communities because this is the level at which we can make a difference. Positive movement in communities depends on the willingness of government, business and non-profit leaders to commit their energies to their local situations.

There has been a downward spiral in relationships between leader and led in recent years. The reciprocal obligation between the person in office and the citizen has been broken. Fewer and fewer good people run because they find the political process demeaning. Citizens see no reason to support their elected officials because they detect no signs of courage or commitment. My favorite story, which may not be true but certainly makes the point, concerns a mayor who had been begged to run for office. She eventually succumbed to pressure. She was elected. The day after she won, she was asked why she was on the take!

In most communities, the vicious circle is still worsening. But there are places where significant efforts are being made to bring people back to a sense of responsibility for their own future. The common factor behind the successful efforts is a commitment to discussion and dialogue. A friend of mine recently told me that he was going to vote for an "honest" political candidate with whom he disagreed but where there was the potential for conversation. He decided at the same time to oppose a person who was grandstanding on an issue in which he believed. He was convinced that progress could only be made if dialogue developed.

Our most basic challenge is to recognize the common humanity of each person. We must learn to judge not by age or sex or race but to listen to what people really say and think. We must commit to supporting those who are willing to stand for office because they want the good of the community rather than because they want power or position for themselves.

My vision of the future is that more and more candidates will agree to accept office despite the strains it creates for them. I am convinced that most people at the local level should serve for only one term, or at a maximum, two. Fresh blood is of enormous benefit. But I do not want to make this a rule, because the greater the number of rules, the lower the flexibility in the culture. Rather I would hope that both candidates and voters would be aware of the advantages of turnover.

Leadership does not, of course, only come from government. The patterns of the United Way, the Chamber of Commerce, the churches and other key non-profits do as much to determine the style of a community as its formal political structure. The commitment of top management in business is also critically important. There are severe problems at many of these levels. One of the trends which has been far too little discussed is the breakdown of locally-based leadership.

As firms and banks are bought by out-of-town organizations and conglomerates, their management becomes part of a revolving door. It is increasingly rare that anybody stays in a community long enough to develop strong local ties. Corporate leadership, which was one of the primary resources of communities, is therefore increasingly denied to them; similarly leadership of key non-profits is often also recruited from out-of-town. It seems unlikely that there will be any short-run reversal of these patterns. The only hope is that organizations will begin to inform managers that a significant part of their evaluation will be based on involvement in their local situations.

The tendency for corporate control to be located outside local communities makes it increasingly difficult to raise money. A colleague who works in Edmonton wrote to me about this reality. He told me that a local grocery executive was very willing to give $50 toward a children's picnic being organized by a local charity. A very large chain with major sales in the area, but with its head office in Calgary, sent only $20. Even when firms outside the community do give generously, bureaucratic requirements are almost inevitably more extensive and time-consuming.

Increasing internal self-sufficiency

The industrial era developed a very strong bias toward central control of economic decision-making. This style has been dominant throughout the world but it has been particularly evident in the United States. The commerce clause of the Constitution, which justifies federal government intervention in state and local decision-making, has been stretched to the limit. In addition, the right to coin currency and to control credit has been managed by the Federal Reserve Board. A community cannot legally develop a local currency without waivers from various national government agencies.

Control of directions is also exercised by the power to tax. About 35% of income is taxed in one way or another. This heavy tax load makes it far more difficult for people to find the resources to support their local communities. Reducing the central tax bite, as proposed in Chapter 5, would make it possible for people to give more and also permit local taxation to be heavier so local needs could be met.

Communities today have few effective decision-making powers. For example, education is theoretically controlled by local school boards. But after all the state mandates have been fulfilled, which in many cases are buttressed by national dynamics, there is little space for real choices. The success of local educational systems is judged on standards set by national testing. School districts which do not achieve high scores are seen as failures. In addition, some states are limiting the powers of local districts to set their own tax rates.

Similarly, communities have very limited powers to stop an unwanted industry or business from moving into its area. For example, even if the building of a large chainstore in a small town will probably result in the bankruptcy of many local merchants, these disadvantages cannot be used as a justification for refusing entry. Some control can be exercised through planning and zoning but this is a blunt tool for those interested in the long-run viability of a community.

Certain steps can nevertheless be taken to promote local enterprise. The first is to support existing merchants by providing better information to citizens and businesses about the types of goods and services which are available within a community. People will then be more likely to buy within the community rather than from outside. This keeps resources within the community and supports its autonomy. It also helps to reduce the costs of transportation. In addition, a strong, supportive local community may also make a major difference when a firm considers if it should move to a location with cheaper labor or other apparent advantages.

In addition, resources could be saved if the failure rate of new businesses could be reduced. The general estimate is that four out of five new businesses fail in the first five years with consequent loss to the owners and to the local economy. There is an urgent need to set up effective advice systems which would discourage people from going into business when they do not have the necessary skills and capital. Marginal entrepreneurs can be provided with the information and knowledge they need to have a better chance. Incubators, which provide more intensive support for new businesses, are also an effective tool in increasing viability.

If communities are to make more decisions for themselves, they must be able to insulate themselves to some degree from national and world dynamics. Unfortunately, the tendency in recent decades has been to integrate communities more and more closely. This is another of the trends which needs to be reversed as Western society emerges from the eye of the hurricane.

The dangers which emerge from the collapse of large interlinked systems, like the savings and loan industry, are much greater than those which result from small local breakdowns. The real issue is whether we should aim to produce structures which "cannot fail" or systems which are resilient when they do "inevitably" fail. Industrial-era structures have been based on the belief that human beings are bright enough to prevent breakdowns. Today everybody is aware that this is all too often untrue.

Local currencies

Banks and banking are usually seen as purely economic concerns. In fact, the decisions made in this area at the time of the American Revolution are one of the primary factors which have led to centralization of the culture. Any attempt to get back to community-based decision-making is impossible until there is a change in the structure of banking.

The traditional economic pattern within countries has been that local economies within a country moved in much the same direction. In the 1980s a profoundly new pattern emerged in the United States, and similar dynamics have occurred elsewhere. A rolling recession developed which hit various parts of the country at different times. While there was overall growth on the national level beginning in the early eighties, most of the regions in the United States had severe corrections one after the other.

The problems started with the old industrial-era rustbelt states. It moved on to affecting the farm and timber areas of the country and then damaged the oil-producing states and much of the South. Negative dynamics then developed in the Northeast. This last set of downturns coincided with the end of the long-running national boom.

Traditional approaches were ineffective in dealing with this rolling recession. While the various regions of the Federal Reserve Board are meant to be responsible for the special needs of their parts of the country, policies are now so centralized that each region has little ability to manage local dynamics. For example, there was no way that the Federal Reserve Boards responsible for the farm states were able to reverse the strong downward pressures in their areas in the early eighties.

The Federal Reserve Board is just one part of the centralizing movement in the twentieth century. In a speech entitled "The Need for National Currencies," Robert Swann made the argument for a return to a decentralized system. He stated:

One of the major arguments against "free banking" in the 18th century, indeed the one that persists today, is that the many small local banks which issued their own money sometimes failed and this hurt many of their small depositors. Some of these banks truly were run by scoundrels who created money for non-productive purposes such as helping their friends buy land for speculation. The feeling was that such abuses could be controlled if money were issued centrally.

But decentralization and diversity have the benefit of preventing large-scale failure. This is as true in banking as it is in the natural world. . . . Today we are facing the failure of the entire system. Consider: by all estimates it is going to cost 60 billion dollars or more for the central deposit insurance system to bail out the savings and loan banks. (This estimate was made in 1988: now the assumed cost is $500 billion and still rising.) When third world countries default on their debts which, in fact, they are already doing—even if it's not called default—billions more will be added to the national debt in order to bail out big banks.

There is a way out of the centralized control imposed by current banking systems. Community financial autonomy can be increased by creating a supplementary local currency. When communities are depressed, and there is open or hidden unemployment, people would be willing to produce additional goods and services which others would buy if the money were there to facilitate exchange. One apparent answer would be for banks to loan more freely. The problem with this approach is that most of the loaned money moves out of town. It does not support local energy and eventually the bank will be forced to retrench.

If banks cannot lend enough, what about the possibility of developing a type of money which could only be used for local interchanges? People might then be willing to sell their goods and services for a mix of moneys, part of which would be national currency and part only good in the immediate area.

Let's consider some simple examples. Let's assume a shop sells shoes. Some of the costs come from buying the shoes and this will usually have to be paid to merchants outside the community. Some of the costs will, on the other hand, result from local activities. Rent and electricity may be paid to nearby companies. Wages will certainly be due to local employees. The shoe seller might therefore put a price on the shoes which would be 75% in national currency and 25% local. At the other extreme, one might imagine somebody who produces crafts which almost all the costs are incurred locally. 75% might then be accepted in local currency and only 25% in national.

Once a local currency became established and had a wide range of uses, people might be willing to increase their percentages of local currency if they knew it was widely accepted within the community. It is also obvious that the larger the size of the community in which the currency circulates, the greater the percentage of local exchanges and the higher the percentage of local money which might circulate. On the other hand, the trust required to support a local currency requires a relatively small community.

It is easy to see the implications of this model for shopping patterns. At the current time, people tend to shop in the larger towns because the price is lower. If, however, the actual federal dollar cost were lower in the small community, the pattern of advantage is changed. People might then shop within their community rather than elsewhere.

Local exchanges may seem totally infeasible. However, currencies of this type have, in fact, circulated in the past and some have functioned successfully in recent years. Sophisticated computer-based approaches, often called LETS (Local Employment and Trade System) systems, have also been developed. There is significant evidence that they can enhance the amount of interchange in a community permitting people to use their time productively instead of being forced into idleness.

There are, of course, several issues which must be resolved before community currencies are anything more than a curiosity. First, the right to coin money is a monopoly of the central government in most countries. Permission has been given for local small-scale experiments in the United States but it is uncertain whether permissions would continue to be granted if there were many requests covering a significant number of communities.

Second, money is tricky stuff. Long ago, Gresham discovered that bad money drives out good. Watching the "exchange rates" between local and national currencies would be a constant struggle. It would be all too easy to set up local systems in ways which caused demand to exceed supply and thus devalue the local currency.

Models

Many of today's community problems stem from the fact that there are not enough leaders for all the tasks that need to be done. When older leaders get tired, younger leaders do not necessarily emerge to take their place. While there are fortunately a growing number of leadership programs, all too often they teach the skills of the current generation of leaders rather than inspiring servant leadership styles which are necessary for periods of fundamental change.

How can communities learn to work together more effectively? There are three basic requirements which must be met under all circumstances. The way they are actually developed will depend upon the pattern of support available in each community. The first is to ensure that people become more aware of the changes which are taking place in the world so they will be ready to move in new directions rather than trying to solve problems using old information and techniques.

The second requirement is to get existing and emerging leaders from various groups to talk and work together. This statement has two implications. All the existing and emerging leadership must be encouraged to be involved. In addition, it should be recognized that not everybody will be ready to be leaders. It is essential to start with those who are most committed rather than try to move a whole community, or organization, at once.

The third normally required element is to have a neutral player in the system. A great deal of distrust exists in most communities and breaking through it requires high levels of skills. It is always challenging and exciting to play this role because there are no rules: one must always look for the specific steps which are appropriate at a particular time.

One of the most exciting community projects I ever observed developed in Pasadena. Denise and John Wood, a husband and wife team, decided that they could improve conditions if they were willing to serve as neutral observers in the sense I have described above. Their commitment to this style over a period of about a decade changed the climate in the city. A large amount of the decision-making in the community now uses this approach. The Woods have now left the city but the process has been institutionalized within the Episcopal church, concentrating particularly on health care for young at-risk kids and on drug issues.

The Woods suggest ten points which they describe as a mindset which will help anybody come to grips with the needs of a city;

1. Hold to the expectancy and the determination that you and others can make a difference in your community.

2. Study the city by listening to its people one-by-one to gain a living picture of the city's needs, strengths and possibilities.

3. Reveal the city to itself—the pain, the facts, the hopes, the moral imperatives you have learned—not in name-calling and blaming but neither in watering down the truth.

4. Think and speak for the whole city,

5. Bring people together, not in confrontation but in trust, to tackle the city's most urgent needs,

6. Build on the agencies and the people who are already at grips with a given issue and, where need be, encourage new initiatives and coalitions.

7. Take care of the care givers of your community so they know they are not alone and can receive the citizens' support they need.

8. Aim to build lasting relationships.

9. Know there is more power in appealing to the very best in people rather than the worst.

10. Persist when everything seems to fall apart, be conscious that it takes patience, perseverance, and passion to move a city.

In some communities, it may be necessary to rebuild trust before moving on to visioning and decision-making. As a result of one of my visits to Anchorage, the city redeveloped an old community model on a slightly more formal basis. In many towns there used to be a table reserved in a local restaurant where the leaders talked once a week or more. Knowledge was shared and ideas were advanced; indeed decisions were often made.

The Alaska model revived this approach. It was called the Wednesday Roundtable, because it met on Wednesdays! Anybody was welcome to come to an early morning continental breakfast and to talk about what their ideas were and what they thought might be important for the community. The group has now been meeting for two years and several specific ideas have been spun off from the group. These have gathered their own support. Similar groups have now been convened in Fairbanks and Juneau. Similar models, with different names, are springing up across America.

In some ways the Wednesday Roundtable is a twenty-first century service club. It is often forgotten that most of the service clubs were created in the late nineteenth and early twentieth centuries to provide specific support to their communities. These groups inevitably adopted both the agendas and the social styles of the societies of their time. They typically invited people from one sex or the other and they also tended to include people from only one class.

Wednesday Roundtables are different. Anybody who wants to be a leader, using influence rather than power, is invited. People do not have to make a long-term commitment: they can miss meetings without penalties. A wide variety of topics are covered. People can be honest because they know that this is not a decision-making body and their statements will not be used to undermine them. Specific ideas are spun off from the group so that the freewheeling discussion can be continued.

There is in a sense only one rule: that there are no rules. But this does not mean that there is no commitment. The commitment is to listen to others and to learn to trust. The Wednesday Roundtable is based on a belief that a value-based culture is a necessity and that the seeds of such a value-based culture need to be planted on a small scale and at a local level. Communication between leaders in various parts of the community has been significantly improved as a result of the Wednesday Roundtable.

This development may move in two obvious directions. One is to encourage other communities in Alaska and elsewhere to adopt the Roundtable model. Ideally, small-scale Roundtables would develop in neighborhoods and interest-groups throughout communities. The overall effect would be to change the dominant style so that people would learn to collaborate rather than fight in order to change their goals.

The other is to imagine what the next stage of such a process might look like. My personal vision is that a meeting place would develop which would become the networking center of the community. The basic approaches of the Roundtable would be preserved but in a broader context. This would be the place where all the information about events, dynamics, trends etc. would be gathered. It would be a place where people could propose projects, find colleagues, discuss directions. It would above all be a place where people could discover what it would be like to work with others in tough, compassionate harmony. Conflict would be recognized and worked through. The commitment would be to manage it so that interpersonal violence was avoided.

Such a "place" could, of course, be developed by members of a Roundtable. It could also develop from the coffee shops which exist in many cities and combine food and discussion. It could be a project of a church which would see the importance of bringing together leaders and information so that the community became more self-aware. It could be developed by one of the social service agencies which understood its mission as supporting interaction between existing and emerging leaders. It could be created by a city council that really wants to serve its constituents. It would be a natural mission for a community college.

It could also be a free-standing club which would be formed for this specific purpose. Such a club would invite all those who wanted to lead and were willing to commit to living on a value-base. It would be sensitive to issues of race, class and gender and would put into place specific policies which showed this commitment. For example, dues might well be based on a percentage of income rather than on an absolute figure.

These places would support the development of the type of activities which I have described earlier. As networks of this type matured, they would significantly affect decision-making in the community. Decisions, however, would not be made on the basis of power but rather through careful dialogue between all those involved in the various questions. Communities would be ready to grasp opportunities when they were available and to manage problems before they became crises.

PART IV

Politics in the Compassionate Era

CHAPTER 10

Beyond Power, Sovereignty and Democracy

Up to this point, the approach in *Turning the Century* will have been somewhat familiar to you, assuming you have kept up with the debates raging about fundamental change over the last thirty years. For example, the need to abandon maximum economic growth policies has been widely discussed, even though it has not yet been accepted nor have its specific implications been widely explored.

Similarly, the arguments for the development of a learning society are increasingly heard, although many of the implications I have raised are new. We are rapidly discovering that we cannot afford to abandon any of the people in our society without damage to everybody. We are giving more effort to improving the opportunities for people to learn and think.

This part of the book will deal with "politics," defined in its broadest sense of "collective decision making." This subject has so far received very little creative attention. Part of the difficulty is that most of us include only the process of voting and the decisions made by elected officials when talking about politics. The overall political process is, however, far wider. Politics determines whether the Chamber of Commerce or the Town Council really calls the shots in a city. Politics decides whether church leaders are significantly involved in making choices. The degree of involvement permitted the poor is also a political question.

Once we recognize the relevance of this broader picture, it is obvious that extraordinary changes are taking place in political structures and the use of power throughout the world. The failure of the coup in the Soviet Union in the summer of 1991 was a direct result of the refusal of crack KGB units to obey orders when confronted with civilian opposition; a dynamic no fiction writer would have been wild enough to use as a plot.

The dynamics of the Yugoslav war were strongly influenced by the increasing tendency of conscripts to refuse induction and to desert, and by civilian opposition to the war. The progressive disintegration of current decision-making structures in the democracies results in large part from the increasing unwillingness of citizens to be forced to act in ways which seem inappropriate, or destructive, to them.

Shifting reactions to the use of power are a critical element in more personal areas also. For example, the public increasingly recognizes that sexual harassment, intimidation and rape have little to do with sex, but result from the desire to dominate. These attitudes shifts have created minefields through which we all have to tread very carefully. Dangers lurk everywhere. For example, many universities have "no touching" codes between faculty and students; this denies our humanity. Others feel that the situation has become so impossible that grappling with the ways we interrelate with each other, either physically or mentally is downright impossible.

An historical overview

The right to be involved in decision making has been increasingly widely shared over the last millennium. The power to make arbitrary choices has been significantly curbed over the same period. Democracy is now the dominant system throughout the world. Many people have come to believe it is the best possible system of government and that it will not change at any time in the future.

Winston Churchill was more realistic. "Democracy, " he said, " is the worst form of government except all the others." While it does support the process of collective decision making better than any other currently available system, it is certainly not adequate to deal with the complexities of the nineties and the twenty-first century.

Our current political systems are an uncomfortable, and incongruous, mix of power and consultation. To understand why politics is conducted as it is, we must look back at how current dynamics developed in the Western world. In the early part of the second millennium, the church held the dominant power. Religious, and superstitious, people paid a large part of their resources to the priestly hierarchy to assure their own salvation. The Pope was the ultimate arbiter of important decisions. Even kings felt unable to ignore or overrule him because of the sanctions he could wield, for example, through an interdict which cut a country off from the rest of the Christian world.

We can get a feel for the Middle Ages by looking at the current situation in the Muslim world. Clerics hold great power. Pilgrimages provide grace in heaven and require respect on earth. People believe that God determines their future and do not expect to make decisions which significantly alter their place in the society or their destiny. The current Muslim worldview would seem "natural" to those who lived as Christians in the first half of the second millennium.

Today, of course, most Christians have a very different viewpoint. In Western churches, absolute authority survives only in the claimed right of the Pope to be infallible when he speaks "ex cathedra." In these circumstances, he claims to transmit God's views and questioning is not "acceptable." Many Catholics today deny even this limited right to enforce obedience and choose to follow their own consciences and beliefs, defying church doctrine if necessary.

Kings, under the Pope's guidance, held the secular power in the Middle Ages. The dominant political philosophy was that rulers "could do no wrong." They made the law; people depended for justice largely on the character and integrity of the individual who held the position. The great kings and queens, like Elizabeth I, commanded obedience because she incarnated the values and beliefs of her subjects. In addition she was able to restrain the greed of those who officially wielded power in her name, a skill often lacking in other rulers of the time.

Kings and queens no longer have significant power, of course. We have not, however, recognized the full implications of the shift which took place as royalty lost the ability to enforce its will. Power moved, at this time, from the "sovereign" to the "sovereign state." The slogan was no longer that the "King could do no wrong" but rather "My country, right or wrong." People were expected to give their loyalty to their nation regardless of its behavior. It was this slogan which led an exasperated Samuel Johnson to exclaim: "Patriotism is the last refuge of a scoundrel."

What powers of the monarch passed to the sovereign state? It has inherited an absolute right to make war. It also has the right, and the duty, to make economic policy to improve the conditions of its citizens. It can determine which activities are illegal. Less obviously, the sovereign state has often demanded the right to monopolize information.

Nations have claimed that they cannot be sued. In the United States, for example, government employees cannot be forced to pay their debts. Successful challenges to many of these sovereign claims in recent years include the Freedom of Information Act in the United States. It gives people the right to discover much of what is in government records. People in Great Britain are still battling to receive this same right.

The dying sovereign state

The nation-state, in its modern form, was a European invention designed to deal with the realities of that area at a particular point in time. It was exported as Europeans dominated the rest of the world but it never proved as suitable for other areas. Today countries can no longer defend their boundaries because of the dangers of mutual destruction. They have also lost control of their economies, because of the extent of financial interrelationships. As a result, the real power of the nation-state is rapidly declining.

Humanity has always divided itself into "insiders" and "outsiders." There has, however, been a steady movement to larger and larger scales of government throughout recorded history. Decision-making was first carried out by tribes, then by cities and city-states, and finally at the national level. Until the coming of modern weaponry and particularly the nuclear arsenal, the ultimate controller of international affairs was the threat of war, and eventually war itself. Clemenceau argued that "War is the continuation of diplomacy by other means." Military adventures cleared the air and produced a new order which held for a time until somebody else tried to change the pattern by force.

This mind-set lay behind the cold war which dominated world thinking from the middle of the nineteen-forties to the end of the eighties. Two heavily armed blocs confronted each other. The resulting stalemate, based on the fear of nuclear weapons, kept the world relatively unchanged for this same period. Both sides were unwilling to provoke the other in a way which might cause nuclear war. A new term, the balance of terror, was coined to describe this reality.

At the end of the eighties, the cost of the military stalemate became excessive for both Russia and America. This led to new patterns of thinking with both nations being willing to sign treaties reducing levels of conventional and nuclear armaments. Later the Russian economy collapsed—apparently leaving the U.S. as the remaining "superpower." The complexity of the new challenges are only now emerging.

Despite America's status, it is forced to make its decisions as part of an increasingly interconnected global network. In a major summary article by Doyle McManus and Robin Wright of the Los Angeles Times Service, former Secretary of State George P. Shultz is quoted as saying that the combined effects of economic globalism on even the strongest nation's freedom of action amount to "the decline of sovereignty." He also says: "The concept of absolute sovereignty is long gone. As national boundaries blur, sovereign power is dispersed and more players vie for international influence."

184 • *Turning the Century*

The same article also quotes Francisco Sagasti of the World Bank:

> Nation-states have become less important as political units in the
> sense of being able to control whatever phenomena—economic,
> social, environmental or technological—take place in the world. This
> is hard to get accustomed to, for all our political systems are geared
> to focus on the nation-state as the locus of power, decision-making
> and as the main unit of political, social and economic analysis. We
> have not yet learned to live with the fact that these phenomena
> transcend national boundaries.

Getting beyond the nation-state model requires a shift at a deeper
level of understanding. I discovered this when I spent some time in the
sixties exploring what would happen if some of us got together and
invented a Martian threat. The times were just crazy enough that it might
have been possible to pull off a stunt of this type. We might have
convinced the world that the "little green men" were coming!

At first sight it seemed to me that such an approach would provide
pure gain. The peoples of the world would continue the insider/outsider
pattern and the non-existent Martians would become the outsiders with
everybody on earth uniting to fight them. Later I realized I was thinking
simplistically. Given that problems would still continue on earth, there
would have to be a scapegoat for failures. As the Martians did not
actually exist, some human beings who did not fit the mold, or who asked
awkward questions, would inevitably be accused of working for the
Martians—or, indeed, of actually being Martians.

The real challenge of the immediate future is to break out of the
insider/outsider model and to discover that we live on a small planet
where we must all cooperate. There are no short cuts. This is why it is
appropriate to talk about the need for the human race to grow out of its
adolescence and into maturity. Either we learn to cooperate with each
other or the conditions on earth become unmanageable.

Moving beyond the dream of a planetary government

The death of the sovereign state is now inevitable. But this change
could theoretically lead humanity in two very different directions. One
route would maintain coercive power but move it to the global level by
developing "world government." Alternatively we can develop totally
new political models which challenge human beings to far higher levels
of responsibility, within their geographical, work and professional
communities.

Many of those who believe that world government is the next
appropriate response look to the United Nations as the great leader of

the future. They point to its role in the Iraq invasion of Kuwait as evidence of its potential. Unfortunately, the U.N. cannot lead us beyond the nation-state model. There are two reasons for this conclusion.

First, the level of competence of those who work for the United Nations is not, in general, equal to the magnitude of the task which must be accomplished. While there are some notable exceptions, most of the people in the UN system are unable to get as lucrative a job anywhere else. They are attracted by the life-long guarantee of employment. It is conceivable that this problem could be overcome but it would be a tremendous hurdle to leap.

I am very much aware of this issue because I worked, when I was young, for a European organization which offered, in effect, total security. Most of my colleagues and friends thought I was crazy because I was willing to throw all this away to come to the United States. Those who want safety tend to stay in bureaucratic systems—people who are more willing to be creative and take risks tend to leave.

The second, and far more serious problem, emerges because many of the issues which must be faced in the nineties and the twenty-first century require the abandonment of the nation-state model. Delegates who are appointed by nation-states cannot be expected to think clearly about issues which can only be resolved by reducing national power.

National governments are not the most appropriate groupings to make decisions about the future because their power must be reduced. The discussions in the European Economic Community continue to be confused by this issue. Great Britain, in particular, hopes to maintain its national sovereignty and denies the fact that it is inevitably vanishing because of trends which have nothing to do with the EEC negotiations.

The future requires fundamental change in political styles. The needed shifts cannot be forced by planetary or regional governments which rely primarily on regulation, law and force. Rather, they will emerge as individuals, communities, firms, churches, organizations and businesses agree on a new story and decide on different priorities as a result. The answer is not to develop global regulation and law but to challenge people to exercise responsible freedom.

The possibility of moving in this direction will become real as we commit to developing learning institutions and societies. People do adopt new priorities if they understand changing realities. Behavior changes are much more likely to be permanent if they are based on perceived self-interest rather than being coerced by regulation.

Setting up learning societies which rely on responsible freedom is often rejected as impossible. We forget that the movement that has already taken place toward democracy was also seen as "impossible" in earlier times. This is not the time to lose our nerve, denying the potential for human growth which has served humanity so well in the past.

Dictatorship will not work

I am aware that many people find my proposals utopian, believing that efficient power structures are necessary and inevitable. Taken to its logical extreme, this viewpoint results in proposals that we should find a wise and benevolent dictator. Given all the problems of today, such a paragon sounds attractive. Indeed, if I could believe in her effectiveness and that of her successors, I'd vote her into office tomorrow even at the cost of my losing the franchise forever!

This approach will not work, however. The reason is very simple. It was suggested by Lord Acton who said that "Power tends to corrupt and absolute power corrupts absolutely." I have struggled with the implications of this statement for a long time. I have always had problems accepting the statement, as it stood, because I have met people with power who have not seemed corrupted. Many of them do the best they can, although the results of their actions are often the opposite of what they hoped.

Adding one word to the Lord Acton statement changes its meaning significantly and makes it a tautology. "Power tends to corrupt information and absolute power corrupts information absolutely." Imagine you are a subordinate. Your natural tendency is to tell your superiors what they want to hear. The more power they use, the less likely it is that you'll take the risk of raising tough issues. A dictator will therefore be deprived of the information needed to make good decisions.

"Power," like almost every word in the English language, has a multitude of meanings. It is a word which some people use in a positive sense and others use negatively. Here, it covers those instances when people have the ability to control behavior and force obedience. I include, in this definition, people who use language, style, coercion and force in ways which require people to do things they would not otherwise choose.

Power, in the definition I have used above, will therefore always tend to distort information and knowledge flows. Lord Acton is normally assumed to have been thinking about the results of power in governmental circles. But exactly the same problems occur in all other systems. Any person who makes decisions, without hearing challenges from others, makes the same type of errors whether he or she is the head of a business firm, a school or college, a non-profit firm, a church or any other institution.

In a recent paper, Herman Bryant Maynard Jr. and Susan E. Mehrtens discuss the problems which prevent most corporations from being effective. They say: "Much of our employees' energy goes into repression, hiding the truth, concealing problems, refusing to face reality. We in business often fall into the Holocaust syndrome, in which people have neither the space nor the awareness of access points to get out of the box in which they find themselves. . . . Inside most corporations there is little tolerance for insubordination or public criticism."

Power always tends to limit honesty and deter effective communication of information. Many people in our culture have the right to use power to force decisions on others. Policemen, judges, schoolteachers, bureaucrats, bosses and many others are able to coerce. Power is sometimes personal, given by position or wealth. More often, in today's world, the ability to use power is primarily controlled by an intricate web of law and regulation, which provides the right to require certain behaviors and avoid others.

An anonymous fable came across my desk just as I was revising this chapter which made the point beautifully.

> In the beginning was the plan, and then came the assumptions, and the assumptions were without form, and darkness was upon the face of the workers, and they spake among themselves saying, "It is a bucket of bull-do and it stinketh."
>
> And the workers went to their Supervisors and sayeth, "It is a pail of dung and none may abide the odor thereof."
>
> And the Supervisors went unto their Managers and sayeth unto them, "It is a container of excrement and it is very strong and none can abide by it."
>
> Then the Managers went unto their Vice-presidents and sayeth, "It is a vessel of fertilizer and none may abide by its strength."
>
> And the Vice-Presidents spake among themselves saying one to another, "It contains that which aids plant growth and it is very strong."
>
> And the Vice-Presidents went unto the President and sayeth unto him: "The plan promotes growth and is very powerful."
>
> And the President went to the Board and proclaimed: "This new plan will actively promote the growth and efficiency of the company."
>
> And the Board looked upon the plan, saw that it was good and were pleased to adopt it."

Gervase R. Bushe, a management consultant, makes the same point in more formal language: "Usually, it is the people at the very 'bottom' of the organization, those least empowered in control-based systems who are the closest to the key sources of information. Due to the tendency of information to distort on the way up in hierarchies, very little of this information gets to those who take the authority to make all the decisions. Eventually, decisions drift further and further away from reality and the organization fails or becomes ripe for a takeover."

According to Tom Englehardt, until recently a senior editor at Pantheon books, a similar pattern caused the collapse of successive Chinese dynasties. He wrote:

> In traditional China, it was believed that dynasties fell, in part, because of the disastrous disparities between names and the things named. The last dynastic ruler, mistaking the reassuring descriptions his courtiers offered him for the actual state of affairs in the imperial domains, found himself, in effect, blinded by names. Sooner or later, the abyss between the named and the real simply swallowed him up.

Hierarchical systems always tend to block negative feedback, which is critically important to long-run success. Negative feedback tells people the things they have forgotten or missed. It provides the opportunity to do better next time and may prevent catastrophic errors. One of the greatest skills in life is making it clear to your friends and colleagues that you will not be angry, let alone damage them, if they tell you things that it may be difficult for you to hear and accept.

Similarly, an unwillingness in potential colleagues or friends to accept negative feedback should be a strong warning signal in setting up your relationships. One of the most hopeful projects with which I was ever associated failed because one of the principals had her staff screen all criticism. As a result, she continued to act in ways which made collaboration impossible.

At the nation-state level, many people believe that the fear which accompanies fascism was one of the basic reasons for Germany's defeat in World War II. From the middle of 1940, the allies read a large proportion of Germany's most confidential messages by breaking her key secret code, which was called Enigma. Although great care was taken in how intercepted messages were used, it seems impossible that nobody ever realized what was happening. Bringing bad news was, however, highly dangerous in the Nazi hierarchy. If somebody had tried to raise the issue, it would almost certainly have been blocked higher up in the system and the messenger killed.

All of us who have dealt with power systems in our theoretical democracy will themselves have had more than a taste of this same problem. There are, however, more ways of dealing with arrogance and stupidity within a democracy than in a dictatorship. You can move out of channels with some hope that you will find somebody prepared to take risks for the sake of justice or effectiveness. But the risks nevertheless remain high and those who are willing to blow the whistle all too often suffer unreasonably.

Challenging inappropriate decisions is made more difficult because all too many human beings and institutions have come to believe that morality and values are not their concern. Many business philosophers have argued that the task of business is profit maximization and that other institutions should look after societal concerns. Similarly, professional groups have often only looked at their own narrow self-interest and been unwilling to censure or control their members. It is therefore not surprising that some people and institutions cut corners and that those who challenge destructive behavior are treated badly.

For example, the medical profession all too often permits irresponsible and incompetent people to continue to practice. The ever-spiralling costs of malpractice insurance are directly related to this failure to punish those who make the most mistakes. Many doctors, particularly those in obstetrics and gynecology, are giving up their practices because insurance costs are spiralling out of control; this is depriving mothers of vitally needed services.

Rebuilding an effective value-based culture will depend on all of us doing what we know we ought, even when it is inconvenient or embarrassing. If we can learn that it is the small steps which make a long-run difference, it will be easier to accept challenges when one would rather "go along." One of the lessons I have learned throughout my life is that one can never know what actions will affect another so they commit to more positive directions. Very often, it is the seemingly trivial which has the greatest impact.

New decision-making patterns

Who should be involved in decision-making and how it should be structured? Given that nation-states do make decisions, who has the right to determine how the powers of the state should be used? This question has bedeviled democracy since its beginning. One of the most vexed questions has been the extension of the franchise.

Every shift toward a broader group of electors has been bitterly fought. It was originally argued that if people without property were able to vote, they would inevitably deprive the rich of their resources. Later, it was argued that women would vote their "emotions." Still later, the right to vote at 18 was challenged on the grounds that people would be too immature to understand the issues. The panic-stricken opposition to more people being involved in government has always been proved wrong; voters have always done better than pessimists feared.

There is a more complex question which cannot be so easily resolved. How should the decision-making process be structured? Should there be one governing body or two? Nebraska is the only state with a unicameral legislature. Can decisions be reviewed for their constitutionality, or not? The United States goes to the Supreme Court to resolve questions of this nature; Britain has no written constitution and parliament is therefore the ultimate decision-maker. How much power should be held at national, regional and local levels? Much experimentation is going on at this time. Indeed, this question is being further complicated by the growth of global organizations, such as the United Nations, and regional groupings, such as the European Economic Community.

Many citizens and organizations are now working to reverse the trend toward centralization which developed during the twentieth-century because all too many communities refused in the past to take the tough decisions which would support equity and social justice. The failure to act responsibly at local levels drove decision-making upwards; it often seemed as though forward movement would only be secured at the federal level. In addition, many state and federal bureaucrats feel they are wiser than the public and should therefore determine the directions of the culture. In addition, most politicians want to point to the legislation they initiated when they stand for re-election.

These pressures for legislation are reinforced by the composition of the Congress and state legislatures. Most politicians are lawyers. Their mind set is based on a belief in the ability of the courts to determine right and wrong. Laws therefore seem to be the best way to achieve justice and change. This bias is enhanced by the fact that the self-interest of lawyers is in complicated legislation which has to be adjudicated.

These factors have prevented any significant movement away from federal control. Indeed, so long as communities, businesses and professional groups are unwilling to take responsibility for their own affairs, and bureaucrats and politicians see power as the way to make their mark, law and regulation will continue to be dominant. In the current climate of opinion, legislation is sought as soon as a majority can be found. It is considered appropriate to force people to obey the will of the majority— or even a vocal minority—if it has the clout to get laws passed.

Where should authority lie in today's complex world? And how is legitimacy assured for this authority? This is always the ultimate question. The key, highly surprising lesson we must learn is that the nation-state cannot be the dominant decision-making organization as we move into the compassionate era. We need to return to the community level.

Four horsemen of the apocalypse

Ever since the end of the Second World War, the dynamics of the world have been dominated by East-West issues. The next decades will be controlled by the ways we manage the relationships between the rich and the poor nations. Unfortunately, the problems of the developing world are still far down on the global agenda. We shall only change perceptions if we recognize both the real potentials and dangers in the current situation. The potentials arise from our ability to increase the standards of those who are most dispossessed among us so they can achieve adequate levels of food, clothing and shelter. The amount of money required to achieve this goal is relatively small, certainly when compared to the amount wasted on weaponry.

One of the real dangers of the nineties is that there may not be enough time left to prevent massive breakdowns in the civil order in more and more of the countries of the world. Only a massive commitment to new ideas will provide the human race with the potential to resolve the immediate crises it faces. The nineties are the time when these new directions must be introduced if progressive breakdown is to be avoided. There is a point of no-return and it can be reached.

In the period which elapsed between starting this book and its final editing, the overall picture in the suffering countries of the world worsened dramatically. There was the mass migration of the Kurds following Iraqi barbarism after the Gulf War. The famine in sub-Saharan Africa killed hundreds of thousands. The cyclone in Bangladesh devastated much of the country and made millions homeless, adding natural disaster to the suffering imposed by overcrowding and inefficient government. There were several major earthquakes and eruptions, particularly in the Philippines.

Confronted with the number and scope of the problems, "donor fatigue" is developing. People are ceasing to give because they feel that they cannot make a difference. It is all too possible that the rich nations, and indeed the primary international organizations, will come to believe that there is nothing to be done for the very poor.

The poor countries of the world will become desperate if they do not receive fairer treatment. There is, however, a major paradox here. The need is not to intensify current activities. Most existing aid policies are damaging nations rather than helping them. Totally new directions must be created which face the reality that there is no chance of the developing countries ever reaching the standards of living of those nations which are already rich. This reality can only be taught, and accepted, if the people of the rich world show a commitment to reducing their unfair draw on the resources of the world.

In addition, vigorous and appropriate efforts must be made to support the poor countries in the patterns of human and community development which are actually feasible, and desirable, for them. The initial requirement here is to face the highly distressing fact that most of the lending and aid to the poor countries has not only been wasted but has even acted against their best interests. A large amount of the money was never even used within these countries; rich individuals within poor countries got hold of the foreign aid and immediately invested it abroad. Most of the developing nations now have such large scale debts that money is flowing away from the poor countries to the rich. Forgiveness of debt is essential; the question is how it can be achieved in the most acceptable, and least disruptive, way.

Future assistance must operate in a very different style, and on a smaller scale, than in the past. It must aim to increase human and socioeconomic viability rather than be targeted narrowly on increasing the standard of living. For example, micro-loans direct to farmers and small entrepreneurs have been dramatically successful. To achieve this, relations between donors and donees will have to be totally different from those which have existed in the past.

The current fall into deeper poverty and degradation which is occurring in many parts of the world is unacceptable and, also, dangerous. I have often heard people from the rich countries argue that the poor cannot harm them. They do not recognize that the rich will suffer from the consequences of the self-interested actions of the poor, which are designed to ensure they do as well as they can in intolerable conditions. There is no possibility that hungry people will preserve the forests needed to let the whole world breathe if they lack fuel to cook their minimal diets. There is no chance that people will refuse to use toxins and poisons which will destroy the quality of the air, land and water on a global scale if they cannot feed themselves without them.

There is one additional way in which the breakdown of the social order in the poor countries will inevitably affect the rich. The potential for the creation of new disease strains from slums in the third and fourth world is obvious, particularly when these conditions are combined with the careless use of antibiotics and other medicines which tend to cause mutations in germs and diseases. The continued spread of AIDS shows that even modern medical techniques and knowledge cannot easily or rapidly prevail over possible diseases. The chances of further illnesses developing which cannot be cured using existing medical knowledge is all too probable; a mutated strain of tuberculosis has recently developed which is immune to drugs.

People who see no danger if the poor countries revolt against the rich fail to recognize just how fragile the current world order actually is. We do not live in robust systems where we can each look after ourselves. We cannot live in our cities without electricity and oil and transportation and water. These are all threatened by terrorism—an ever-present possibility if enough poor countries become sufficiently angry about the actions of the more powerful than they are in terms of conventional weaponry. If enough rage develops, the rich countries cannot protect themselves from terrorism, without destroying the freedoms that are necessary for the development of responsible freedom and long-run survival.

Any dramatic increase in terrorism would almost certainly be accompanied by a breakdown of the civil order in the rich countries. If the world polarizes between the white and the non-white nations of the world—a result that is certainly feasible—there would be both violence generated from outside the rich world and in the poor sections of cities.

Terrorism is the poor nation's "power." It is understandable that the rich countries see this technique of violence as intolerable. Little useful dialogue will develop, however, until there is an honest recognition of the real role terrorism plays. One can see this pattern most clearly in the evolution of thinking in Israel. When Israel was trying to become a state in the 1940s, terrorism against Britain which controlled the "promised land," was the only available weapon. It was widely and effectively used. Now that Israel is herself a state, she has joined most other nations in condemning terrorism. I detest terrorism. But this does not mean that it makes sense to deny the link between terrorism and the unwillingness of those with power to listen to the beliefs and concerns of those without it. Willful blindness to reality is no solution to problems.

Terrorism has been primarily state-sponsored up to the current time. The leaders of certain nation-states have believed that this was the only way to damage the rich countries, which they saw as unwilling to meet the reasonable aspirations of people in various parts of the world. If the world continues to divide between the rich and the poor countries as seems all too possible, then terrorism could eventually become the technique of choice of a very large number of people and groups. The Gulf War significantly increased these dangers as did the break-up of the

Soviet Union; there is today a significant prospect of nuclear scientists selling themselves to the highest bidder.

The situation in many poor countries is desperate and getting worse each year. At the beginning of the nineties a special report was put out by the *Wall Street Journal* on the economic prospects for the world. The report stated baldly that nothing could be done for the vast majority of countries in Africa. Such a statement is accurate given current conditions. It was the calm acceptance of this reality as unalterable which was both chilling, and totally unacceptable.

A new sense of global solidarity is the only hope to deal with the growing gap between the rich and the poor and to avoid an unsustainable move toward authoritarian government. Tensions between the rich and the poor, both internally and internationally, are always high. The middle-class and the rich have an interest in stability. Poor people and poor nations, if driven far enough, can become desperate and tear down their structures even if this causes severe damage to their own situation.

The standard of living in many of the poor countries has declined significantly in the eighties. By 1988, the number of people living in households too poor to obtain the food necessary to maintain energy levels sufficient for work had risen to one billion, or 20 percent of the world's population.

People who have never encountered the poverty of the Third and Fourth World can hardly imagine it. What we call poverty in the United States is unbelievable wealth to many who live in the slums of the poor countries. They are always hungry, and usually desperate. People live from the garbage of the rich, they squat on land in hovels built from scraps. Many of them are permanently sick. Will we be bright enough, and sufficiently compassionate, to grasp this reality before it destroys us?

Money is not the problem, the sums involved are manageable. Intelligence, creativity and compassion are the critical missing elements.

CHAPTER 11 —————————————————————————————

Creating the Compassionate Era

THE ADVERSARIAL STRUCTURES CURRENTLY DOMINATING OUR CULTURE were appropriate as long as we believed that we could find truth through debate and argument. Now we know that truth is perceptual, the challenge is to find open processes which gently encourage each of us to rethink our existing understandings.

Some of the implications of a shift from closed to open systems can be demonstrated by looking at two major crises which occurred during Kennedy's presidency. A small group of like-minded individuals carried out the planning for the Bay of Pigs invasion in Cuba. The planners refused to listen to those who challenged their assumptions about the vulnerability of the island and the results were catastrophic.

Patterns differed widely when the Soviet Union tried to install missiles in the same country. Kennedy assembled a far more diverse group of advisors. Long and careful discussions led to a plan very different from the original. While the approach did bring America to the brink of war, careful diplomacy finally avoided the dangers.

Open systems will always be more effective in times of rapid change and crisis than closed groups. Dealing with a wide range of views, however, requires high levels of commitment. It is easier to narrow one's sources of information than to keep checking on what is really necessary and desirable. The possibility of missing critically important information is particularly high at the current time because, despite the extraordinarily large number of channels for moving information, a very narrow interpretation exists defining what ideas are "acceptable" and "publishable" in most of the media.

Creating open systems for the twenty-first century

The challenge of the nineties and the twenty-first century is to

195

complete the movement toward responsible freedom which started with the Greeks. While the movement has often been halting and has sometimes been reversed, the overall direction has been unmistakable. Now we must move further.

The Civil War, a remarkable mini-series on PBS, gathered very large audiences because it showed the positive directions which emerged in the middle of the nineteenth century but also reminded us of the incompleteness of the American Revolution. The current challenge is to make the same quantum leap in commitments to freedom as those which developed during the 1860s. This time we must carry through the necessary mindquakes without frustrating people to the point where violence seems the only possible response.

We need to develop "responsible freedom." These words cover the concept I wish to express as well as any phrase I have been able to devise. The difficulty with the word "freedom," of course, is that it covers a broad range of meanings. At one extreme, it implies "license" which is defined by Webster as "liberty that consists in breaking laws or rules either as an abuse or an exercise of special privilege."

At the other end of its spectrum of meanings, "freedom" already contains the idea of responsibility. Used in this way, it provides the right to do what one wishes without outside constraint, while remaining aware of the consequences of one's actions. If freedom is used in this latter sense, the addition of the word "responsible" is unnecessary. But in current conditions, where freedom if often the rationale for irresponsible or anti-social behavior, joining the two words "responsible freedom" together seems essential if the essence of my thought is to be communicated.

Responsible freedom is not possible without reducing the degree of control in today's culture. The appropriate balance between personal choice, and coercion through law and regulation, depends on the maturity of each culture and the people in it. Legislation can be reduced as people begin to develop a deeper and more spiritual sense of what their self-interest really is. Edmund Burke, a British political philosopher, caught this tension beautifully in the following statement: "Men are qualified for civil liberty in exact proportion to their disposition to put moral chains upon their appetites. Society cannot exist unless a controlling power upon will and appetite is placed somewhere, and the less there is within, the more there must be without."

What can be done to reverse the trend to overcontrol of people and systems, which is currently so pervasive? One of the primary issues which arises when answering this question is the degree to which society can and should protect people from their own irresponsibility. For example, the dangers of riding a motorcycle without a helmet are very great; doctors and nurses dread the type of head injuries that occur all too frequently. Legislators have therefore required use of a helmet in many parts of the world for dangerous activities such as motorcycle and horse riding. The next step, in many areas, has been to require seat belts in automobiles, for they too can be shown to reduce death and injuries.

The people who make individual liberty their primary concern have fought these steps, claiming that coercion is inappropriate in cases where people are only damaging themselves. The problem, of course, is that when people are not wearing seat-belts, human bodies can become projectiles and damage others. Those who favor legislation also argue that because the costs of accidents are borne eventually by the whole society, the society has the right to impose regulations.

The problem is that this approach places humanity on a very slippery slope. A great many behaviors can be shown, statistically, to increase the costs to the total society. Does society have the right, and the ability, to control all of them? For example, the health problems of the obese are certainly far more severe than those of people whose weights are around the average. Would society be justified in aiming to control weight? And how would it to do so? Should a weighing machine be placed at the entry to restaurants and those who were above their normal weight be required to eat salads?

When I wrote the paragraph above, I saw my idea as a science-fiction nightmare. I did not recognize that there was already a mechanism in place to create this sort of pattern. To my surprise, it was being created by private institutions which want to improve the health of their employees in order to reduce insurance costs. Businesses and non-profit corporations are demanding unparalleled control over human behavior.

Corporations are traumatized by the increase in their medical costs and are looking for ways to limit them by controlling costly behavior patterns. An article in the *Juneau Empire* by Alan Spiress stated: "Some (companies), such as Cable News Network, won't even hire someone who smokes an occasional cigarette at home. Others such as U-Haul, have begun fining their employees for off-hours smoking and being overweight. And a few companies have begun to regulate the amount of cholesterol, saturated fats, coffee and even fast food their workers eat."

The company town with its paternalistic policies was largely banished at the beginning of the twentieth-century. Should we permit a new form of company strategy to grow up which controls the behavior of employees not only on the job, but also at home? What should be the limits of the contract between the employer and the employee? The answers we develop to these questions will have implications far beyond those which are obvious.

Health insurance debates are normally concentrated on controlling costs. But the real question we must answer is who has the right to make decisions? Some of the most critical problems cluster around the issue of pregnancy. For example, drug abuse of all kinds—smoking, alcohol, legal and illegal drugs—results in problems for the fetus; the number of babies born addicted to crack is already appalling and is still increasing. Some, maybe most, addicted babies suffer from a continuing imbalance which causes them to crave drugs all their lives.

There have been efforts to charge mothers who damage their unborn children with various legal offenses; this trend seems likely to grow but it is unlikely it will be effective. Those who abuse their unborn children normally suffer from a basic lack of self-respect. The only way this form of destructive behavior is going to be limited is by bringing up human beings so they know how to love and be loved. We need to find ways to break through the negative dynamics which perpetuate anger and hostility in the culture.

Moving toward responsible freedom and an open society will demand that people have the following opportunities:

■ the chance to learn the values of honesty, responsibility, humility and love,

■ the ability to live with uncertainty,

■ equality of opportunity so those who have been disadvantaged in the past have a chance to reach an equal starting point,

■ systems which are diverse enough for each person to develop himself or herself to the fullest extent possible,

■ majority rule and minority rights,

■ socioeconomic equity and social justice,

■ methods to ensure environmental balance for as far into the future as we can see,

■ a commitment to reduce violence at all levels from the individual to the global.

Reducing legislation

My theme throughout this book has been the need to bring about change through learning rather than power. I have so far discussed how we can develop the learning side of the equation. I shall now propose that it should be made more difficult to pass laws and introduce regulations. Instead of a simple majority being enough to force others to behave in a particular way, we should move forward to a point where legislation *which restricts freedom* requires a two-thirds majority.

A two-thirds majority seems realistic as the percentage required to pass legislation which restricts freedom. On the other hand, repealing legislation of this type should require only a 40% vote. The bias should always be toward freeing people, communities and groups from control. The laws which do exist should be supported by such a strong consensus that people are unwilling to break the law because they will incur the displeasure of their peers, rather than because the police will penalize them if they disobey. People do have a right to make their own choices unless a strong case can be made for a particular law or regulation.

I am aware that my proposal for changing the percentage of votes to pass and repeal legislations would probably require a constitutional amendment and the chance of getting it passed would currently be low. Thinking about such a constitutional amendment would, however, force each of us to consider the key issues of the twenty-first century. What sort of society do we want to live in? Do we want to drift toward ever-greater controls? Or are we prepared to commit to more responsible decision-making for ourselves and our society? How much internal control will be developed and how much external control must be imposed?

Such regulations and laws as are essential should be passed in a form which emphasizes the result and not the means, so as to leave as much space for creativity as possible. Suppose, for example, that there is an agreed need to increase the energy efficiency of buildings. The regulations should state the degree to which heat loss and gain should be restricted and not the building processes which must be used. If this approach is not employed, appropriate technologies will often be unintentionally excluded. For example, passive solar has often been prohibited, and still is in some jurisdictions, although it might well use less energy than other approaches.

Limiting the amount of government control seems frightening to many people. Some of those who have seen my arguments believe I am eliminating the only efficient approach to bring about rapid changes. Those who challenge my approach ignore the clear-cut evidence which shows that legislation, ahead of agreement, often leads to backlash. Indeed, there is an inherent flaw in the logic of bringing about major positive change through legislation. Legislators tend to lag public opinion rather than move ahead of it. It will therefore be quicker to encourage change using citizen energy than to push for government decision-making.

Moral judgments which restrict the behavior of others should only be made when the case is overwhelming. Our attempts to legislate morality emerged at the time when we thought absolute answers existed. Today we know that we must live in the questions and apply the values of honesty, responsibility, humility and love to each situation. This requires that we leave people freer to make their own choices. "Murder" will still be outlawed but each of us must learn to face up to the dilemmas which exist around life and death issues, given today's high technologies.

Greater self-responsibility will require that each of us be more supportive of the laws enacted for our protection. For example, modern traffic patterns depend entirely on the willingness of people to obey the traffic code. Most people do so most of the time and the roads are therefore relatively safe but some communities are seeing a growing tendency to run yellow lights. A breakdown in traffic discipline would make life far more stressful than it already is.

In addition, we must recognize that the legal system breaks down if too many activities are defined as crimes. As the burden of law and regulation increases, people obey the law only when they are afraid they may be caught and penalized. We have long since passed this danger point; obedience to society's norms is now based on fear of being caught rather than on social consensus.

There is a lesson to be learned from the different patterns in the United States and Japan. A foreigner was observing how the Japanese police force operated. An individual began to jaywalk, the police cruiser turned on its siren and the individual scuttled back to the sidewalk. The obvious question was then asked: "What are the penalties for jaywalking?" The response was, "There are no penalties for jaywalking. It is enough for us to remind people of their civic duty."

Finding a way back to knowing our duty is the primary challenge that confronts all of us. The required shift toward responsible behavior must affect individuals, work and professional groups, communities and those who make large-scale decisions. Fortunately giving people greater freedom does result in more effective decision-making. The feedback loop which causes this result is self-evident once one looks for it.

Ed Lindaman, a futurist whose early death deprived us of his wisdom, told a story which demonstrates this point. He worked at one of the large aircraft companies and was involved when an office of quality control was set up with two people. A year later, 200 people were in the office but everybody agreed that standards had declined. Personal and group responsibility had been replaced by an intrusive bureaucracy.

It must also be remembered that breaking the law is sometimes a challenge, particularly for young people. On a visit to Oklahoma, I was discussing the level of losses from community college libraries. At that time, the loss from an open stack system was lower than from one with higher levels of security. People saw no challenge in taking books from the open stacks but were delighted to show that they were smarter than the systems set up to prevent theft.

Margaret Mead once questioned how society could reverse the downward slide which starts when people steal milk-bottles off the stoop. Today cities throughout the world, confronted with major increases in violence and murder, are asking the same question with far more urgency. The only possibility is for citizens, communities, work and professional groups to reestablish standards and norms which are accepted, and enforced, by their members individually and collectively.

This is the point where responsible freedom and duty come together. There is a highly relevant biblical text: "In the service of God is perfect freedom." If one thinks clearly and widely, what one needs to do and what one wants to do and what one can do all come together in a single clear-cut direction. Only saints reach this level. The rest of us must do the best we can!

Developing leaders

Consumption has taken the place of citizenship. The psychic link between communities and their representatives is broken. People feel that most politicians are on the take. Politicians believe that most of their constituents have no interest in good governance. Campaigns get dirtier and dirtier as candidates point out the flaws in the other person rather than the positive reasons why people should vote for them.

The ever-growing drive to limit terms in office results from a profound sense of alienation. But if politicians are not able to remain in office for a significant period, decision-making power will move to bureaucracies. It seems highly unlikely that this will produce an improvement in patterns of decision-making. Today's problems will not be fixed by moving the deck-chairs around on the Titanic; the need is to change systems.

Two challenges are most critical at the current time. First, good people feel it does not make sense for them to run for office. They object to the constant suspicion which surrounds them and the negative reactions to their best efforts. Citizens are also unwilling to spend time supporting their elected representatives. Most messages which reach politicians are from those people who want special treatment or favors as well as from the "antis" and the "crazies." There is little communication, or support, from those who understand the nature of the compassionate era and the need for new directions.

I was in Washington several years ago talking to members of the Senate and Congress. I told them that there were many people who shared my belief that positive changes were both necessary and possible. The response was: "We'd like to believe you. But our mail does not reflect your point of view." Those of us who are change agents have a responsibility to inform leaders of our points of view.

We can rebuild the trust system which ought to surround politics at two levels. First, we can act at an individual level in ways which can make a difference. Second, we can make fundamental alterations in the ways society structures political activities. We need to develop compassionate attitudes toward each other. We need to learn to cooperate. Until we internalize these values, no changes in technical approaches to election procedures will make a difference. Specifically, this means that the electorate must turn, as a matter of principle, away from those who use negative messages and toward those who stand for something. Penalization for negativity should become automatic.

We must also commit to a rhetoric which is frequently used and abused—that decisions should be placed as close to the people as possible. Neighborhoods, communities and communities of interest can resolve many questions without involving national, let alone international, decision-makers. Certain global directions must be adopted by all. The specific approaches which can ensure their implementation can only be designed in the light of each local situation.

As time goes by, we must become more aware of the danger of passing legislation at the state and national level which has unwanted effects at the local. I have become increasingly conscious of the way in which higher levels of government have been imposing mandates and requirements on localities which restrict the exercise of responsible freedom. In earlier times when communities were isolated, it was reasonable to assume that there was more knowledge in legislatures than locally. This is no longer necessarily true.

The next step is to enlarge how we think about politics. The meaning of the word politics has been narrowed so that, for most people, it only brings to mind issues of governance. Indeed, politics is defined by many as the way that elections are won and lost. We have essentially forgotten the broader definition which is "the total complex of relations between people in society."

While it is certainly important to elect the right people to city and county councils and school boards, it is even more vital to make sure that the interconnections between all the parts of communities are creative and positive. As we move in this direction, and partnerships become the dominant mode in decision-making rather than power, the roles played by elected officials will shift dramatically. They will neither expect, nor be allowed to, make arbitrary decisions which do not reflect the will of the public. They will be linked far more closely with their constituents who will support them, and also hold them liable for their actions.

What steps can be taken to move in this direction at the current time? No magic bullets exist. The breakdown in political participation has taken place over many years and any recovery cannot therefore be expected to be rapid. The first necessary step is for people to support those leaders who do choose to operate in a cooperative and compassionate style.

Such an approach is particularly important at the current time. This sort of approach ensures a victory whether the candidate gets the most votes or not. If the candidate wins, he or she reaches office with a committed citizenry who will be supportive of the changes which are necessary in the immediate future. If the candidate loses, then a process of education has been started which will make it easier for the next person to do well, and eventually win.

Effective campaigning is personal. It is designed to excite voters and gain their commitment to volunteering. The primary requirement for this approach to work is a clear, convincing message which involves people rather than a large amount of money. Surprisingly this approach can work even at a state level. Two of the surprises of the 1988 election, the successes of Paul Wellstone for Minnesota Senator and Lawton Chiles for Florida Governor, emerged from strategies of this type.

Choices in a pluralistic universe

Almost all adults grew up believing that the "right" answer could be known and society would then be able to force this answer on its citizens. We are now moving into a pluralistic world with very different belief patterns. People are no longer willing to be dominated by thinking which does not fit their own viewpoints. Western cultures, which have tried to control others for centuries, find it difficult to come to grips with this new reality.

How can different groups and viewpoints learn to live with each other without forcing shifts either by coercion or, more subtly, by imposing expectations that others have to accept? Many years ago I read *The Helping Hand* by Poul Anderson. It told the story of negotiations between earth and two planets which had been at war. Earth was willing to help because of the long-run benefits it would receive from the economic recovery of both systems. Each planet sent negotiators who were told to get the best terms they could, both of them instructed their ambassadors to do anything necessary to get help. The Ambassador of one planet did exactly what he was told and resources were promised. The negotiator from the other planet disobeyed instructions. He insulted the people of earth who turned against him and refused help, came home in disgrace and refused to explain his actions.

The short-run results of these planetary choices were what would have been expected. The planet which got aid flourished. It was able to restore its standard of living relatively rapidly. It became a tourist destination. Earthpeople found themselves increasingly "at home" because hotels and eating places provided familiar standards and foods. Industry moved ahead because it was able to use existing earth technologies.

The planet without aid found it immensely difficult to pull itself up by its bootstraps. It was isolated and had to depend on its own resources because it had bankrupted itself during the war. Necessities were in short supply for years and many died. There was little commerce or exchange with earth because there was no real mesh between the thinking of the conquered planet and earth's ideas.

In the long-run, however, the picture was very different. The planet which got aid stagnated. In order to fit in with the styles of earth, it had to abandon the wellsprings of its culture and the way it had previously been organized. There had been no conscious imperialism which demanded that things be done the same way as on earth. But if the conquered planet wanted to take advantage of what was being so "generously" offered, the only way it could do so was to manage its affairs in the same way as earth.

The planet which refused aid was forced to restudy its roots and to discover its own deepest learnings and knowledge. It examined the achievements of earth and found that their planet's traditions made it possible to surpass them. It developed methods of space flight which baffled earth scientists because they came out of a totally different cultural structure. Earth became allied with the planet which refused aid, while the other planet was essentially relegated to being a colony. Just before his death, the thinking and actions of the Ambassador who had anticipated these developments were made public and he was honored as a hero rather than reviled as a traitor.

The Ambassador who refused aid forced his planet toward pluralism. The Ambassador who accepted aid unconsciously opted for an imposed uniformity. This is the same choice which the world, and particularly the poor countries, faces at the current time. Will there be a commitment to building out of the strengths of each of the cultures of the globe or will there be a continued effort to impose the viewpoints of the West?

Historically, each area throughout the world has believed in the superiority of its way of life. Other traditions are seen as inferior and dangerous. If you think in this way, it inevitably follows that real progress can only be achieved if your ideas continue to dominate. This attempt to maintain superiority is then buttressed and reinforced by distortions, half-truths and outright lies about the attitudes of other nations and religions.

Colonial powers have been totally convinced that their worldview was the right one—and indeed it was very often perceived as the only way to look at events. A slow erosion of this form of narrow-minded thinking is today taking place. Unfortunately, rhetorics like those coined by Bush when he talks about "the American century," suggest that there is a possibility of slipping back into patterns of understanding which are obsolete. There is little difference between twentieth-century "American century" rhetoric and nineteenth century European expansionism.

An alternative way of looking at cultural norms does exist already. We can recognize the seeds of positive directions in all areas of the world. We should nurture positive processes wherever they are found. It will be easier to build from deeply-rooted indigenous beliefs than to graft ideas onto a culture from the outside. The difficulty with this approach is that the West has undercut the wellsprings of most cultures; whether the blocks are temporary or permanent is one of the most critical questions of our time.

How should poor areas and countries, which still have significantly different cultures, think and act at this time? Instead of rushing to adopt the styles which have emerged in the countries now rich, they should dig back into their traditions. They need to ask how their religious, moral and ethical systems will help them preserve ecological systems and eliminate violence. They also need to find out how responsible freedom can be achieved by building on their own traditions.

The province of Kerala in India has been one of the success stories. Committed to social justice, it has developed hybrid forms, between capitalism and socialism. These have produced significant movement toward better health, education and a high quality of life despite severe limits on the availability of goods and services. Living in Louisiana, I am increasingly aware that the same issue applies to the dynamics of this state. There has been a tendency for Louisiana to adopt the styles of the

North. But this denies both the uniqueness which attracts people to the state and also the potential of a new and vibrant synthesis.

One of the most depressing aspects of my work is the level of negativity which exists in many geographical areas. I did a great deal of work in Nebraska in the eighties. One of the exercises we carried out was to get people involved in two exercises. One of them asked for the list of adjectives that should be used to promote business and industry in the state—this task was found to be very difficult by many participants. The other was to develop descriptors which could be used to stereotype the region and might be used as a basis for a sitcom; most people found it far easier to come up with a large number of negative words.

Developing local value-based cultures will undercut the development of fundamentalism, which is a primary threat to the world's future. Fundamentalism is strengthened when people perceive that the certainties of their lives are being undermined and they feel a desperate need to find some rock which will support them. The easiest place to find the certainty they want is in the sacred texts of their culture. The texts are then treated as absolutes which must be accepted exactly as they are written.

When new truths are drawn out of old cultures, on the other hand, individuals feel their past is still being honored. The stress which inevitably follows from change still remains, of course, but it will be far more limited because people feel they are following in the footsteps of their ancestors. They will find it easier to accept new approaches which honor old beliefs but can be adapted to modern conditions.

We must honor the many views which exist in the world. Diverse societies are the basis for a healthy world culture in just the same way as healthy ecologies require a complex balance of organisms, none of which dominates the others. Many reject the relevance of pluralism, however, arguing that other traditions are too flawed to enable positive growth. The best cure for this negative attitude is to face the extent and depth of the difficulties of using even one's own culture as the basis for moving toward more compassionate values. Others will reject pluralism because it is not efficient but rather profoundly messy and untidy. The message of chaos theory, however, is that untidiness is healthy rather than destructive.

The problem with pluralism, of course, is that it makes effective communication very difficult, and also guarantees high levels of conflict. There will be a need for very careful dialogue if conflicts are not to escalate into violence. The central requirement for the future, therefore, is not "efficiency" but "resiliency." It is critically important that a large number of approaches are tried so that humanity can discover which ones work best. Adaptability is supported by a wide range of diversification. Overspecialization, on the contrary, leads to rigidity and increased vulnerability.

Ethnic pluralism

Much of the tension, and violence, in the world today stems from the inclusion within nation-states of ethnic minorities. There has been a strong tendency for the heritage of these ethnic minorities, and their rights, to be abridged by dominant majorities. Ethnic tensions have been endemic throughout the world during the second half of the twentieth-century, particularly in Africa and Asia. They have threatened the break-up of countries like Nigeria and have caused large-scale loss of life in such countries as Cambodia.

This issue has become dramatically visible as Communist power has disintegrated and past hatreds have resurfaced. The civil war in Yugoslavia has shown the dangers of massive fragmentation. More and more provinces have declared themselves independent of the center and their sovereignty has been recognized. Similarly, the break-up of the Soviet Union has already restored Estonia, Latvia and Lithuania to nationhood. Many other republics now want their freedom and so do ethnic groups within the Republic of Russia and other Republics.

Solutions to ethnic issues require that the redefinition of sovereignty, discussed in the last chapter, be constantly kept in mind. Current definitions of "absolute" sovereignty cause two destructive patterns. One has been a largely unconscious assumption of superiority, causing the majority group to believe it has the "right" answers. The fact that others might see the world in a different way has been ignored. This was the primary pattern of the colonial powers who assumed they were bringing the gift of progress and order to "the lesser breeds without the law."

The other process is totally conscious. It is the deliberate use of power to ensure that one ethnic group—which has an electoral majority, or economic or military superiority—gets what it wants at the cost of others. This pattern has been all too common in both Africa and Southeast Asia. Instead of recognizing the need for majority rule and minority rights, the majority all too often uses its power to dominate.

The tragic, long-running Sri Lankan civil war emerged from majority pressure. In 1983, the Presidential campaign promised "Sinhalese in 24 hours," if an election was won. The language of the dominant majority was made official, replacing English which had been more effectively learned by the Tamils. The Tamils naturally felt that this was unfair and responded with the violence which has resulted in thousands of deaths and gravely damaged the development dynamics of a nation which were previously very promising.

The ethnic issue is often deliberately downplayed by those who believe in nation-state models because recognition of its importance challenges current structures. For decades, and indeed centuries, the goal has been to break down and eliminate ethnic differences. Living in Scotland as we do for part of the year, the success of this approach has been all too clear. By the mid-seventies, the uniqueness of the Scottish culture was well on its way to being lost.

Given that the nation-state is not a viable organizational form for the twenty-first century, the nature of the ethnic question shifts in critical ways. We can no longer assume that the nation-state will be strong enough to suppress ethnic vitality nor that it will be wise for it to do so. Moving from nation-state dominance to the reemergence of ethnic strengths is going to raise very difficult questions. Ethnic memories are very long. Violence tends to develop as each group tries to take revenge for past "injustices." Because all sides have their own tragedies to avenge, the potentials for escalation are enormous.

Cultures all too often define their experiences in terms of their past tragedies rather than by looking at their own unique strengths. Only as each ethnic group regains pride in its own history, and moves beyond defining itself as superior to its past enemies, can societies grow beyond violence. If ethnic groups can regain their self-respect, then they will learn to collaborate. Violence is the resort of the weak, not of the strong.

Fortunately, more progress has been made toward positive images than is commonly realized. Referring again to our Scottish experience, dance, music and the Gaelic have been revived, together with a sense that Scotland can be proud of its own heritage rather than angry with the English. Other ethnic groups have moved in similar directions. They are coming to see their history as something which provides values to the world.

Ethnic strength could provide a reservoir of strength and solidarity to the world if we are willing to tap into it rather than being afraid of it. The roots of ethnic groups go back deep into the soil rather than being supported by nationalistic rhetoric. Each area also supports its own vision and its own humor. I remember walking to our home in Scotland with one of the old-fashioned vacuum-cleaners with hoses sprouting from every part of it. A passer-by saw its resemblance to the bagpipes and told me; "You'll never got a tune out of that, laddy!" He assumed that I would get the joke because the bagpipe is central to Scottish culture.

We need to move beyond the anger of the past and towards a recognition of the need for diversity. The appropriate image for the future is that of a tapestry with a very rich pattern rather than a melting pot in which all differences are submerged. The tapestry image encourages each group to develop its own primary colors while committing to a total picture of which each person and culture can be part.

Patterns of intervention

If we are to provide greater local freedom, we must also ask what happens when local dynamics go wrong. Given that more rights and responsibilities will be held close to the people, when do other groups have a right, and responsibility to intervene? There are several different aspects to this question. What's appropriate when a community is harming its members? What about the region who uses so much water that its down-stream neighbors are deprived? What about the nation-state which fails to live within its resource base?

It is extraordinarily difficult to get our heads around these questions. Because of our history, there is an assumption that not only does government know best but it will always be effective when it tries to control problems. The idea that "masterly inaction" may be a healthy policy is almost always a subject of ridicule. Thus the first natural reaction, when things get out of line, is for an outside group to come in and straighten things out.

We forget that there is another possible model. This aims to challenge people to organize themselves to produce the direction which they want. One of Robert Heinlein's stories deals with this issue at a very different scale. The plot of the story, *Glory Road*, assumes that there is a government which covers a myriad of galaxies. Its leader is imprinted with the wisdom of those who have held power before. The main lesson that has been learned from millennia of history is that intervention usually makes things worse. Letting things work themselves out, however messy and unsatisfactory this may be, often proves to be the best course.

The real choice which lies before us is whether to concentrate on the negative or to accentuate the positive. Western societies have spent much of their time drawing attention to the weaknesses and failures of people and institutions. Far less effort has been made to inform people about the positive and to spread information about what can be done. There is far more chance of making the necessary transformations if all of us concentrate on what is possible than on bemoaning the seriousness of the current crises.

Negativity and whining disempower. They make people feel that things are hopeless. Change agents need to help individuals and groups believe it is possible to deal with issues. While there will be times when intervention is required to prevent totally unacceptable dynamics, we should always remember that spending time fighting the negative takes energy away from developing the positive. Building is always tougher than tearing down and it takes great persistence to stick with it.

Any decisions to intervene should be tested using several criteria. The first is to be sure that the standards being upheld are really applicable in the situation rather than resulting from one's own cultural background. Given the desirability of creative actions throughout the culture, one must be absolutely certain that those who are acting contrary to one's own instincts are not pioneering a possible new route into the future. During the industrial era, the tendency has been for those at "higher" levels to believe that they (almost) always know better. In the compassionate era, the bias must be exactly the opposite.

The second need is to apply the message of the serenity prayer, which demands that we distinguish between what can be changed and what cannot. Some interventions are possible and there are others which will not work or may be counterproductive. All too many people still feel it is enough to do the "right" thing; they feel justified in shrugging off any undesirable second and third level consequences which result from their interventions. This approach is intolerable in the compassionate era.

The third need is to remember what will *not* be thought about or done as a result of choosing to intervene. Resources are always scarce. The decision to be active in one area implies that one will pay less attention to other issues and questions. It is relatively easy to see that it would be desirable to do something. It is far harder to weigh whether one area of activity is more helpful than another. Attention is also a scarce commodity. If it is used for one purpose, other potentials and dangers will be treated less seriously or ignored.

Finally, one must ask whether a community is more likely to be effective in the future if an outside intervention takes place. In the long run, the only way to develop a self-governing community is to encourage people to become committed citizens. If people come to believe that outsiders are willing to make the tough decisions for them, they will be less likely to make an effort of their own. If they find that outsiders are unwilling to let them make their own choices, on the grounds that they are inappropriate or wrong, they will simply back off and become uninterested in leadership.

Good decision-making in the twenty-first century requires that we learn to think and act despite our inability to be certain. We must learn to focus our gut-feelings and intuition rather than hope to find hard data. We need to rely on knowledge rather than information.

Population issues

In more and more parts of the world, population is growing beyond the carrying-capacity of the land, water and air to support it. To what extent can, and should, the global community deal with the consequences of this situation. Alternatively, should problems of this type be confined within national boundaries?

In the poor countries, the most urgent need is to provide birth control information to all those who want it. Failure to move in these directions will force compulsory efforts to limit births in wider and wider areas of the world. Even the most immediate action in this area will not prevent crises in a number of countries, the most obvious of which are Bangladesh, China and some of the Saharan nations.

Many years ago, Garrett Hardin tried to deal with the issue of inadequate resources. He proposed that there should be a conscious adoption of "a lifeboat ethic." He argued that if a lifeboat was full already, those in it were justified in keeping others out even though this resulted in people drowning. His parallel was with the world which he claimed was approaching the limits of its carrying capacity and that keeping people alive through aid would only worsen the problem. His thesis was very simple. If people get food, they will keep on having babies. The only way to prevent them from doing so is to permit starvation to occur when a country is unable to support its population, thus bringing the area back to an equilibrium position.

Population experts have feared overpopulation ever since the traditional high birth-rate and high death-rate pattern was broken at the end of World War II. Medical care led to the survival of more and more children in the poor countries as well as rapid lengthening of the average lifespan. Population has grown rapidly in the second half of the twentieth-century and the world-wide total of births in 1990 was the highest ever.

Garrett Hardin was right to draw our attention to the emerging problem. However, I have always felt that Hardin's model doesn't work even at the level of the image. Suppose a lot of white people are in a lifeboat and a lot of non-whites outside. Suppose further that the non-whites feel that the whites gained their position in the lifeboat unjustly. In this case, they are likely to try to upset the lifeboat even at the risk that nobody will be saved at all.

Unfortunately, the fact that the image is flawed does not get rid of the validity of the question. When conditions become intolerable people are likely to try to flee their situation. Are other countries responsible for taking them in? There are three significantly different situations. One is in Europe. A conference called by the Council of Europe to look at the possibility of massive migration from Eastern to Western Europe estimated it might reach as high as 30 million people.

According to the report in the *Wall Street Journal,* "there was unanimous agreement, according to delegates, that a strict separation must be made between genuine refugees as defined by the 1951 Geneva convention—those fleeing wars or religious or political persecution—and so-called economic refugees, people seeking to migrate for better economic opportunities." The United States uses the same distinction to exclude many people from Latin America while letting in most Europeans claiming the same status without serious challenge. Refugees, however, find such a distinction highly theoretical, because the very act of fleeing a country will often be seen as a political act which makes return highly dangerous.

Bangladesh forms a second type of case. What is the appropriate response to the ever-worsening population pressure in this area of the world? Should more and more resources be provided from outside? Should outward migration be permitted? Or should the area be warned that it cannot expect continuing aid from the rest of the world? And what would this mean?

The third type of question emerges because overcrowded, over-extended cities may break down in the nineties. The most immediately challenging problem for the United States is Mexico City. There is growing evidence that the combination of environmental damage and poverty is leading to the potential for a massive collapse. Can the United States do anything significant to help prevent this possibility and, if it did occur, what would be the correct attitudes?

Limiting violence

How are areas of the world which use very different approaches to governance going to be able to avoid wars during the next half-century when communication failures will make conflicts difficult to resolve? This is a key question which must be faced if the number and intensity of wars are to be reduced. How are the wounds of centuries and millennia to be healed not only in the Middle East, but in many other parts of the world?

President Bush was right when he argued that a new world order is required in the world today, but the lessons to be learned are quite different from those he suggested. The core needs are:

■ *to avoid building up tyrants for reasons of realpolitik.* (Realpolitik is a word used to imply that moral values must take a back seat to pragmatic issues.) The time has come for the world community to demand certain basic standards. Saddam Hussein and Hitler have often been compared. The real parallel with Hitler is that neither he nor Hussein would have become major threats if the world community had been willing to deal with them before they built up their power. Hitler was willing to withdraw his invading armies if European countries had reacted strongly to his early breaches of the Versailles treaty; the failure to protest encouraged his future conduct. Similarly, the decision of the Western powers to build up Iraq in order to prevent a victory by Iran produced the invasion of Kuwait.

Future directions should be chosen in terms of whether they will lead to a world order of responsible freedom. While realpolitik will still sometimes be more important than the long-run need to build toward a value-based culture, positive stands should only be abandoned when the case for doing so is overwhelming. In our rapidly changing, and heavily interconnected world, the consequences of realpolitik decisions will haunt the future. The forces which support responsible freedom should be encouraged wherever they surface throughout the world.

■ *to prevent tyrants from gaining possession of modern weaponry.* Unfortunately, the international sale of weapons, particularly to countries in the third world, has been a major factor in achieving rich-country economic growth. Almost all the governments of the world support arms sales. Businesses have all too often been willing to break the few regulations which have been imposed by governments.

In the thirties, there was an outcry against "merchants of death," companies who sold weapons to any purchaser who could pay. Today, more and more countries are destroying the quality of life of their citizens by spending an increasing percentage of their budgets on arms. In their own long-run self-interest, all countries need to de-escalate tensions and reduce arms expenditures. Global public opinion must demand that countries cease using weaponry exports as a prime means of supporting economic growth and balancing foreign trade. Citizens should also support treaties which lead to disarmament rather than the constant increase in the destructive potential of regional enemies. Japan, for example, has decided that the military policies of developing countries will be a factor in deciding how much aid they receive. This is the type of government initiative which can help shift priorities.

■ *to reduce the vulnerability of nations to behavior they cannot control.* Disruptions in the Middle East are intolerable to the United States because of its excessive dependence on oil. This is, in turn, a result of past policy failures. If America had done as much as Japan, and many European countries, to develop energy efficiency the importance of the Middle East to the U.S. would be far more limited. Indeed the view of the Gulf crisis was very different in Japan, precisely because it was less vulnerable to disruptions of its oil supply. The debate over how to reduce energy demand, and the right mix of sources for the energy still required, must now take center-stage.

The United States used massive power following the invasion of Kuwait because it feared interruptions in the supply of oil. This danger was greatly overstated. Most Middle East countries can no more afford a stoppage in their oil exports than importing countries can cope with a significant decrease in availability. The world is increasingly tied together in a web where disruptions cause damage all around. We can only flourish if others do well.

In the industrial era, humanity thought in win-lose terms. "If I do better, then you will do worse." In the new compassionate era, we are understanding that life is a seamless web. John Donne knew this centuries ago when he said: "Do not ask for whom the bell tolls, it tolls for thee."

Building a transnational web

Some of the most visible of the existing coordination groups work on international transportation, both sea and air, weather, telecommunications and mail. Nations are also just beginning to collaborate around environmental issues.

Ceding considerable decision-making authority to transnational organizations now seems essential. The Universal Postal Union facilitates the movement of the mail throughout the world. Every country has an interest in a common set of patterns which facilitate sea and air transportation. Transnational rules are seen as a way of supporting the concerns of everybody involved and relatively few tense disagreements therefore develop. There is a growing commitment to clear, understandable rules. It was the lack of sufficient clarity which caused the crash of a South American plane in the early nineties. Its intention was to land at Kennedy Airport but they did not know the protocols for informing controllers of their potentially critical shortage of fuel.

Weather is another area where better knowledge is recognized as critically important by all nations. Indeed, this information is now perceived as so vital that reporting often continues despite wars. Weather reporting has indeed become "transnational" in nature.

Telecommunications pose far more difficult problems. The number of bands for electronic communication are fixed. While the supply is being stretched by technological innovation which permits more efficient usage, it is still finite. The question of which countries, and indeed which areas of the world, get what shares of the limited pie involves difficult and tough negotiations. Discussions in this area are, indeed, models for the decision-making processes which will have to take place as more and more of the products and services in the world have to be fairly allocated. Southern Nations believe that the North already has too large a share and will inevitably strive for reallocation.

Another area where changes have been taking place in the last decades is around the issues of the seas and oceans. Transnational agreements on limitation of whaling and fishing have been given more and more "teeth" as the seriousness of the situation has become visible. As a result, nation-states have ceded authority not to a transnational government but rather to ecological realities where the self-interest of everybody is today seen differently than in the past. The international treaty on the use of the oceans has brought some sanity to many aspects of this shared international resource, despite the failure of the United States to ratify the treaty.

The agreement to phase out the use of chlorofluorocarbons and to report progress to a supranational body represents a new level of transnational cooperation. Indeed, some of the rich countries agreed that the need to ban CFCs rapidly was so important that they have committed to providing technological support to the poor countries to aid the process of phasing out these products. The loss of ozone over temperate zones speeded up commitments significantly.

We can expect transnational agreements to continue to develop as we recognize our interconnected self-interest. This is one of the routes into the compassionate era.

How to Sing Our Story

WE HAVE LOST OUR SENSE OF CELEBRATION of ourselves and the universe. Human survival does not only depend on getting our thinking right. We are all "artists" who need to create a cultural picture, or story, which will satisfy our souls. Joy is as much a part of a good life as rationality.

Each culture has a "story." This story is normally invisible because, in stable times, most people take their beliefs for granted. They act within set norms and do not even recognize that there are other options. Today all of us being forced to deal with mindquakes. We are half-way through a revolutionary shift.

One of the primary causes of the sudden fundamental changes which are taking place at this time is that human relationships with the planet are coming full circle. In hunting and gathering religions, people saw themselves as supported by the land. Their rituals continuously reminded them of the need to be thankful for the benefits they received from earth's bounty. Population rose and fell as a result of high fertility, on the one hand, and the toll of war, famine, pestilence and plagues, on the other. It rarely reached the level where it could significantly impact even on local environments.

Dynamics changed dramatically as animals were domesticated and crops cultivated. Local environmental damage started in the Middle East over two millennia ago when populations grew and human beings became more and more convinced that they could outpower nature. Damage began to affect planetary systems in the twentieth-century as industrial production increased to the point that it interfered with global balancing systems.

What approaches should we now develop to reintegrate human beings into natural systems? One step has been stressed again and again in this book: the need to move beyond the current commitment to maximum economic growth. However, this change will not be sufficient unless there is also a sharp shift in the way that human beings and organizations think and relate to the world around us.

Garrett Hardin wrote the classic article many years ago with the title "The Tragedy of the Commons." He explored the reason why European common land, where everybody could put animals, was often destroyed by overgrazing. He pointed out that each person would place additional animals on the land because the impact of their flock was not large enough, by itself, to do damage. But the overall impact of all the grazing beasts was disastrous. Similar problems have emerged in Africa as tribes, which count their welfare in cattle, have destroyed the habitats on which they count for survival.

Hardin argued convincingly that this same phenomenon was developing on a very broad scale throughout the world. The "commons" of the air, water and land were being despoiled because they were "nobody's business" and everybody saw their own contribution to the damage as marginal. Having posed the question, he provided no answer to the dilemma. As people have struggled with this question in the years since he wrote, two answers have emerged at different ends of the spectrum.

One group believes that the only hope is to increase the amount of power that nation-states have over individuals and institutions. For example, Donella Meadows, who has been one of the most creative people in the movement toward a sustainable society, supports limiting the amount of CO_2 in the atmosphere in order to reduce the greenhouse effect. She then makes the following suggestion.

> The amount of human-generated carbon emission the planet can take without being clinically deranged is perhaps one billion tons per year. That requires an eighty percent cut from present emissions— to about zero point two tons per person on earth. Now suppose that we allocate to every nation the right to emit zero point two tons per person of that nation's 1990 population.
>
> Any nation that wants to burn more fuel or cut more forest than that would have to buy emission rights from a nation that won't or can't use up its allowance. The price per ton of emission would be set in an open market. It would undoubtedly be high enough to eliminate any need for foreign aid, to pay off third world debts, and to settle the problem of economic inequity forever. It would also be a powerful incentive to practice energy efficiency, to develop solar energy, and to preserve and replant forests.
>
> Here's an important kicker. Since total emission rights would be set at what the planet can ever tolerate, each nation's allocation

would be fixed forever. If the population of that nation grows, that's too bad—its emissions per person would have to shrink. If the population slowly decreases, as some European populations are now doing, then each person's share would increase.

Stop and think for a moment, at this point, about how you feel about this proposal. According to Meadows, the first reaction of those at a meeting in Denmark where this idea was surfaced was rejection and, after a while, a belief that it would be fair. I understand the temptation to adopt a model of this type but I would suggest to you that, hidden within its logic, is the inevitability of a terrifying police state.

It all sounds so easy. But who is going to collect the statistics? And how are people going to be compelled to do what they must to reduce the amount of CO_2? In addition, once this type of regulatory principle has been agreed for CO_2 emissions, there are inevitably going to be quotas set for other noxious products. We would therefore move further and further into a controlled society with "thought police" everywhere. And because there would be increasing law and regulation, people would try to cheat.

This approach represents the exact opposite of the directions I have been proposing throughout this book. The conclusion from all my arguments is that people must learn the need to preserve natural systems. Many different patterns can be combined to create this result. Support can emerge from an instinctive negative reaction to the smell of chemicals and the sight of garbage.

It can also result from a highly sophisticated understanding of the dangers which will arise if natural cycles are interrupted to the point that the long-run climate on earth is drastically changed. As this value-shift occurs, each one of us will need to reexamine our lifestyles and life-choices. Preventing damage to nature and ecological systems will be higher on our personal priorities, our institutional, economic and societal agendas. The more open the political system, the more rapidly these new choices will impact on current structures.

This argument also throws new light on the issue of private property. An enormous amount of damage has been done in the past as people have claimed that ownership of land and resources has given them the right to destroy the land and use resources carelessly. As the human race moves toward an understanding of ecological necessities, the rights inherent in private property can make it possible to ensure that the land, water and air is once again seen as a sacred trust.

The costs of destructive use of private property by a few can again be exceeded by the benefits of responsible decisions by the many. We can redevelop a belief in "usufruct," where people had the right to benefit from the fruitfulness of the land but were required by tribal ethics to pass it on undamaged and, indeed, improved. This requires that not only private individuals but also corporations and governments recognize that they have responsibilities to the land.

The central challenge our societies face is to rethink our fundamental attitudes. Traditional Christianity believed that human beings had a right to subdue nature. There are a growing number of biblical scholars who believe, on the contrary, that Genesis has been misunderstood and that human beings are meant to be stewards of nature rather than controllers of it. Lynn White sums up the challenge:

> Since the roots of our trouble are so largely religious, the remedy must also be religious, whether we call it that or not. We must think and re-feel our nature and destiny. The profoundly religious, but heretical, sense of the primitive Fransiscans for the spiritual autonomy of all parts of nature may point a direction. I propose Francis as a patron saint for ecologists.

We are forced back to the question posed by Bacon. Is the control on our appetites to be placed within us or outside of us? I believe that the human adventure can only continue if we commit ourselves to a process of education which will help us all make responsible choices about our own lives and the planet.

Seeing everything as politics

The essential revolution which has to take place if we are to resolve the crisis of governance now afflicting us is to broaden our definition of politics. Politics should not be thought of only as the thoughts and actions of our elected officials. Rather we must understand it is the sum total of our actions as they affect our collective decision-making. Our purchases are political. Our commitment to our church, and feelings about its involvement in the world, are political. Our activities to support, or ignore, education are political. Our attitudes toward the poor, and the dispossessed, are political.

Citizens, moving together, make the waves which define political options. Politicians merely ride them, often changing their opinions to make sure they are re-elected. The critical part of the political process is not the decisions on issues which have already been surfaced. Rather it is the effort which is given to surfacing new questions. The movement to ban smoking has been a highly significant political effort. So has the recognition that our health and education systems are deeply flawed.

For too long, we have been concentrating on what happens in Washington, DC and the various state capitols. Our challenge today is to learn how to help people change their ideas of appropriate directions and their self-interest. All of us who are interested in developing a better world need to discover how to help people move beyond their current definitions of their self-interest.

The division between "learning" and "politics" will vanish over time. If I were writing about these topics in the middle of the twenty-first century, there would be no difference between them. For the moment, we are so accustomed to putting these two activities into separate boxes that it will be easier to understand them if I continue the tradition. I have already dealt with learning in Part III of this book, politics has been the subject of Part IV.

There are three primary necessary steps as we move from industrial-era to compassionate-era institutions and communities. The first is to build trust and relationships. Industrial-era systems are meant to operate on logic, structure and hierarchy. Compassionate-era systems operate on hunch, perception and, even, "magic." At a recent meeting, where companies were taking the first steps toward a supplier council and talking to each other about how to cooperate, the word "magic" was frequently used to describe the effectiveness of interactions after trust had developed.

As people learn to work and play together, levels of activity and performance rise dramatically. Many people are today ready to commit to trust and relationships but there are few places in our current society where they can "try their wings." We are all sufficiently different in our thoughts and action that even when we are aiming to support others, we shall disappoint them. It is easy for people to see these failures as deliberate, rather than the result of different perceptions and understandings.

Industrial-era systems deny the importance of trust. Today's systems, as we have already seen, are adversarial. We believe that the only way to make forward progress is to fight those with whom we disagree. The idea that we could get more done by working with people—rather than disagreeing with them—is foreign to us. Even our forms of discussion tend to be in the "but" rather than the "and" style.

Those people who are in the minority therefore tend to be permanently embittered. They are constantly put down and overruled. The validity of their ideas is continually denied. We shall only build trust if we make people feel that they have been listened to and heard. Then they may be willing to listen to others. This approach is critically important both when setting up small groups and in working with continuing political processes.

In a recent meeting in Renton, a small town outside Seattle, the need to think seriously about these dynamics became very clear. Both the Council and the Planning Board were basically destroying themselves because there was no trust within the groups. In a long discussion, a few of us agreed that the key task was to help people understand that they would be listened to even if all of their ideas would not necessarily be adopted. It is amazing how much wisdom can be garnered once one admits that it can come from a large variety of sources rather than only one's friends.

The second step is to create the new ideas and structures which are needed for the future. When people trust each other, they are willing to say what they really think and believe. This is the raw material for new ways of seeing the world. Creativity provides the potential for totally novel understandings of how we can create equity in the world. It permits us to break out of the obsolete ideologies which are still controlling our world and preventing us from seeing the new opportunities, and dangers, which surround us.

In recent years we have tended to assume that "brainstorming" and creativity are the same thing. When we need to come up with new ideas we bring out flip charts and let people state their ideas. After this process has taken place, we classify all that has been said and assume that this represents the best thinking of those in the group.

We often fail to remember that most people, for obvious reasons, tend to raise the issues which they think are acceptable—this is particularly true when the results of an activity will affect the credibility and power of those involved. If one wants individuals to talk about their real ideas, this can only take place after trust has been built. The specific requirement is that those involved in a creativity process know that the results of their thinking will not be held against them.

People must not lose brownie points because they say things which are not "politically" correct. The purpose of a creativity session if to find new ways of dealing with tough questions—the only way this can be done is by raising all the critical issues. Wild ideas must also be encouraged. Some of the thoughts which occur to people in this process will be "stupid." But they may trigger better ideas down the road. Individuals need to be clear about the expectations for this type of activity for otherwise they will be excessively careful.

In today's world when people are so fearful for their future, the problems in ensuring creativity are even more difficult. All too often, it is the person who goes along who gets promoted rather than the person who takes risks. We need to learn to support those who challenge the status quo rather than those who support the inertia of current systems.

The third step is to create effective action. "Partnerships" are a good way to support new directions. The various "players" in a situation get together and decide to come up with action steps they can all accept. These partnership models are only effective if people have already been through the stages of trust-building and creativity within their own systems. Partnerships require that people are honest with each other in terms of what they want and what the politics of their systems are. In addition, partnerships demand that people know how to look for novel solutions rather than be blocked by their current ideological thinking.

There are a growing number of partnerships in place across the United States. They involve public, private and non-profit groups. They would spread more rapidly if the law could be redesigned to make cooperation between these groups easier. All too often, collaboration is restricted by fears of liability and legal suits. We need a new legal form which is a hybrid of public, private and governmental. We also need to recognize that the ideal of a "riskless" and "perfect" society which underlies much of our legislation is totally unrealistic.

Despite all the problems of our times, a very large number of successes are developing around the United States, and across the world. We need to ask why it is so difficult to learn about the many exciting ways in which people are seizing opportunities and dealing with problems. There are two primary reasons. The first is that the media still define news as "bad news." There are few slots for the positive events.

One evening each week, however, the NBC Evening News Show has a segment which describes "What's Working." As I travel, I suggest that local radio and TV stations adopt parallel local programming so that people get a sense that everything is not hopeless. This idea is often seen as a "natural" and is spreading across the United States.

Unfortunately, many of the groups which have been creative feel no responsibility to spread the word about their efforts. There seem to a number of motivations for this failure. Some people do not want to take time away from their local work. Some don't want to be seen as blowing their own horn too loudly. Some don't want to give away the results of their work for free.

I suspect that there may be, in addition, one overarching block to communication. Many of the most exciting programs and processes cut across the current success criteria of our industrial-era culture. People are therefore not sure that what they are doing is important. But even if they are personally convinced that their activities are valuable, they may fear they will be attacked by those who still want to preserve the old-style culture. This is particularly true in the field of education. There are a lot of people who don't want significant educational change. They are often extraordinarily vocal and even violent. People may not want to expose themselves to the dangers which come with going "public."

One of the most critical needs of our time is to make it clear within each system, and the culture as a whole, that innovators and leaders will be respected and honored. This change of emphasis would be of great value to those who have devoted their lives to bringing about fundamental change. Perhaps one can look forward to the day when those who have struggled to build a just society will get as much attention as athletes!

New measures of success

One way to improve communication among those who are creating positive changes is to make people feel that their efforts are in the mainstream, rather than isolated on the frontier or even running against the dynamic of the culture. Healthy human beings and societies want to succeed. If we can show individuals and groups that what they are doing is valued, they are more likely to be open about their activities.

The success criteria which dominate behavior vary from era to era. The primary success criterion for the industrial era was maximum economic growth. One purpose of this book has been to propose new images of success, many of them have been described in various parts of this book. The next challenge is to find ways to measure how successful we have been.

It is a basic truth that what cultures measure, they will also value. Once a measurement has been established, and is seen as having consequences, efforts will be made to move it in positive directions. For example, schools have recently been fixated on improving SAT scores. Doctors try to reduce death rates. Capitalist firms focus on increasing profits. Government organizations aim to meet targets. And countries want to increase Gross Domestic Product (GDP).

Some goals are valuable. Some are neutral. Some are positively damaging. Many of the measures we have inherited from the industrial era fall into this last category. The GDP is one of the most seriously flawed. GDP figures were created to measure industrial productivity. They are totally unsuitable for determining whether the social welfare of a culture is improving or worsening. In particular, they do not take into account the implications of extreme poverty.

In looking at the flaws of the current approaches and examining future potentials I cannot do better than state the measurements proposed at a meeting on "Redefining Wealth and Progress" held in Caracas in 1989. It started from the approaches which could be used to measure success in countries where the level of poverty is today so desperate that calculations must be simple. The primary suggested measures were:

■ the percentage of population below the poverty level;

■ success in completing first grade in school in the allotted time;

■ levels of pollution and the degree of destruction of natural resources;

■ the infant mortality index of children under five;

■ the number of children born with low birth weight; and

■ the weight and height measurements in relation to age.

This is suggested as minimum basic information. The report then proposed that countries with larger data bases study public safety, nutrition, health, education, basic services, shelter, child development, employment and the status of women.

As we move away from money measures to broader social indices, we need to decide whether we should aim to ensure comparability between areas and nations or to create measures which are particularly suitable for each geographical area. In the industrial era, the emphasis was always placed on comparability. In the compassionate era, the need will be to concentrate on the specifics of a local situation. Thus, an arid area needs to pay particular attention to its success in water conservation while one with lots of water will see this as unimportant. Similarly, an area with a mild and equable climate will have very different views about housing than one with temperature extremes.

Planetary networking

New images of success change our self-perceptions. In the fifties, for example, many companies throughout the world had murals which featured clouds of black smoke because this was seen as a symbol of prosperity. As people became more aware of the environmental issues, smoke became a negative. Murals were then repainted to show a clean, pastoral scene with cows and factories coexisting. Some people deny the importance of this change in images, dismissing it as mere public relations and image-making. They fail to understand that when images change, they create a different set of priorities. The environment is now a potent force in transnational decision-making.

The really critical struggle is always for the hearts and minds of people. The fundamental, although largely unnoticed, debate in the second half of the twentieth-century has been around the "success criteria" each person should adopt for themselves and their societies. Major changes in thought patterns have taken place since World War II and action priorities in the nineties differ significantly from those of the fifties. People are demanding more of themselves and of their cultures.

As people become more comfortable with their potentials, they link with others who are also working toward new and positive directions on a world-wide basis. Teilhard de Chardin, a great Catholic theologian, grasped the importance of this process at the beginning of the twentieth-century. He developed the concept of the "noosphere" which would tie together all those who were being creative about the direction of the world. He saw it as a set of invisible threads which would connect thinking people everywhere. Today his concept is being created as millions of people throughout the world are interconnected through thousands of networks.

The operation of networks is based on very different approaches from those which control bureaucratic systems. Networks are held together by the common interests of those involved rather than by the power over resources which is available to the people at the top of bureaucratic systems. Networks last as long as common interests can be clearly enough articulated to attract time and resources from their members.

In the fifties, Charles Merrifield, who was one of my mentors, made me aware that the ever-growing number of networking non-governmental organizations (NGOs) were a key element in the development of the noosphere. These organizations, which cover every conceivable field, pull together the creative energy of people throughout the world and develop bonds which are often stronger than those which link people to their nation-state. Non-governmental organizations have little power but they do have great influence and authority.

They have already served to reduce some of the worst abuses against human dignity in the world. For example, Amnesty International, through its reputation and the energy of its members, has ended many political imprisonments and curbed torture in a wide range of countries. Their concentration on individual cases has led to releases of prisoners, even in countries which pay least attention to world public opinion. Increasingly, the reports of this organization affect the standing of a country in global opinion.

NGOs have been highly effective because they help to change the views and behavior of people. Unfortunately, however, they often limit their own potential by seeing their work as preparatory to the passage of legislation. Many of them believe that only the shifts in legal structures which they create will make them successful. In reality, the noosphere will only become truly effective when those within it devote their efforts to providing citizens with the skills to make decisions for themselves rather than working primarily with governments to coerce behavior.

Why is this issue critical? One way to understand it is by considering the questions which underlay the U.N. Conference on the Environment and Development in Brazil in June 1992. There were two ways to structure the debate. One was to concentrate on governmental agreements which would force changes in behavior. The other was to educate people to understand the critical importance of preserving environmental balance for their own lives and succeeding generations. The argument of this book leads inescapably to the conclusion that the largest part of the effort should have been educational and the smaller part regulatory—unfortunately the process had exactly the opposite priorities.

The rhetorics of democracy no longer suffice. We must move toward the reality of responsible freedom. It will be extraordinarily difficult to make this shift because most existing socioeconomic systems function using coercive power. If we really believed in our democratic rhetoric, the freeing implications of the noosphere would be easy to grasp. Because our pragmatic commitment is to the power of large institutions, networking seems naive and unbelievable to most people.

The old story by which people live and the new one which is now emerging are in conflict. The old story assumes that order must be imposed by power. The new story is based on "chaos theory" which argues that well-balanced and strong systems will show a surface disorder which conceals a deeper order.

One of the most interesting ways of understanding this reality is to learn about the operation of the body. Given the implications of chaos theory, doctors are taking more notice of the very wide range of fluctuations in such indicators as pulse and blood pressure. They are discovering that balance is preserved as movement around an "ideal" state takes place. They are also discovering that when the body does not show fluctuations, for example in pulse rates, this may be a predictor of heart attacks.

The fact that our bodies maintain stability at all is, in a very real sense, a "miracle." The task of humanity today is to discover how to design cultures to mimic the complex feedback loops in the body—or more broadly in environmental systems. Fluctuations always need to exist in healthy societies. It's a commonplace that military units are in trouble when the griping stops.

Confusion and argument in democracies is a sign of health as long as everybody respects the position of others and is honest, rather than manipulative, when stating their positions. Automatic feedback loops based on broadly conceived self-interest and positive self-image will then lead in creative directions.

Moving up the involvement ladder

How does one choose where to put one's effort? What patterns of action, creation and communication are most valuable? The answer to this question will be unique to the person, group or institution which is considering what it should be doing. There is no single key to the puzzle which confronts us at the current time. We need many initiatives which all lead toward a more value-based society.

Your challenge is to find an activity which inspires you and gives you energy. When you connect with your personal concerns, and the need of the world, you are noticed and your opportunities develop. There are always further levels of opportunity and these will emerge to the degree that you are successful in discovering your own skills and energies and how they link to the challenges of our time.

This is a progressive process. Robert Burns, the great Scottish poet, wrote:

> Oh wad some Pow'r the giftie gie us
> To see ourselves as others see us.
> It would from many a blunder free us
> And foolish notion.

The challenge we face is to become aware of how our actions and activities are perceived by others. As we do this, we are able to be more effective. The fundamental challenge of the nineties is to live the "examined" life. Each of us needs to learn about ourselves and the world around us. I hope I have moved you in this direction.

A Very Short Resource List

All of us have so much to read that I no longer believe in extended bibliographies. The titles given below have been most helpful to me in my personal growth.

Bateson, Gregory, *Steps Toward an Ecology of Mind,* Ballantine, New York, 1975

Bennis, Warren and Burt Nanus, *Leaders,* Harpers, New York, 1985.

Campbell, Joseph and Bill Moyers, *The Power of Myth,* Doubleday, New York, 1988.

Erdmann, Erika and David Stover, *Beyond a World Divided,* Shambala, Boston, 1991.

Gleick, James, *Chaos,* Viking, New York, 1987.

Greenleaf, Robert K., *Servant Leadership,* Paulist Press, New York, 1977.

Harman, Willis and John Hormonn, *Creative Work,* Knowledge Systems, Indianapolis, 1990.

Henderson, Hazel, *The Politics of the Solar Age,* Knowledge Systems, Indianapolis, 1992.

Johnston, Charles M, *The Creative Imperative,* Celestial Arts, Berkeley, 1984.

Land, George and Beth Jarman, *Breakpoint and Beyond,* HarperCollins, New York, 1992.

Lux, Kenneth, *Adam Smith's Mistake,* Shambala, Boston, 1990.

Milbraith, Lester W, *Envisioning a Sustainable Society,* State University of New York Press, Albany, 1989.

Russell, Peter, *The White Hole in Time,* Harper: San Francisco, 1992.

Robertson, James, *Future Work,* Universe Books, New York, 1985.

Schmookler, Andrew Bard, *Sowings and Reapings,* Knowledge Systems, Indianapolis, 1989.

Periodicals

Humankind Advancing, RR I, Lockeport, Nova Scotia, Canada, BOT 1L0.

In Context, 712 Cherry Avenue NE., Bainbridge Island, WA 98010.

Skole, 72 Philip Street, Albany, NY 12202.

Index